TRAVELING JAPAN'S DEEP INTERIOR

TRAVELING JAPAN'S DEEP INTERIOR

ISABELLA LUCY BIRD

EDITED BY WILLIAM DE LANGE

TOYO REFERENCE SERIES

First edition, 2017

Originally published as *Unbeaten Tracks in Japan*

Published by TOYO PRess
Visit us at: **www.toyopress.com**

ISBN 978-94-92722-04-1

Contents

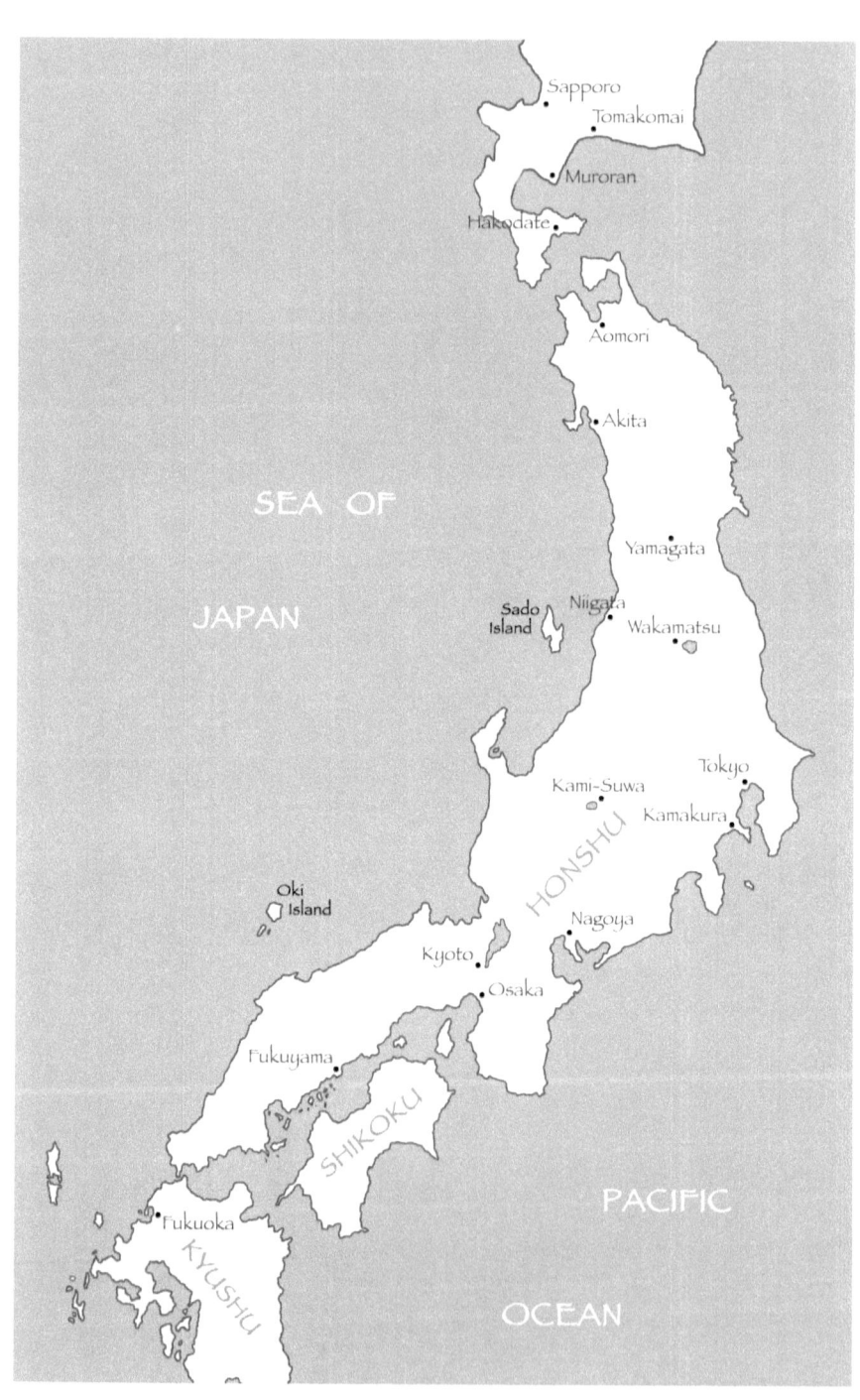

SEA OF

JAPAN

Sapporo

Tomakomai

Muroran

Hakodate

Aomori

Akita

Yamagata

Sado
Island

Niigata

Wakamatsu

Tokyo

Kami-Suwa

Kamakura

HONSHU

Oki
Island

Nagoya

Kyoto

Osaka

Fukuyama

SHIKOKU

Fukuoka

KYUSHU

PACIFIC

OCEAN

First Views of Japan

Oriental Hotel, Yokohama, May 21, 1878
Eighteen days of unintermitted rolling over desolate rainy seas brought the city of Tokyo early yesterday morning to Cape King, and by noon we were steaming up Edo Bay, quite near the shore. The day was soft and grey with a little faint blue sky, and, though the coast of Japan is much more prepossessing than most coasts, there were no startling surprises either of color or form. Broken wooded ridges, deeply cleft, rise from the water's edge, gray, deep-roofed villages cluster about the mouths of the ravines, and terraces of rice cultivation, bright with the greenness of English lawns, run up to a great height among dark masses of upland forest.

The populousness of the coast is very impressive, and the bay everywhere was equally peopled with fishing boats, of which we passed not only hundreds, but thousands, in five hours. The coast and sea were pale, and the boats were pale too, their hulls being unpainted wood, and their sails pure white duck. Now and then a high-sterned *bezaisen* drifted by like a phantom galley, then we slackened speed to avoid exterminating a fleet of triangular-looking fishing boats with white square sails, and so on through the grayness and dumbness hour after hour.

For long I looked in vain for Fuji-*san*, and failed to see it, though I heard ecstasies all over the deck, till, accidentally looking heavenwards instead of earthwards, I saw far above any possibility of height, as one would have thought, a huge, truncated cone of pure snow, 13,080 feet above the sea, from which it sweeps upwards in a glorious curve, very wan, against a very pale blue sky, with its base and the intervening country veiled in a pale grey mist. It was a wonderful vision, and shortly, as a vision, vanished. Except the cone of Tristan d'Acunha—also a cone of snow—I never saw a mountain rise in such lonely majesty, with nothing near or far to detract from its height and grandeur. No wonder that it is a sacred mountain, and so dear to the Japanese that their art is never weary of representing it. It was nearly fifty miles off when we first saw it.

The air and water were alike motionless, the mist was still and pale, grey clouds lay restfully on a bluish sky, the reflections of the white sails of the fishing boats scarcely quivered. It was all so pale, wan, and ghastly, that the turbulence of crumpled foam which we left behind us, and our noisy, throbbing progress, seemed a boisterous intrusion upon sleeping Asia.

The gulf narrowed, the forest-crested hills, the terraced ravines, the pic-turesque grey villages, the quiet beach life, and the pale blue masses of the mountains of the interior, became more visible. Fuji-*san* retired into the mist in which he enfolds his grandeur for most of the summer. We passed Reception Bay, Perry Island, Webster Island, Cape Saratoga, and Mississippi Bay—American nomenclature which perpetuates the successes of American diplomacy—and not far from Treaty Point came upon a red lightship with the words "Treaty Point" in large letters upon her. Outside of this no foreign vessel may anchor.[1]

The bustle among my fellow passengers, many of whom were returning home, and all of whom expected to be met by friends, left me at leisure, as I looked at unattractive, unfamiliar Yokohama and the pale grey land stretched out before me, to speculate somewhat sadly on my destiny on these strange shores, on which I have not even an acquaintance. On mooring we were at once surrounded by crowds of *bezaisen*, called by foreigners sampan, and Dr. Gulick, a near relation of my Hilo friends, came on board to meet his daughter, welcomed me cordially, and relieved me of all the trouble of disembarkation. These *bezaisen* are very clumsy-looking, but are managed with great dexterity by the boatmen, who gave and received any number of bumps with much good nature, and without any of the shouting and swearing in which competitive boatmen usually indulge.

1 All these names have long since been replaced with Japanese ones. Reception Bay is now the port of Kurihama, Perry Island is Sarushima, Webster Island is Hakkejima, Cape Saratoga is Futtsu Misaki, much of Missisippi Bay has been reclaimed and Treaty Point is now the western landing point of the Tokyo Bay Aqua Line. Indeed, it is questionable wether the Japanese ever used these names.

The partially triangular shape of these boats approaches that of a salmon-fisher's punt used on certain British rivers. Being floored gives them the appearance of being absolutely flat-bottomed. Though they tilt readily, they are very safe, being heavily built and fitted together with singular precision with wooden bolts and a few copper cleats. They are *sculled*, not what we should call rowed, by two or four men with very heavy oars made of two pieces of wood working on pins placed on outrigger bars. The men scull standing and use the thigh as a rest for the oar. They all wear a single, wide-sleeved, scanty, blue cotton garment, not fastened or girdled at the waist, straw sandals, kept on by a thong passing between the great toe and the others, and if they wear any headgear, it is only a wisp of blue cotton tied round the forehead. The one garment is only an apology for clothing, and displays lean concave chests and lean muscular limbs. The skin is very yellow, and often much tattooed with mythical beasts. The charge for *bezaisen* is fixed by tariff, so the traveller lands without having his temper ruffled by extortionate demands.

The first thing that impressed me on landing was that there were no loafers, and that all the small, ugly, kindly-looking, shrivelled, bandy-legged, round-shouldered, concave-chested, poor-looking beings in the streets had some affairs of their own to mind. At the top of the landing steps there was a portable restaurant, a neat and most compact thing, with charcoal stove, cooking and eating utensils complete. It looked as if it were made by and for dolls, and the mannikin who kept it was not five feet high. At the custom house we were attended to by minute officials in blue uniforms of European pattern and leather boots. They were very civil creatures, who opened and examined our trunks carefully, and strapped them up again, contrasting pleasingly with the insolent and rapacious officials who perform the same duties at New York.

Outside were about fifty of the now well-known *kuruma*, or *jinrikisha*, and the air was full of a buzz produced by the rapid reiteration of this uncouth word by fifty tongues. This conveyance is a feature of Japan, growing in importance every day. It was only invented seven years ago, and already there are nearly 23,000 in one city, and men can make so much more by drawing them than by almost any kind of skilled labour, that thousands of fine young men desert agricultural pursuits and flock into the towns to make draught-animals of themselves, though it is said that the average duration of a man's life after he takes to running is only five years, and that the runners fall victims in large numbers to aggravated forms of heart and lung disease. Over tolerably level ground a good runner can trot forty miles a day, at a rate of about four miles an hour. They are registered and taxed at eight shillings. a year for one carrying two persons, and four shillings. for one which carries one only, and there is a regular tariff for time and distance.

The *kuruma* consists of a light perambulator body, an adjustable hood of oiled paper, a velvet or cloth lining and cushion, a well for parcels under the seat, two high slim wheels, and a pair of shafts connected by a bar at the ends. The body is usually lacquered and decorated according to its owner's taste. Some show little except polished brass, others are altogether inlaid with shells known as Venus's ear, and others are gaudily painted with contorted dragons, or groups of peonies, hydrangeas, chrysanthemums, and mythical personages. They cost from two pounds upwards. The shafts rest on the ground at a steep incline as you get in—it must require much practice to enable one to mount with ease or dignity—the runner lifts them up, gets into them, gives the body a good tilt backwards, and goes off at a smart trot. They are drawn by one, two, or three men, according to the speed desired by the occupants. When rain comes on, the man puts up the hood, and ties you and it closely up in a covering of oiled paper, in which you are invisible.

At night, whether running or standing still, they carry prettily painted circular paper lanterns eighteen inches long. It is most comical to see stout, florid, solid-looking merchants, missionaries, male and female, fashionably dressed ladies, armed with card cases, Chinese compradores, and Japanese peasant men and women flying along Main Street, which is like the decent respectable high street of a dozen forgotten country towns in England, in happy unconsciousness of the ludicrousness of their appearance. Racing, chasing, crossing each other, their lean, polite, pleasant runners in their great hats shaped like inverted bowls, their incomprehensible blue tights, and their short blue overshirts with badges or characters in white upon them, tearing along, their yellow faces streaming with perspiration, laughing, shouting, and avoiding collisions by a mere shave.

4

After a visit to the consulate I entered a *kuruma* and, with two ladies in two more, was bowled along at a furious pace by a laughing little mannikin down Main Street—a narrow, solid, well-paved street with well-made side walks, kerbstones, and gutters, with iron lampposts, gas lamps, and foreign shops all along its length—to this quiet hotel recommended by Sir Wyville Thomson, which offers a refuge from the nasal twang of my fellow voyagers, who have all gone to the caravanserais on the Bund. The host is a Frenchman, but he relies on a Chinaman. The servants are Japanese "boys" in Japanese clothes. And there is a Japanese "groom of the chambers" in faultless English costume, who perfectly appals me by the elaborate politeness of his manner.

Almost as soon as I arrived I was obliged to go in search of Mr. Fraser's office in the settlement. I say *search*, for there are no names on the streets. Where there are numbers they have no sequence, and I met no Europeans on foot to help me in my difficulty. Yokohama does not improve on further acquaintance. It has a dead-alive look. It has irregularity without pic-turesqueness, and the grey sky, grey sea, grey houses, and grey roofs, look harmoniously dull.

No foreign money except the Mexican dollar passes in Japan, and Mr. Fraser's compradore soon metamorphosed my English gold into Japanese *satsu* or paper money, a bundle of yen nearly at par just now with the dollar, packets of fifty, twenty, and ten *sen* notes, and some rolls of very neat copper coins. The initiated recognize the different denominations of paper money at a glance by their differing colors and sizes, but at present they are a distracting mystery to me. The notes are pieces of stiff paper with Chinese characters at the corners, near which, with exceptionally good eyes or a magnifying glass, one can discern an English word denoting the value. They are very neatly executed, and are ornamented with the chrysanthemum crest of the emperor and the interlaced dragons of the empire.

I long to get away into real Japan. Hiram Shaw Wilkinson, the acting British consul, called yesterday, and was extremely kind. He thinks that my plan for travelling in the interior is rather too ambitious, but that it is perfectly safe for a lady to travel alone, and agrees with everybody else in thinking that legions of fleas and the miserable horses are the great drawbacks of Japanese travelling.

Kurumaya

Today has been spent in making new acquaintances, instituting a search for a servant and a pony, receiving many offers of help, asking questions and receiving from different people answers which directly contradict each other. Hours are early. Thirteen people called on me before noon. Ladies drive themselves about the town in small pony carriages attended by running footmen called *bettō*. The foreign merchants keep *kuruma* constantly standing at their doors, finding a willing, intelligent *kurumaya* much more serviceable than a lazy, fractious, capricious Japanese pony, and even the dignity of an Ambassador Extraordinary and minister Plenipotentiary is not above such a lowly conveyance, as I have seen today. My last visitors were Sir Harry and Lady Parkes, who brought sunshine and kindliness into the room, and left it behind them. Sir Harry is a young-looking man scarcely in middle life, slight, active, fair, blue-eyed, a thorough Saxon, with sunny hair and a sunny smile, a sunshiny geniality in his manner, and bearing no trace in his appearance of his thirty years of service in the East, his sufferings in prison at Beijing, and the various attempts upon his life in Japan. He and Lady Parkes were most truly kind, and encourage me so heartily in my largest projects for travelling in the interior, that I shall start as soon as I have secured a servant. When they went away they jumped into *kuruma*, and it was most amusing to see the representative of England hurried down the street in a perambulator with a tandem of *kurumaya*.

As I look out of the window I see heavy, two-wheeled man carts drawn and pushed by four men each, on which nearly all goods, stones for building, and all else, are carried. The two men who pull press with hands and thighs against a crossbar at the end of a heavy pole, and the two who push apply their shoulders to beams which project behind, using their thick, smooth-ly-shaven skulls as the motive power when they push their heavy loads uphill. Their cry is impressive and melancholy. They draw incredible loads, but, as if the toil which often makes every breath a groan or a gasp were not enough, they shout incessantly with a coarse, guttural grunt, something like "*Ha huida, ho huida, wa ho, ha huida*."

Edo and Tokyo

British legation, Tokyo, May 24

I have dated my letter Edo, according to the usage of the British legation, but popularly the new name of Tokyo, or Eastern Capital, is used. Kyoto, the emperor's former residence, has received the name of Saikyo, or Western Capital, though it has now no claim to be regarded as a capital at all.[1] Tokyo belongs to the old regime and the Shogunate, Tokyo to the new regime and the Restoration, with their history of ten years. It would seem an incongruity to travel to Tokyo by railway, but quite proper when the destination is Tokyo.

The journey between Yokohama and Tokyo is performed in an hour by an admirable, well-metalled, double track railroad, eighteen miles long, with iron bridges, neat stations, and substantial roomy termini, built by English engineers at a cost known only to government, and opened by the emperor in 1872. The Yokohama station is a handsome and suitable stone building, with a spacious approach, ticket offices on our plan, roomy waiting rooms for different classes— uncarpeted in consideration of Japanese clogs, or *geta*—and supplied with the daily papers. There is a department for the weighing and labelling of luggage, and on the broad, covered, stone platform at both termini a barrier with turnstiles, through which, except by special favor, no ticketless person can pass. Except the ticket clerks, who are Chinese, and the guards and engine drivers, who are English, the officials are Japanese in European dress. Outside the stations, instead of cabs, there

---

1 In 1868 the old capital was named Saikyō to distinguish it from the new capital of Tōkyō (without macrons in the text), yet the name was soon dropped again in favor of the former name.

are *kuruma*, which carry luggage as well as people. Only luggage in the hand is allowed to go free; the rest is weighed, numbered, and charged for, a corresponding number being given to its owner to present at his destination. The fares are—third class, an *ichibu*, or about one shilling; second class, sixty *sen*, or about two shillings and four pence; and first class, a *yen*, or about three shillings and eight pence. The tickets are collected as the passengers pass through the barrier at the end of the journey. The English-built cars differ from ours in having seats along the sides, and doors opening on platforms at both ends. On the whole, the arrangements are continental rather than British. The first class cars are expensively fitted up with deeply-cushioned, red morocco seats, but carry very few passengers, and the comfortable seats, covered with fine matting, of the second class are very scantily occupied. But the third class vans are crowded with Japanese, who have taken to railroads as readily as to *kuruma*. This line earns about eight million dollars a year.

The Japanese look most diminutive in European dress. Each garment is a misfit, and exaggerates the miserable physique and the national defects of concave chests and bow legs. The lack of "complexion" and of hair upon the face makes it nearly impossible to judge of the ages of men. I supposed that all the railroad officials were striplings of seventeen or eighteen, but they are men from twenty-five to forty years old.

It was a beautiful day, like an English June day, but hotter, and though the *sakura* (wild cherry) and its kin, which are the glory of the Japanese spring, are over, everything is a young, fresh green yet, and in all the beauty of growth and luxuriance. The immediate neighborhood of Yokohama is beautiful, with abrupt wooded hills, and small picturesque valleys. After passing Kanagawa the railroad enters upon the immense plain of Tokyo, said to be ninety miles from north to south, on whose northern and western boundaries faint blue mountains of great height hovered dreamily in the blue haze, and on whose eastern shore for many miles the clear blue wavelets of Edo Bay ripple, always as then, brightened by the white sails of innumerable fishing boats. On this fertile and fruitful plain stand not only the capital, with its million of inhabitants, but a number of populous cities, and several hundred thriving agricultural villages. Every foot of land which can be seen from the railroad is cultivated by the most careful spade husbandry, and much of it is irrigated for rice. Streams abound, and villages of grey wooden houses with grey thatch, and grey temples with strangely curved roofs, are scattered thickly over the landscape. It is all homelike, liveable, and pretty, the country of an industrious people, for not a weed is to be seen, but no very striking features or peculiarities arrest one at first sight, unless it be the crowds everywhere.

You don't take your ticket for Tokyo, but for Shinagawa or Shinbashi, two of the many villages which have grown together into the capital. Tokyo is hardly seen before Shinagawa is reached, for it has no smoke and no long chimneys. Its temples and public buildings are seldom lofty; the former are often concealed among thick trees, and its ordinary houses seldom reach a height of twenty feet. On the right a blue sea with fortified islands upon it, wooded gardens with massive retaining walls, hundreds of fishing boats lying in creeks or drawn up on the beach. On the left a broad road on which *kuruma* are hurrying both ways, rows of low, grey houses, mostly teahouses and shops.

As I was asking "Where is Tokyo?" the train came to rest in the terminus, the Shinbashi railroad station, and disgorged its two hundred Japanese passengers with a combined clatter of four hundred *geta*—a new sound to me. These *geta* add three inches to their height, but even with them few of the men attained five feet inches, and few of the women five feet two inches. But they look far broader in the national costume, which also conceals the defects of their figures. So lean, so yellow, yet so pleasant-looking, so wanting in color and effectiveness. The women so very small and tottering in their walk; the children so formal-looking and such dignified burlesques on the adults, I feel as if I had seen them all before, so like are they to their pictures on trays, fans, and teapots. The hair of the women is all drawn away from their faces, and is worn in chignons, and the men, when they don't shave the front of their heads and gather their back hair into a quaint queue drawn forward over the shaven patch, wear their coarse hair about three inches long in a refractory undivided mop.

Davies, an orderly from the legation, met me,—one of the escort cut down and severely wounded when Sir Harry Parkes was attacked in the street of Kyoto in March 1868 on his way to his first audience of the emperor. Hundreds of *kuruma*, and covered carts with four wheels drawn by one miserable horse, which are the omnibuses of certain districts of Tokyo, were waiting outside the station, and an English brougham for me, with a running *bettō*. The legation stands in Kojimachi on very elevated ground above the inner moat of the historic Edo castle. On my way there I saw miles of dark, silent, barrack-like buildings, with highly ornamental gateways, and long rows of projecting windows with screens made of reeds—the feudal mansions of Edo—and miles of moats with lofty grass embankments or walls of massive masonry fifty feet high, with kiosk-like towers at the corners, and curious, roofed gateways, and many bridges, and acres of lotus leaves.

Turning along the inner moat, up a steep slope, there are, on the right, its deep green waters, the great grass embankment surmounted by a dismal wall overhung by the branches of coniferous trees which surrounded the palace of the *shōgun*, and on the left sundry *yashiki*, as the mansions of the *daimyō* were called, now in this quarter mostly turned into hospitals, barracks, and government offices.

On a height, the most conspicuous of them all, is the great red gateway of the *yashiki*, now occupied by the French military mission, formerly the residence of Ii Naosuke, one of the great actors in recent historic events, who was assassinated not far off, outside the Sakaruda gate of the castle. Besides these, barracks, parade grounds, policemen, *kuruma*, carts pulled and pushed by kurumaya, packhorses in straw sandals, and dwarfish, slatternly-looking soldiers in European dress, made up the Tokyo that I saw between Shinbashi and the legation.

The british legation has a good situation near the Foreign Office, several of the government departments, and the residences of the ambassadors, which are chiefly of brick in the English suburban villa style. Within the compound, with a brick archway with the royal arms upon it for an entrance, are the ambassador's residence, the chancery, two houses for the two English secretaries of legation, and quarters for the escort.

It is an English house and an English home, though, with the exception of a venerable nurse, there are no English servants. The butler and footman are tall Chinamen, with long pigtails, black satin caps, and long blue robes. The cook is a Chinaman, and the other servants are all Japanese, including one female servant, a sweet, gentle, kindly girl about four feet five in height, the wife of the head "housemaid." None of the servants speak anything but the most aggravating pidgin English, but their deficient speech is more than made up for by the intelligence and service of the orderly in waiting, who is rarely absent from the neighborhood of the hall door, and attends to the visitors' book and to all messages and notes. There are two English children of six and seven, with great capacities for such innocent enjoyments as can be found within the limits of the nursery and garden. The other inmate of the house is a beautiful and attractive terrier called Rags, a Skye dog, who unbends in the bosom of his family, but ordinarily is as imposing in his demeanor as if he, and not his master, represented the dignity of the British empire.

The Japanese secretary of legation is Ernest Satow, whose reputation for scholarship, especially in the department of history, is said by the Japanese themselves to be the highest in Japan. Often in the later months of my residence in Japan, when I asked educated Japanese questions concerning their history, religions, or ancient customs, I was put off with the answer, "You should ask Mr. Satow, he could tell you"—an honorable distinction for an Englishman, and won by the persevering industry of fifteen years.

The scholarship connected with the British Civil Service is not monopolized by Ernest Satow, for several gentlemen in the consular service, who are passing through the various grades of student interpreters, are distinguishing themselves not alone by their facility in colloquial Japanese, but by their researches in various departments of Japanese history, mythology, archaeology, and literature. Indeed it is to their labours, and to those of a few other Englishmen and Germans, that the Japanese of the rising generation will be indebted for keeping alive not only the knowledge of their archaic literature, but even of the manners and customs of the first half of this century.

A Solemn Contract

I went to Yokohama for a week to visit the Hepburns on the Bluff. Bishop and Mrs. Burdon of Hong Kong were also guests, and it was very pleasant.

One cannot be a day in Yokohama without seeing quite a different class of orientals from the small, thinly-dressed, and usually poor-looking Japanese. Of the 2500 Chinamen who reside in Japan, over 1100 are in Yokohama, and if they were suddenly removed, business would come to an abrupt halt.

Here, as everywhere, the Chinese immigrant is making himself indispensable. He walks through the streets with his swinging gait and air of complete self-complacency, as though he belonged to the ruling race. He is tall and big, and his many garments, with a handsome brocaded robe over all, his satin pantaloons, of which not much is seen, tight at the ankles, and his high shoes, whose black satin tops are slightly turned up at the toes, make him look even taller and bigger than he is. His head is mostly shaven, but the hair at the back is plaited with a quantity of black purse twist into a queue which reaches to his knees, above which, set well back, he wears a stiff, black satin skullcap, without which he is never seen. His face is very yellow, his long dark eyes and eyebrows slope upwards towards his temples, he has not the vestige of a beard, and his skin is shiny. He looks thoroughly "well-to-do." He is not unpleasing-looking, but you feel that as a celestial he looks down upon you. If you ask a question in a merchant's office, or change your gold into *satsu*, or take your railroad or steamer ticket, or get change in a shop, the inevitable Chinaman appears. In the street he swings

13

past you with a purpose in his face; as he flies past you in a *kuruma* he is bent on business; he is sober and reliable, and is content to "squeeze" his employer rather than to rob him—his one aim in life is money. For this he is industrious, faithful, self-denying; and he has his reward.

Several of my kind new acquaintances interested themselves about the (to me) vital matter of a servant interpreter, and many Japanese came to "see after the place." The speaking of intelligible English is a *sine qua non*, and it was wonderful to find the few words badly pronounced and worse put together, which were regarded by the candidates as a sufficient qualification. Can you speak English? "Yes." What wages do you ask? "Twelve dollars a month." This was always said glibly, and in each case sounded hopeful. Whom have you lived with? A foreign name distorted out of all recognition, as was natural, was then given. Where have you travelled? This question usually had to be translated into Japanese, and the usual answer was, "The Tokaidō, the Nakasendō, to Kyoto, to Nikkō," naming the beaten tracks of countless tourists. Do you know anything of Northern Japan and Hokkaido? "No," with a blank wondering look.

At this stage in every case Dr. Hepburn compassionately stepped in as interpreter, for their stock of English was exhausted. Three were regarded as promising. One was a sprightly youth who came in a well-made European suit of light-colored tweed, a laid-down collar, a tie with a diamond (?) pin, and a white shirt, so stiffly starched, that he could hardly bend low enough for a bow even of European profundity. He wore a gilt watch chain with a locket, the corner of a very white cambric pocket handkerchief dangled from his breast pocket, and he held a cane and a felt hat in his hand. He was a Japanese dandy of the first water. I looked at him ruefully. To me starched collars are to be an unknown luxury for the next three months. His fine foreign clothes would enhance prices everywhere in the interior, and besides that, I should feel a perpetual difficulty in asking menial services from an exquisite. I was therefore quite relieved when his English broke down at the second question.

The second was a most respectable-looking man of thirty-five in a good Japanese dress. He was highly recommended, and his first English words were promising, but he had been cook in the service of a wealthy English official who travelled with a large retinue, and sent servants on ahead to prepare the way. He knew really only a few words of English, and his horror at finding that there was "no master," and that there would be no woman-servant, was so great, that I hardly know whether he rejected me or I him.

The third, sent by Wilkinson, wore a plain Japanese dress, and had a frank, intelligent face. Though Dr. Hepburn spoke with him in Japanese, he thought that he knew more English than the others, and that what he knew would come out when he was less agitated. He evidently understood what I said, and, though I had a suspicion that he would turn out to be the "master," I thought him so prepossessing that I nearly engaged him on the spot. None of the others merit any remark.

However, when I had nearly made up my mind in his favor, a creature appeared without any recommendation at all, except that one of Dr. Hepburn's servants was acquainted with him. He is only eighteen, but this is equivalent to twenty-three or twenty-four with us, and only four feet ten inches in height, but, though bandy-legged, is well proportioned and strong-looking. He has a round and singularly plain face, good teeth, much elongated eyes, and the heavy droop of his eyelids almost caricatures the usual Japanese peculiarity. He is the most stupid-looking Japanese I have seen, but, from a rapid, furtive glance in his eyes now and then, I think that the stolidity is partly assumed. He said that he had lived at the American legation, that he had been a clerk on the Osaka railroad, that he had travelled through northern Japan by the eastern route, and in Ezo with Charles Maries, a botanical collector, that he understood drying plants, that he could cook a little, that he could write English, that he could walk twenty-five miles a day, and that he thoroughly understood getting through the interior!

This would-be paragon had no recommendations, and accounted for this by saying that they had been burned in a recent fire in his father's house. Maries was not forthcoming, and more than this, I suspected and disliked the boy. However, he understood my English and I his, and, being very anxious to begin my travels, I engaged him for twelve dollars a month, and soon afterwards he came back with a contract, in which he declares by all that he holds most sacred that he will serve me faithfully for the wages agreed upon, and to this document he affixed his seal and I my name. The next day he asked me for a month's wages in advance, which I gave him, but Dr. Hepburn consolingly suggested that I should never see him again!

Ever since the solemn night when the contract was signed I have felt under an incubus, and since he appeared here yesterday, punctual to the appointed hour, I have felt as if I had a veritable "old man of the sea" upon my shoulders. He flies up stairs and along the corridors as noiselessly as a cat, and already knows where I keep all my things. Nothing surprises or abashes him, he bows profoundly to Sir Harry and Lady Parkes when he encounters them, but is obviously quite at home in a legation, and only allowed one of the orderlies to show him how to put on a Mexican saddle and English bridle out of condescension to my wishes. He seems as sharp or smart as can be, and has already arranged for the first three days of my journey. His name is Itō, and you will doubtless hear much more of him, as he will be my good or evil genius for the next three months.

As no English lady has yet travelled alone through the interior, my project excites a very friendly interest among my friends, and I receive much warning and dissuasion, and a little encouragement. The strongest, because the most intelligent, dissuasion comes from Dr. Hepburn, who thinks that I ought not to undertake the journey, and that I shall never get through to the Tsugaru Strait. If I accepted much of the advice given to me, as to taking tinned meats and soups, claret, and a Japanese maid, I should need a train of at least six packhorses! As fleas, there is a lamentable concensus of opinion that they are the curse of Japanese travelling during the summer, and some people recommend me to sleep in a bag drawn tightly round the throat, others to sprinkle my bedding freely with insect powder, others to smear the skin all over with carbolic oil, and some to make a plentiful use of dried and powdered flea-bane. All admit, however, that these are but feeble palliatives. Hammocks unfortunately cannot be used in Japanese houses.

The "food question" is said to be the most important one for all travellers, and it is discussed continually with startling earnestness, not alone as regards my tour. However apathetic people are on other subjects, the mere mention of this one rouses them into interest. All have suffered or may suffer, and every one wishes to impart his own experience or to learn from that of others. Foreign ambassadors, professors, missionaries, merchants— all discuss it with becoming gravity as a question of life and death, which by many it is supposed to be. The fact is that, except at a few hotels in popular resorts which are got up for foreigners, bread, butter, milk, meat, poultry, coffee, wine, and beer, are unattainable, that fresh fish is rare, and that unless one can live on rice, tea, and eggs, with the addition now and then of some tasteless fresh vegetables, food must be taken, as the fishy and vegetable abominations known as Japanese food can only be swallowed and digested by a few, and that after long practice.

Another, but far inferior, difficulty on which much stress is laid is the practice common among native servants of getting a squeeze out of every money transaction on the road, so that the cost of travelling is often doubled, and sometimes trebled, according to the skill and capacity of the servant. Three gentlemen who have travelled extensively have given me lists of the prices which I ought to pay, varying in different districts, and largely increased on the beaten track of tourists, and Wilkinson has read these to Itō, who offered an occasional remonstrance. Wilkinson remarked after the conversation, which was in Japanese, that he thought I should have to "look sharp after money matters"—a painful prospect, as I have never been able to manage anybody in my life, and shall surely have no control over this clever, cunning Japanese youth, who on most points will be able to deceive me as he pleases.

On returning here I found that Lady Parkes had made most of the necessary preparations for me, and that they include two light baskets with covers of oiled paper, a travelling bed or stretcher, a folding-chair, and an india-rubber bath, all which she considers as necessaries for a person in feeble health on a journey of such long duration. This week has been spent in making acquaintances in Tokyo, seeing some characteristic sights, and in trying to get light on my tour. Foreigners seem to know little of northern Japan, and a government department, on being applied to, returned an itinerary, leaving out 140 miles of the route that I dream of taking, on the ground of "insufficient information," on which Sir Harry cheerily remarked, "You will have to get your information as you go along, and that will be all the more interesting." Ah! but how?

Kannon Temple

British legation, Tokyo, June 9
Once for all I will describe a Buddhist temple, and it shall be the popular temple of Asakusa, which keeps fair and festival the whole year round, and is dedicated to the "thousand-armed" Kannon, the goddess of mercy. Writing generally, it may be said that in design, roof, and general aspect, Japanese Buddhist temples are all alike.

The sacred architectural idea expresses itself in nearly the same form always. There is a single or double-roofed gateway, with highly-colored figures in niches on either side; the paved temple-court, with more or fewer stone or bronze lanterns; *amainu*, or heavenly dogs, in stone on stone pedestals; stone sarcophagi, roofed over or not, for holy water; a flight of steps; a portico, continued as a verandah all round the temple; a roof of tremendously disproportionate size and weight, with a peculiar curve; a square or oblong hall divided by a railing from a chancel with a high and low altar, and a shrine containing Buddha, or the divinity to whom the chapel is dedicated; an incense-burner, and a few ecclesiastical ornaments.

The symbols, idols, and adornments depend upon the sect to which the temple belongs, or the wealth of its votaries, or the fancy of the priests. Some temples are packed full of gods, shrines, banners, bronzes, brasses, tablets, and ornaments, and others, like those of the Monto sect, are so severely simple, that with scarcely an alteration they might be used for Christian worship tomorrow.

The foundations consist of square stones on which the uprights rest. These are of elm, and are united at intervals by longitudinal pieces. The great size and enormous weight of the roofs arise from the trusses being formed of one heavy frame being built upon another in diminishing squares till the top is reached, the main beams being formed of very large timbers put on in their natural state. They are either very heavily and ornamentally tiled, or covered with sheet copper ornamented with gold, or thatched to a depth from one to three feet, with fine shingles or bark. The casing of the walls on the outside is usually thick elm planking either lacquered or unpainted, and that of the inside is of thin, finely-planed and bevelled planking of the beautiful cypress. The lining of the roof is in flat panels, and where it is supported by pillars they are invariably circular, and formed of the straight, finely-grained stem of the cypress. The projecting ends of the roof-beams under the eaves are either elaborately carved, lacquered in dull red, or covered with copper, as are the joints of the beams. Very few nails are used, the timbers being very beautifully joined by mortices and dovetails, other methods of junction being unknown.

Basil Hall Chamberlain and I went in a *kuruma* hurried along by three liveried kurumaya, through the three miles of crowded streets which lie between the legation and Asakusa, once a village, but now incorporated with this monster city, to the broad street leading to the Azuma bridge over the Sumida River, one of the few stone bridges in Tokyo, which connects east Tokyo, an uninteresting region, containing many canals, storehouses, timber yards, and inferior *yashiki*, with the rest of the city. This street, marvellously thronged with pedestrians and *kuruma*, is the terminus of a number of city "stage lines." Twenty wretched-looking covered waggons, with still more wretched ponies, were drawn up in the middle, waiting for passengers. Just there plenty of real Tokyo life is to be seen, for near a shrine of popular pilgrimage there are always numerous places of amusement, innocent and vicious, and the vicinity of this temple is full of restaurants, teahouses, minor theatres, and the resorts of dancing and singing girls.

A broad-paved avenue, only open to foot passengers, leads from this street to the grand entrance, a colossal two-storied double-roofed *mon*, or gate, painted a rich dull red. On either side of this avenue are lines of booths—which make a brilliant and lavish display of their contents—toy shops, shops for smoking apparatus, and shops for the sale of ornamental hair-pins predominating. Nearer the gate are booths for the sale of rosaries for prayer, sleeve and bosom idols of brass and wood in small shrines, amulet bags, representations of the jolly-looking Daikoku, the god of wealth, the most popular of the household gods of Japan, shrines, memorial tablets, cheap ex votos, sacred bells, candlesticks, and incense-burners, and all the endless and various articles connected with Buddhist devotion, public and private. Every day is a festival-day at Asakusa. The temple is dedicated to the most popular of the great divinities. It is the most popular of religious resorts. And whether he be Buddhist, Shintoist, or Christian, no stranger comes to the capital without making a visit to its crowded courts or a purchase at its tempting booths. Not to be an exception, I invested in bouquets of firework flowers, fifty flowers for two *sen*, each of which, as it slowly consumes, throws off fiery coruscations, shaped like the most beautiful of snow crystals. I was also tempted by small boxes at two *sen* each, containing what look like little slips of withered pith, but which, on being dropped into water, expand into trees and flowers.

Down a paved passage on the right there is an artificial river, not very clean, with a bridge formed of one curved stone, from which a flight of steps leads up to a small temple with a magnificent bronze bell. At the entrance several women were praying. In the same direction are two fine bronze Buddhas, seated figures, one with clasped hands, the other holding a lotus, both with "The light of the world" upon their brows. The grand red gateway into the actual temple courts has an extremely imposing effect. It is the portal to the first great heathen temple that I have seen, and it made me think of another temple whose courts were equally crowded with buyers and sellers, and of a "whip of small cords" in the hand of One who claimed both the temple and its courts as His "Father's House." Not with less righteous wrath would the gentle founder of Buddhism purify the unsanctified courts of Asakusa.

Hundreds of men, women, and children passed to and fro through the gateway in incessant streams, and so they are passing through every daylight hour of every day in the year, thousands becoming tens of thousands on the great *matsuri* (festival) days, when the *mikoshi*, or portable shrine, containing certain symbols of the god, is exhibited, and after sacred mimes and dances have been performed, is carried in a magnificent, antique procession to the shore and back again.

Under the gateway on either side are the *Niō*, or two kings, gigantic figures in flowing robes, one red and with an open mouth, representing the Yang, or male principle of Chinese philosophy, the other green and with the mouth firmly closed, representing the Yin, or female principle.[1] They are hideous creatures, with protruding eyes, and faces and figures distorted and corrupted into a high degree of exaggerated and convulsive action. These figures guard the gates of most of the larger temples, and small prints of them are pasted over the doors of houses to protect them against burglars. Attached to the grating in front were a number of straw sandals, hung up by people who pray that their limbs may be as muscular as those of the *Niō*.

Passing through this gate we were in the temple court proper. In front of the temple itself was a building of imposing height and size, of a dull red color, with a grand roof of heavy iron grey tiles, with a sweeping curve which gives grace as well as grandeur. The timbers and supports are solid and of great size, but, in common with all Japanese temples, whether Buddhist or Shinto, the edifice is entirely of wood. A broad flight of narrow, steep, brass-bound steps lead up to the porch, which is formed by a number of circular pillars supporting a very lofty roof, from which hang paper lanterns ten feet long. A gallery runs from this round the temple, under cover of the eaves. There is an outer temple, unmatted, and an inner one behind a grating, into which those who choose to pay for the privilege of praying in comparative privacy, or of having prayers said for them by the priests, can pass.

In the outer temple the noise, confusion, and perpetual motion, are bewildering. Crowds on clattering *geta* pass in and out. Pigeons, of which hundreds live in the porch, fly over your head, and the whirring of their wings mingles with the tinkling of bells, the beating of drums and gongs, the high-pitched drone of the priests, the low murmur of prayers, the rippling laughter of girls, the harsh voices of men, and the general buzz of a multitude. There is very much that is highly grotesque at first sight. Men squat on the floor selling amulets, rosaries, printed prayers, incense sticks,

---

1 In fact, the right statue, called Misshaku Kongō, has its mouth open, representing the vocalization of the first grapheme of the Sanskrit alphabet, which is pronounced "a." The left statue, called Naraen Kongō, has its mouth closed, representing the vocalization of the alphabet's last grapheme, which is pronounced "un." Thus the two characters together symbolize the birth and death of all things.

and other wares. Ex votos of all kinds hang on the wall and on the great round pillars. Many of these are rude Japanese pictures. The subject of one is the blowing-up of a steamer in the Sumidagawa with the loss of one hundred lives, when the donor was saved by the grace of Kannon. Numbers of memorials are from people who offered up prayers here, and have been restored to health or wealth. Others are from *bezaisen* sailors whose lives have been in peril. There are scores of men's queues and a few dusty braids of women's hair offered on account of vows or prayers, usually for sick relatives, and among them all, on the left hand, are a large mirror in a gaudily gilt frame and a framed picture of the P.M.S. China! Above this incongruous collection are splendid wood carvings and frescoes of angels, among which the pigeons find a home free from molestation.

Near the entrance there is a superb incense-burner in the most massive style of the older bronzes, with a mythical beast rampant upon it, and in high relief round it the Japanese signs of the zodiac—the rat, ox, tiger, rabbit, dragon, serpent, horse, goat, monkey, cock, dog, and hog. Clouds of incense rise continually from the perforations round the edge, and a black-toothed woman who keeps it burning is perpetually receiving small coins from the worshippers, who then pass on to the front of the altar to pray. The high altar, and indeed all that I should regard as properly the temple, are protected by a screen of coarsely-netted iron wire. This holy of holies is full of shrines and gods, gigantic candlesticks, colossal lotuses of gilded silver, offerings, lamps, lacquer, litany books, gongs, drums, bells, and all the mysterious symbols of a faith which is a system of morals and metaphysics to the educated and initiated, and an idolatrous superstition to the masses. In this interior the light was dim, the lamps burned low, the atmosphere was heavy with incense, and amidst its fumes shaven priests in chasubles and stoles moved noiselessly over the soft matting round the high altar on which Kannon is enshrined, lighting candles, striking bells, and murmuring prayers. In front of the screen is the treasury, a wooden chest fourteen feet by ten, with a deep slit, into which all the worshippers cast copper coins with a ceaseless clinking sound.

There, too, they pray, if that can be called prayer which frequently consists only in the repetition of an uncomprehended phrase in a foreign tongue, bowing the head, raising the hands and rubbing them, murmuring a few words, telling beads, clapping the hands, bowing again, and then passing out or on to another shrine to repeat the same form. Merchants in silk clothing, soldiers in shabby French uniforms, farmers, kurumaya in "vile raiment," mothers, maidens, swells in European clothes, even the samurai policemen, bow before the goddess of mercy. Most of the prayers were offered rapidly, a mere momentary interlude in the gurgle of careless talk, and without a pretense of reverence; but some of the petitioners obviously brought real woes in simple faith.

In one shrine there is a large idol, spotted all over with pellets of paper, and hundreds of these are sticking to the wire netting which protects him. A worshipper writes his petition on paper, or, better still, has it written for him by the priest, chews it to a pulp, and spits it at the divinity. If, having been well aimed, it passes through the wire and sticks, it is a good omen, if it lodges in the netting the prayer has probably been unheard. The *Niō* and some of the gods outside the temple are similarly disfigured.

On the left there is a shrine with a screen, to the bars of which innumerable prayers have been tied. On the right, accessible to all, sits Binzuru, one of Buddha's original sixteen disciples. His face and appearance have been calm and amiable, with something of the quiet dignity of an elderly country gentleman of the reign of George III. But he is now worn and defaced, and has not much more of eyes, nose, and mouth than the Sphinx. The polished, red lacquer has disappeared from his hands and feet, for Binzuru is a great medicine god, and centuries of sick people have rubbed his face and limbs, and then have rubbed their own.

A young woman went up to the statue, rubbed the back of its neck, and then rubbed her own. Then a modest-looking girl, leading an ancient woman with badly inflamed eyelids and paralysed arms, rubbed its eyelids, and then gently stroked the closed eyelids of the crone. Then a laborer, with a swelled knee, applied himself vigorously to Binzuru's knee, and more gently to his own. This is the great temple of the populace, and not many rich, not many noble, not many mighty, enter its dim, dirty, crowded halls. I visited this temple alone many times afterwards, and each visit deepened the interest of my first impressions. There is always enough of change and novelty to prevent the interest from flagging, and the mild, but profoundly superstitious, form of heathenism which prevails in Japan is nowhere better represented.

But the great temple to Kannon is not the only sight of Asakusa. Outside it are countless shrines and temples, huge stone *amainu*, or heavenly dogs, on rude blocks of stone, large cisterns of stone and bronze with and without canopies, containing water for the ablutions of the worshippers, cast iron Amainu on hewn stone pedestals—a recent gift—bronze and stone lanterns, a stone prayer-wheel in a stone post, figures of Buddha with the serene countenance of one who rests from his labours, stone idols, on which devotees have pasted slips of paper inscribed with prayers, with sticks of incense rising out of the ashes of hundreds of former sticks smouldering before them, blocks of hewn stone with Chinese and Sanskrit inscriptions, an eight-sided temple in which are figures of the Five Hundred Disciples of Buddha, a temple with the roof and upper part of the walls richly colored, the circular Shinto mirror in an inner shrine, a bronze treasury outside with a bell, which is rung to attract the god's attention, a striking, five-storied pagoda, with much red lacquer, and the ends of the roof-beams very boldly carved, its heavy eaves fringed with wind bells, and its uppermost roof terminating in a graceful copper spiral of great height, with the sacred pearl surrounded by flames for its finial. Near it, as near most temples, is an upright frame of plain wood with tablets, on which are inscribed the names of donors to the temple, and the amount of their gifts.

There is a handsome stone-floored temple to the south-east of the main building, to which we were the sole visitors. It is lofty and very richly decorated. In the centre is an octagonal revolving room, or rather shrine, of rich red lacquer most gorgeously ornamented. It rests on a frame of carved black lacquer, and has a lacquer gallery running round it, on which several richly decorated doors open. On the application of several shoulders to this gallery the shrine rotates. It is, in fact, a revolving library of the Buddhist Scriptures, and a single turn is equivalent to a single pious perusal of them. It is an exceedingly beautiful specimen of ancient decorative lacquer work. At the back part of the temple is a draped brass figure of Buddha, with one hand raised—a dignified piece of casting. All the Buddhas have Hindoo features, and the graceful drapery and oriental repose which have been imported from India contrast singularly with the grotesque extravagances of the indigenous Japanese conceptions.

In the same temple are four monstrously extravagant figures carved in wood, life-size, with clawed toes on their feet, and two great fangs in addition to the teeth in each mouth. The heads of all are surrounded with flames, and are backed by golden circlets. They are extravagantly clothed in garments which look as if they were agitated by a violent wind. They wear helmets and partial suits of armour, and hold in their right hands something between a monarch's sceptre and a priest's staff. They have goggle eyes and open mouths, and their faces are in distorted and exaggerated action. One, painted bright red, tramples on a writhing devil painted bright pink. Another, painted emerald green, tramples on a sea-green devil, an indigo blue monster tramples on a sky-blue fiend, and a bright pink monster treads under his clawed feet a flesh-colored demon. I was much inclined to sympathize with the more innocent-looking fiends whom they were mal-treating. They occur very frequently in Buddhist temples, and are said by some to be assistant-torturers to Enma, the lord of hell, and are called by others "The gods of the Four Quarters."

The temple grounds are a most extraordinary sight. No English fair in the palmiest days of fairs ever presented such an array of attractions. Behind the temple are archery galleries in numbers, where girls, hardly so mod-est-looking as usual, smile and smirk, and bring straw-colored tea in dainty cups, and tasteless sweetmeats on lacquer trays, and smoke their tiny pipes, and offer you bows of slender bamboo strips, two feet long, with rests for the arrows, and tiny cherry-wood arrows, bone-tipped, and feathered red, blue, and white, and smilingly, but quite unobtrusively, ask you to try your skill or luck at a target hanging in front of a square drum, flanked by red cushions. A click, a boom, or a hardly audible thud, indicate the result. Nearly all the archers were grown-up men, and many of them spend hours at a time in this childish sport.

All over the grounds booths with the usual charcoal fire, copper boiler, iron kettle of curious workmanship, tiny cups, fragrant aroma of tea, and winsome, graceful girls, invite you to drink and rest, and more solid but less inviting refreshments are also to be had. Rows of pretty paper lanterns decorate all the stalls. Then there are photograph galleries, mimic tea gardens, tableaux in which a large number of groups of life-size figures with appropriate scenery are put into motion by a creaking wheel of great size, matted lounges for rest, stands with saucers of rice, beans and peas for offerings to the gods, the pigeons, and the two sacred horses, Albino ponies, with pink eyes and noses, revoltingly greedy creatures, eating all day long and still craving for more. There are booths for singing and dancing, and under one a professional story-teller was reciting to a densely packed crowd one of the old, popular stories of crime. There are booths where for a few *rin* you may have the pleasure of feeding some very ugly and greedy apes, or of watching mangy monkeys which have been taught to prostrate themselves Japanese fashion.

This letter is far too long, but to pass over Asakusa and its novelties when the impression of them is fresh would be to omit one of the most interesting sights in Japan. On the way back we passed red mail carts like those in London, a squadron of cavalry in European uniforms and with European saddles, and the carriage of the minister of Marine, an English brougham with a pair of horses in English harness, and an escort of six troopers—a painful precaution adopted since the assassination of Ōkubo Toshimichi, the Home Minister, three weeks ago. So the old and the new in this great city contrast with and jostle each other.

The emperor and his ministers, naval and military officers and men, the whole of the civil officials and the police, wear European clothes, as well as a number of dissipated-looking young men who aspire to represent "young Japan." Carriages and houses in English style, with carpets, chairs, and tables, are becoming increasingly numerous, and the bad taste which regulates the purchase of foreign furnishings is as marked as the good taste which everywhere presides over the adornment of the houses in purely Japanese style. Happily these expensive and unbecoming innovations have scarcely affected female dress, and some ladies who adopted our fashions have given them up because of their discomfort and manifold difficulties and complications.

The empress on state occasions appears in scarlet satin *hakama*, and flowing robes, and she and the court ladies invariably wear the national costume. I have only seen two ladies in European dress, and this was at a dinner party here. They were the wives of Mori Arinori, the Senior Vice-minister for Foreign Affairs, and of the Japanese consul at Hong Kong. Both by long residence abroad have learned to wear it with ease. The wife of

Saigo Takamori, the Minister of Education, called one day in an exquisite Japanese dress of dove-colored silk crepe, with a pale pink under-dress of the same material, which showed a little at the neck and sleeves. Her girdle was of rich dove-colored silk, with a ghost of a pale pink blossom hovering upon it here and there. She had no frills or fripperies of any description, or ornaments, except a single pin in her chignon, and, with a sweet and charming face, she looked as graceful and dignified in her Japanese costume as she would have looked exactly the reverse in ours.

Their costume has one striking advantage over ours. A woman is perfectly *clothed* if she has one garment and a girdle on, and perfectly *dressed* if she has two. There is a difference in features and expression—much exaggerate by Japanese artists—between the faces of high-born women and those of the middle and lower classes. I decline to admire fat-faces, pug noses, thick lips, long eyes, turned up at the outer corners, and complexions which owe much to powder and paint. The habit of painting the lips with a reddish-yellow pigment, and of heavily powdering the face and throat with pearl powder, is a repulsive one. But it is hard to pronounce any unfavorable criticism on women who have so much kindly grace of manner.

The Inn at Kasukabe

Kasukabe, June 10

I have started on my long journey, though not upon the unbeaten tracks, which I hope to take after leaving Nikkō, and my first evening alone in the midst of this crowded Asian life is strange, almost fearful. I have suffered from nervousness all day—the fear of being frightened, of being rudely mobbed, as threatened by John Francis Campbell, of giving offense by transgressing the rules of Japanese politeness. Itō is my sole reliance, and he may prove a "broken reed." I often wished to give up my project, but was ashamed of my cowardice when, on the best authority, I received assurances of its safety.

The preparations were finished yesterday, and my outfit weighed 110 pounds, which, with Itō's weight of 90 pounds, is as much as can be carried by an average Japanese horse. My two painted wicker boxes lined with paper and with waterproof covers are convenient for the two sides of a packhorse. I have a folding-chair—for in a Japanese house there is nothing but the floor to sit upon, and not even a solid wall to lean against—an air-pillow for *kuruma* travelling, an india-rubber bath, sheets, a blanket, and last, and more important than all else, a canvas stretcher on light poles, which can be put together in two minutes; and being two and a half feet high is supposed to be secure from fleas. The "Food Question" has been solved by a modified rejection of all advice! I have only brought a small supply of Liebig's extract of meat, 4 pounds of raisins, some chocolate, both for eating and drinking, and some brandy in case of need. I have my own Mexican saddle and bridle, a reasonable quantity of clothes, including a loose wrapper for wearing in the evenings, some candles, Richard Henry Brunton's large map of Japan, volumes of the Transactions of the English Asiatic Society, and Satow's *Anglo-Japanese Dictionary*. My travelling dress is a short costume of dust-colored striped tweed, with strong laced boots of unblacked leather, and a Japanese hat, shaped like a large inverted bowl, of light bamboo plait, with a white cotton cover, and a very light frame inside, which fits round the brow and leaves a space of one and a half inches between the hat and the head for the free circulation of air. It only weighs two and a half ounces, and is infinitely to be preferred to a heavy pith helmet, and, light as it is, it protects the head so thoroughly, that, though the sun has been unclouded all day and the mercury at 86 degrees, no other protection has been necessary. My money is in bundles of fifty yen, and fifty, twenty, and ten *sen* notes, besides which I have some rouleaux of copper coins. I have a bag for my passport, which hangs to my waist. All my luggage, with the exception of my saddle, which I use for a footstool, goes into one *kuruma*, and Itō, who is limited to twelve pounds, takes his along with him.

I have three *kuruma*, which are to go to Nikkō, ninety miles, in three days, without change of runners, for about eleven shillings each.

Passports usually define the route over which the foreigner is to travel, but in this case Sir Harry Parkes has obtained one which is practically unrestricted, for it permits me to travel through all Japan north of Tokyo and in Ezo without specifying any route. This precious document, without which I should be liable to be arrested and forwarded to my consul, is of course in Japanese, but the cover gives in English the regulations under which it is issued. A passport must be applied for, for reasons of "health, botanical research, or scientific investigation." Its bearer must not light fires in woods, attend fires on horseback, trespass on fields, enclosures, or game-preserves, scribble on temples, shrines, or walls, drive fast on a narrow road, or disregard notices of "No thoroughfare." He must "conduct himself in an orderly and conciliating manner towards the Japanese authorities and people;" he "must produce his passport to any officials who may demand it," under pain of arrest. While in the interior, he "is forbidden to shoot, trade, to conclude mercantile contracts with Japanese, or to rent houses or rooms for a longer period than his journey requires."

Nikkō, June 13

This is one of the paradises of Japan! It is a proverbial saying, "He who has not seen Nikkō must not use the word *kekkō*" (splendid, delicious, wonderful); but of this more hereafter. My attempt to write at Kasukabe failed, owing to the onslaught of an army of fleas, which compelled me to retreat to my stretcher, and the last two nights, for this and other reasons, writing has been out of the question.

I left the legation at 11 a.m. on Monday and reached Kasukabe at five p.m., the runners keeping up an easy trot the whole journey of twenty-three miles. But the halts for smoking and eating were frequent.

These *kuruma*-runners wore short blue cotton drawers, girdles with tobacco pouch and pipe attached, short blue cotton shirts with wide sleeves, and open in front, reaching to their waists, and blue cotton handkerchiefs knotted round their heads, except when the sun was very hot, when they took the flat flag discs, two feet in diameter, which always hang behind *kuruma*, and are used either in sun or rain, and tied them on their heads. They wore straw sandals, which had to be replaced twice on the way. Blue and white towels hung from the shafts to wipe away the sweat, which ran profusely down the lean, brown bodies. The upper garment always flew behind them, displaying chests and backs elaborately tattooed with dragons and fishes. Tattooing has recently been prohibited; but it was not only a favorite adornment, but a substitute for perishable clothing.

Most of the men of the lower classes wear their hair in a very ugly fashion—the front and top of the head being shaved, the long hair from the back and sides being drawn up and tied, then waxed, tied again, and cut short off, the stiff queue being brought forward and laid, pointing forwards, along the back part of the top of the head. This topknot is shaped much like a short clay pipe. The shaving and dressing the hair thus require the skill of a professional barber. Formerly the hair was worn in this way by the samurai, in order that the helmet might fit comfortably, but it is now the style of the lower classes mostly and by no means invariably.

Blithely, at a merry trot, the *kurumaya* hurried us away from the kindly group in the legation porch. They hurried us across the inner moat and along the inner drive of the castle, past gateways and retaining walls of Cyclopean masonry, across the second moat, along miles of streets of sheds and shops. All were grey, thronged with foot-passengers and *kuruma*, with packhorses loaded two or three feet above their backs, the arches of their saddles red and gilded lacquer, their frontlets of red leather, their straw sandals, their heads tied tightly to the saddle-girth on either side, great white cloths figured with mythical beasts in blue hanging down loosely under their bodies. They were thronged with laborers dragging heavy loads to the guttural cry of *Hai! huida!* and children whose heads were shaved in hideous patterns. Now and then, as if to point a moral lesson in the midst of the whirling diorama, a funeral passed through the throng, with a priest in rich robes, mumbling prayers, a covered barrel containing the corpse, and a train of mourners in blue dresses with white wings.

Then we came to the fringe of Tokyo, where the houses cease to be continuous, but all that day there was little interval between them. All had open fronts, so that the occupations of the inmates, the domestic life in fact, were perfectly visible. Many of these houses were roadside *chaya*, or teahouses, and nearly all sold sweetmeats, dried fish, pickles, *mochi*, or uncooked cakes of rice dough, dried persimmons, rain hats, or straw shoes for man or beast. The road, though wide enough for two carriages (of which we saw none), was not good, and the ditches on both sides were frequently neither clean nor sweet. Must I write it? The houses were mean, poor, shabby, often even squalid, the smells were bad, and the people looked ugly, shabby, and poor, though all were working at something or other.

The country is a dead level, and mainly an artificial mud flat or swamp, in whose fertile ooze various aquatic birds were wading, and in which hundreds of men and women were wading too, above their knees in slush. For this plain of Tokyo is mainly a great rice field, and this is the busy season of rice-planting. There are eight or nine leading varieties of rice grown in Japan, all of which, except an upland species, require mud, water, and much puddling and nasty work. Rice is the staple food and the wealth of Japan. Its revenues were estimated in rice. Rice is grown almost wherever irrigation is possible.

The rice fields are usually very small and of all shapes. A quarter of an acre is a good-sized field. The rice crop planted in June is not reaped till November, but in the meantime it needs to be "puddled" three times, i.e. for all the people to turn into the slush, and grub out all the weeds and tangled aquatic plants, which weave themselves from tuft to tuft, and puddle up the mud afresh round the roots. It grows in water till it is ripe, when the fields are dried off. An acre of the best land produces annually about fifty-four bushels of rice, and of the worst about thirty.

On the plain of Tokyo, besides the nearly continuous villages along the causewayed road, there are islands, as they may be called, of villages surrounded by trees, and hundreds of pleasant oases on which wheat ready for the sickle, onions, millet, beans, and peas, were flourishing. There were lotus ponds too, in which the glorious lily is being grown for the sacrilegious purpose of being eaten! Its splendid classical leaves are already a foot above the water.

After running cheerily for several miles my men bowled me into a teahouse, where they ate and smoked while I sat in the garden, which consisted of baked mud, smooth stepping-stones, a little pond with some goldfish, a deformed pine, and a stone lantern. Observe that foreigners are wrong in calling the Japanese houses of entertainment indiscriminately "teahouses." A teahouse or *chaya* is a house at which you can obtain tea and other refreshments, rooms to eat them in, and attendance. That which to some extent answers to an hotel is a *yadoya*, which provides sleeping accommodation and food as required. The licenses are different.

Tea-houses are of all grades, from the three-storied erections, gay with flags and lanterns, in the great cities and at places of popular resort, down to the roadside teahouse, as represented in the engraving, with three or four lounges of dark-colored wood under its eaves, usually occupied by naked laborers in all attitudes of easiness and repose. The floor is raised about eighteen inches above the ground, and in these teahouses is frequently a matted platform with a recess called the *doma*, literally "earth space," in the middle, round which runs a ledge of polished wood called the *itama*, or "board space," on which travellers sit while they bathe their soiled feet with the water which is immediately brought to them; for neither with soiled feet nor in foreign shoes must one advance one step on the matted floor. On one side of the *doma* is the kitchen, with its one or two charcoal fires, where the laborers lounge on the mats and take their food and smoke, and on the other the family pursue their avocations. In even the smallest teahouse there are one or two rooms at the back, but all the life and interest are in the open front. There is only an *irori*, a square hole in the floor, full of sand or white ash, on which the live charcoal for cooking purposes is placed, and small racks for food and eating utensils. In the large ones there is a row of charcoal stoves, and the walls are garnished up to the roof with shelves, and the lacquer tables and lacquer and china ware used by the guests. The large teahouses contain the possibilities for a number of rooms which can be extemporized at once by sliding paper panels, called *fusuma*, along grooves in the floor and in the ceiling or cross-beams.

When we stopped at wayside teahouses the runners bathed their feet, rinsed their mouths, and ate rice, pickles, salted fish, and "broth of abominable things," after which they smoked their tiny pipes, which give them three whiffs for each filling. As soon as I got out at any of these, one smiling girl brought me the *tabakobon*, a square wood or lacquer tray, with a china or bamboo charcoal-holder and ash-pot upon it, and another presented me with a *zen*, a small lacquer table about six inches high, with a tiny teapot with a hollow handle at right angles with the spout, holding about an English tea-cupful, and two cups without handles or saucers, with a capacity of from ten to twenty thimblefuls each. The hot water is merely allowed to rest a minute on the tea-leaves, and the infusion is a clear straw-colored liquid with a delicious aroma and flavor, grateful and refreshing at all times. If Japanese tea "stands," it acquires a coarse bitterness and an unwholesome astringency. Milk and sugar are not used. A clean-looking wooden or lacquer pail with a lid is kept in all teahouses, and though hot rice, except to order, is only ready three times daily, the pail always contains cold rice, and the laborers heat it by pouring hot tea over it. As you eat, a teahouse girl, with this pail beside her, squats on the floor in front of you, and fills your rice bowl till you say, "Hold, enough!" On this road it is expected that you leave three or four *sen* on the tea tray for a rest of an hour or two and tea.

All day we travelled through rice swamps, along a much-frequented road, as far as Kasukabe, a good-sized but miserable-looking town, with its main street like one of the poorest streets in Tokyo, and halted for the night at a large *yadoya*, with downstairs and upstairs rooms, crowds of travellers, and many evil smells. On entering, the house master or landlord, folded his hands and prostrated himself, touching the floor with his forehead three times. It is a large, rambling old house, and fully thirty servants were bustling about in the *daidokoro*, or great open kitchen. I took a room upstairs (i.e. up a steep step-ladder of dark, polished wood), with a balcony under the deep eaves.

The front of the house upstairs was one long room with only sides and a front, but it was immediately divided into four by drawing sliding screens or panels, covered with opaque wall papers, into their proper grooves. A back was also improvised, but this was formed of frames with panes of translucent paper, like our tissue paper, with sundry holes and rents. This being done, I found myself the possessor of a room about sixteen feet square, without hook, shelf, rail, or anything on which to put anything—nothing, in short, but a matted floor.

Do not be misled by the use of the word "matting." Japanese house mats, or *tatami*, are as neat, refined, and soft a covering for the floor as the finest Axminster carpet. They are five feet nine inches long, three feet broad, and two and a half inches thick. The frame is solidly made of coarse straw, and this is covered with very fine woven matting, as nearly white as possible, and each mat is usually bound with dark blue cloth. Temples and rooms are measured by the number of mats they contain, and rooms must be built for the mats, as they are never cut to the rooms. They are always level with the polished grooves or ledges which surround the floor. They are soft and elastic, and the finer qualities are very beautiful. They are as expensive as the best Brussels carpet, and the Japanese take great pride in them, and are much aggrieved by the way in which some thoughtless foreigners stamp over them with dirty boots. Unfortunately they harbour myriads of fleas.

Outside my room an open balcony with many similar rooms ran round a forlorn aggregate of dilapidated shingle roofs and water-butts. These rooms were all full. Itō asked me for instructions once for all, put up my stretcher under a large mosquito net of coarse green canvas with a fusty smell, filled my bath, brought me some tea, rice, and eggs, took my passport to be copied by the house master, and departed, I know not whither. I tried to write, but fleas and mosquitoes prevented it. Besides, the *fusuma* were frequently noiselessly drawn apart, and several pairs of dark, elongated eyes surveyed me through the cracks; for there were two Japanese families in the room to the right, and five men in that to the left. I closed the sliding windows, with translucent paper for window panes, called *shōji*, and went to bed, but the lack of privacy was fearful, and I have not yet sufficient trust in my fellow-creatures to be comfortable without locks, walls, or doors!

Eyes were constantly applied to the sides of the room, a girl twice drew aside the *shōji* between it and the corridor. A man, who I afterwards found was a blind man, offering his services as a shampooer, came in and said some (of course) unintelligible words, and the new noises were perfectly bewildering. On one side a man recited Buddhist prayers in a high key; on the other a girl was twanging a *shamisen*, a species of sitar. The house was full of talking and splashing, drums and tom-toms were beaten outside. There were street cries, and the whistling of the blind shampooers, and the resonant clap of the fire watchman who perambulates all Japanese villages, and beats two pieces of wood together in token of his vigilance, were intolerable. It was a life of which I knew nothing, and the mystery was more alarming than attractive. My money was lying about, and nothing seemed easier than to slide a hand through the *fusuma* and appropriate it. Itō told me that the well was badly contaminated, the odors fearful. Illness was to be feared as well as robbery! So unreasonably I reasoned!

My bed is merely a piece of canvas nailed to two wooden bars. When I lay down the canvas burst away from the lower row of nails with a series of cracks, and sank gradually till I found myself lying on a sharp-edged pole which connects the two pair of trestles, and the helpless victim of fleas and mosquitoes. I lay for three hours, not daring to stir lest I should bring the canvas altogether down, becoming more and more nervous every moment, and then Itō called outside the *shōji*, "It would be best, Miss Bird, that I should see you." What horror can this be? I thought, and was not reassured when he added, "Here's a messenger from the legation and two policemen want to speak to you." On arriving I had done the correct thing in giving the house master my passport, which, according to law, he had copied into his book, and had sent a duplicate copy to the police-station, and this intrusion near midnight was as unaccountable as it was unwarrantable. Nevertheless the appearance of the two mannikins in European uniforms, with the familiar batons and bull's-eye lanterns, and with manners which were respectful without being deferential, gave me immediate relief. I should have welcomed twenty of their species, for their presence assured me of the fact that I am known and registered, and that a government which, for special reasons, is anxious to impress foreigners with its power and omniscience is responsible for my safety.

While they spelt through my passport by their dim lantern I opened the Tokyo parcel, and found that it contained a tin of lemon sugar, a most kind note from Sir Harry Parkes, and a packet of letters. While I was attempting to open the letters, Itō, the policemen, and the lantern glided out of my room, and I lay uneasily till daylight, with the letters and telegram, for which I had been yearning for six weeks, on my bed unopened!

Already I can laugh at my fears and misfortunes. A traveller must buy his own experience, and success or failure depends mainly on personal idiosyncrasies. Many matters will be remedied by experience as I go on, and I shall acquire the habit of feeling secure. But lack of privacy, bad smells, and the torments of fleas and mosquitoes are, I fear, irremediable evils.

By seven the next morning the rice was eaten, the room as bare as if it had never been occupied, the bill of eighty *sen* paid, the house master and servants had prostrated themselves with many *sayōnara*s, and we were away in the *kuruma* at a rapid trot. At the first halt my runner, a kindly, good-natured creature, but absolutely hideous, was seized with pain and vomiting, owing, he said, to drinking the bad water at Kasukabe, and was left behind. He pleased me much by the honest independent way in which he provided a substitute, strictly adhering to his bargain, and never asking for a gratuity on account of his illness. He had been so kind and helpful that I felt quite sad at leaving him there ill—a laborer, to be sure, only an atom among the thirty-four million of the empire.

It was a brilliant day, with the mercury 86 degrees in the shade, but the heat was not oppressive.

At noon we reached the Tone River, and I rode on a laborer's tattooed shoulders through the shallow part, and then, with the *kuruma*, some ill-disposed packhorses, and a number of travellers, crossed in a flat-bottomed boat. The boatmen, travellers, and cultivators, were nearly or altogether without clothes, but the richer farmers worked in the fields in curved bamboo hats as large as umbrellas, *kimono* with large sleeves not girt up, and large fans attached to their girdles.

Many of the travellers whom we met were without hats, but shielded the front of the head by holding a fan between it and the sun. Probably the inconvenience of the national costume for working men partly accounts for the general practice of getting rid of it. It is such a hindrance, even in walking, that most pedestrians have their loins girded up by taking the middle of the hem at the bottom of the *kimono* and tucking it under the girdle. This, in the case of many, shows woven, tight-fitting, elastic, white cotton pantaloons, reaching to the ankles. After ferrying another river at a village from which a steamer plies to Tokyo, the country became much more pleasing, the rice fields fewer, the trees, houses, and barns larger, and, in the distance, high hills loomed faintly through the haze. Much of the wheat, of which they don't make bread, but noodles, is already being carried. You see wheat stacks, ten feet high, moving slowly, and while you are wondering, you become aware of four feet moving below them; for all the crop is carried on horses' if not on human backs.

I went to see several threshing floors—clean, open spaces outside barns—where the grain is laid on mats and threshed by two or four men with heavy revolving flails. Another method is for women to beat out the grain on racks of split bamboo laid lengthwise; and I saw yet a third practised both in the fields and barnyards, in which women pass handfuls of stalks backwards through a sort of carding instrument with sharp iron teeth placed in a slanting position, which cuts off the ears, leaving the stalk unbruised. The ears are then rubbed between the hands. In this region the wheat was winnowed altogether by hand, and after the wind had driven the chaff away, the grain was laid out on mats to dry. Sickles are not used, but the reaper takes a handful of stalks and cuts them off close to the ground with a short, straight knife, fixed at a right angle with the handle. The wheat is sown in rows with wide spaces between them, which are utilised for beans and other crops, and no sooner is it removed than *daikon* (radish), cucumbers, or some other vegetable, takes its place, as the land under careful tillage and copious manuring bears two, and even three, crops, in the year. The soil is trenched for wheat as for all crops except rice, not a weed is to be seen, and the whole country looks like a well-kept garden.

The barns in this district are very handsome, and many of their grand roofs have that concave sweep with which we are familiar in the pagoda.

The eaves are often eight feet deep, and the thatch three feet thick. Several of the farm-yards have handsome gateways like the ancient lychgates of some of our English churchyards much magnified. As animals are not used for milk, draught, or food, and there are no pasture lands, both the country and the farmyards have a singular silence and an inanimate look; a mean-looking dog and a few fowls being the only representatives of domestic animal life. I long for the lowing of cattle and the bleating of sheep.

At six we reached Tochigi, a large town, formerly the castle town of a *daimyō*. Its special manufacture is rope of many kinds, a great deal of hemp being grown in the neighborhood. Many of the roofs are tiled, and the town has a more solid and handsome appearance than those that we had previously passed through. But from Kasukabe to Tochigi was from bad to worse. I nearly abandoned Japanese travelling altogether, and, if last night had not been a great improvement, I think I should have gone ignominiously back to Tokyo.

The *yadoya* was a very large one, and, as sixty guests had arrived before me, there was no choice of accommodation, and I had to be contented with a room enclosed on all sides not by *fusuma* but *shōji*, and with barely room for my bed, bath, and chair, under a fusty green mosquito net which was a perfect nest of fleas. One side of the room was against a much-frequented passage, and another opened on a small yard upon which three opposite rooms also opened, crowded with some not very sober or decorous travellers. The *shōji* were full of holes, and often at each hole I saw a human eye.

Privacy was a luxury not even to be recalled. Besides the constant application of eyes to the *shōji*, the servants, who were very noisy and rough, looked into my room constantly without any pretext. The host, a bright, pleasant-looking man, did the same. Jugglers, musicians, blind shampooers, and singing girls, all pushed the screens aside. I began to think that Campbell was right, and that a lady should not travel alone in Japan. Itō, who had the room next to mine, suggested that robbery was quite likely, and asked to be allowed to take charge of my money, but did not decamp with it during the night

I lay down on my precarious stretcher before eight, but as the night advanced the din of the house increased till it became truly diabolical, and never ceased till after one. Drums, tom-toms, and cymbals were beaten.

Koto and *shamisen* screeched and twanged. Geisha (professional women with the accomplishments of dancing, singing, and playing) danced— accompanied by songs whose jerking discords were most laughable. Story- tellers recited tales in a high key, and the running about and splashing close to my room never ceased. Late at night my precarious *shōji* were accidentally thrown down, revealing a scene of great hilarity, in which a number of people were bathing and throwing water over each other.

The noise of departures began at daylight, and I was glad to leave at seven. Before you go the *fusuma* are slidden back, and what was your room becomes part of a great, open, matted space—an arrangement which effectually prevents fustiness. Though the road was up a slight incline, and the men were too tired to trot, we made thirty miles in nine hours. The kindliness and courtesy of the *kurumaya* to me and to each other was a constant source of pleasure to me. It is most amusing to see the elaborate politeness of the greetings of men clothed only in hats and *fundoshi*. The hat is invariably removed when they speak to each other, and three profound bows are never omitted.

Soon after leaving the *yadoya* we passed through a wide street with the largest and handsomest houses I have yet seen on both sides. They were all open in front; their highly-polished floors and passages looked like still water; the *kakemono*, or wall-pictures, on their side-walls were extremely beautiful; and their mats were very fine and white. There were large gardens at the back, with fountains and flowers, and streams, crossed by light stone bridges, sometimes flowed through the houses. From the signs I supposed them to be *yadoya*, but on asking Itō why we had not put up at one of them, he replied that they were all teahouses of disreputable character—a very sad fact.

As we journeyed the country became prettier and prettier, rolling up to abrupt wooded hills with mountains in the clouds behind. The farming villages are comfortable and embowered in wood, and the richer farmers seclude their dwellings by closely-clipped hedges, or rather screens, two feet wide, and often twenty feet high. Tea grew near every house, and its leaves were being gathered and dried on mats. Signs of silk culture began to appear in shrubberies of mulberry trees, and white and sulphur yellow cocoons were lying in the sun along the road in flat trays. Numbers of women sat in the fronts of the houses weaving cotton cloth fifteen inches wide, and cotton yarn, mostly imported from England, was being dyed in all the villages—the dye used being a native indigo. Old women were spinning, and young and old usually pursued their avocations with wise-looking babies tucked into the backs of their dresses, and peering cunningly over their shoulders. Even little girls of seven and eight were playing at children's games with babies on their backs, and those who were too small to carry real ones had big dolls strapped on in similar fashion. Innumerable villages, crowded houses, and babies in all, give one the impression of a very populous country.

As the day wore on in its brightness and glory the pictures became more varied and beautiful. Great snow-slashed mountains looked over the foothills, on whose steep sides the dark blue green of pine and cryptomeria was lighted up by the spring tints of deciduous trees. There were groves of cryptomeria on small hills crowned by Shinto shrines, approached by grand flights of stone stairs. The red gold of the harvest fields contrasted with the fresh green and exquisite leafage of the hemp. Rose and white azaleas lighted up the copse-woods. And when the broad road passed into the colossal avenue of cryptomeria which overshadows the way to the sacred shrines of Nikkō, and tremulous sunbeams and shadows flecked the grass, I felt that Japan was beautiful, and the mud flats of Tokyo only an ugly dream!

Two roads lead to Nikkō. I avoided the one usually taken by Utsunomiya, and by doing so lost the most magnificent of the two avenues, which extends for nearly fifty miles along the great highway called the Ōshū Kaidō. Along the Reiheishi Kaidō, the road by which I came, it extends for thirty miles, and the two, broken frequently by villages, converge upon the village of Imaichi, eight miles from Nikkō, where they unite, and only terminate at the entrance of the town. They are said to have been planted as an offering to the buried *shōguns* by a man who was too poor to place a bronze lantern at their shrines. A grander monument could not have been devised, and they are probably the grandest things of their kind in the world. The avenue of the Reiheishi Kaidō is a good carriage road with sloping banks eight feet high, covered with grass and ferns. At the top of these are the cryptomeria, then two grassy walks, and between these and the cultivation a screen of saplings and brushwood. A great many of the trees become two at four feet from the ground. Many of the stems are twenty-seven feet in girth. They do not diminish or branch till they have reached a height of from fifty to sixty feet, and the appearance of altitude is aided by the longitudinal splitting of the reddish colored bark into strips about two inches wide. The trees are pyramidal, and at a little distance resemble cedars. There is a deep solemnity about this glorious avenue with its broad shade and dancing lights, and the rare glimpses of high mountains. Instinct alone would tell one that it leads to something which must be grand and beautiful like itself. It is broken occasionally by small villages with big bells suspended between double poles; by wayside shrines with offerings of rags and flowers; by stone effigies of Buddha and his disciples, mostly defaced or overthrown, all wearing the same expression of beatified rest and indifference to mundane affairs. And by temples of lacquered wood falling to decay, whose bells sent their surpassingly sweet tones far on the evening air.

Imaichi, where the two stately aisles unite, is a long uphill street, with a clear mountain stream enclosed in a stone channel, and crossed by hewn stone slabs running down the middle. In a room built over the stream, and commanding a view up and down the street, two policemen sat writing. It looks a dull place without much traffic, as if oppressed by the stateliness of the avenues below it and the shrines above it, but it has a quiet *yadoya*, where I had a good night's rest, although my canvas bed was nearly on the ground. We left early this morning in drizzling rain, and went straight uphill under the cryptomeria for eight miles. The vegetation is as profuse as one would expect in so damp and hot a summer climate, and from the prodigious rainfall of the mountains. Every stone is covered with moss, and the roadsides are green with algae and several species of liverwort.

We were among the foothills of Mount Nantai at a height of a thousand feet, abrupt in their forms, wooded to their summits, and noisy with the dash and tumble of a thousand streams. The long street of Hachiishi, with its steep-roofed, deep-eaved houses, its warm coloring, and its steep roadway with steps at intervals, has a sort of Swiss picturesqueness as you enter it, as you must, on foot, while your *kuruma* are hauled and lifted up the steps. Nor is the resemblance given by steep roofs, pines, and mountains patched with coniferae, altogether lost as you ascend the steep street, and see wood carvings and quaint baskets of wood and grass offered everywhere for sale. It is a truly dull, quaint street, and the people come out to stare at a foreigner as if foreigners had not become common events since 1870, when Sir Harry and Lady Parkes, the first Europeans who were permitted to visit Nikkō, took up their abode in the Imperial Honbō. It is a doll's street with small low houses, so finely matted, so exquisitely clean, so finically neat, so light and delicate, that even when I entered them without my boots I felt like a bull in a china shop, as if my mere weight must smash through and destroy. The street is so painfully clean that I should no more think of walking over it in muddy boots than over a drawing-room carpet. It has a silent mountain look, and most of its shops sell specialties, lacquer work, boxes of sweetmeats made of black beans and sugar, all sorts of boxes, trays, cups, and stands, made of plain, polished wood, and more grotesque articles made from the roots of trees.

It was not part of my plan to stay at the beautiful *yadoya* which receives foreigners in Hachiishi, and I sent Itō half a mile farther with a note in Japanese to the owner of the house where I now am, while I sat on a rocky eminence at the top of the street, unmolested by anybody, looking over to the solemn groves upon the mountains, where the two greatest of the *shōguns* sleep in glory. Below, the rushing Daiya River, swollen by the night's rain, thundered through a narrow gorge. Beyond, colossal flights of stone stairs stretch mysteriously away among cryptomeria groves, above which tower the Nikkō Mountains. Just where the torrent finds its impetuosity checked by two stone walls, it is spanned by a bridge, eighty-four feet long by eighteen wide, of dull red lacquer, resting on two stone piers on either side, connected by two transverse stone beams. A welcome bit of color it is amidst the masses of dark greens and soft grays, though there is nothing imposing in its structure, and its interest consists in being the Mihashi, or Sacred Bridge, built in 1636, formerly open only to the *shōguns*, the envoy of the emperor, and to pilgrims twice a year. Both its gates are locked. Grand and lonely Nikkō looks, the home of rain and mist. *Kuruma* roads end here, and if you wish to go any farther, you must either walk, ride, or be carried.

Itō was long away, and the kurumaya kept addressing me in Japanese, which made me feel helpless and solitary, and eventually they shouldered my baggage, and, descending a flight of steps, we crossed the river by the secular bridge, and shortly met my host, Kanaya, a very bright, pleasant-looking man, who bowed nearly to the earth. Terraced roads in every direction lead through cryptomerias to the shrines. This one passes many a stately enclosure, but leads away from the temples, and though it is the highway to Chūzenji, a place of popular pilgrimage, Yumoto, a popular resort, and several other villages, it is very rugged, and, having flights of stone steps at intervals, is only practicable for horses and pedestrians.

At the house, with the appearance of which I was at once delighted, I regretfully parted with my kurumaya, who had served me kindly and faithfully. They had paid me many little attentions, such as always beating the dust out of my dress, inflating my air pillow, and bringing me flowers, and were always grateful when I walked up hills. Just now, after going for a frolic to the mountains, they called to wish me good-bye, bringing branches of azaleas.

Kanaya and his Household

I don't know what to write about my house. It is a Japanese idyll; there is nothing within or without which does not please the eye, and, after the din of *yadoya*, its silence, musical with the dash of waters and the twitter of birds, is truly refreshing. It is a simple but irregular two-storied pavilion, standing on a stone-faced terrace approached by a flight of stone steps. The garden is well laid out, and, as peonies, irises, and azaleas are now in blossom, it is very bright. The mountain, with its lower part covered with red azaleas, rises just behind, and a stream which tumbles down it supplies the house with water, both cold and pure, and another, after forming a miniature cascade, passes under the house and through a fish-pond with rocky islets into the river below. The grey village of Irimichi lies on the other side of the road, shut in by the rushing Daiya, and beyond it are high, broken hills, richly wooded, and slashed with ravines and waterfalls.

Kanaya's sister, a very sweet, refined-looking woman, met me at the door and divested me of my boots. The two verandahs are highly polished, so are the entrance and the stairs which lead to my room, and the mats are so fine and white that I almost fear to walk over them, even in my stockings. The polished stairs lead to a highly polished, broad verandah with a beautiful view, from which you enter one large room, which, being too large, was at once made into two. Four highly polished steps lead from this into an exquisite room at the back, which Itō occupies, and another polished staircase into the bathhouse and garden. The whole front of my room is composed of *shōji*, which slide back during the day. The ceiling is of light wood crossed by bars of dark wood, and the posts which support it are of dark polished wood. The panels are of wrinkled sky-blue paper splashed with gold. At one end are two alcoves with floors of polished wood, called tokonoma. In one hangs a *kakemono*, or scroll, a painting of a blossoming branch of the cherry on white silk—a perfect piece of art, which in itself fills the room with freshness and beauty. The artist who painted it painted nothing but cherry blossoms, and fell in the rebellion. On a shelf in the other alcove is a very valuable cabinet with sliding doors, on which peonies are painted on a gold ground. A single spray of rose azalea in a pure white vase hanging on one of the polished posts, and a single iris in another, are the only decorations. The mats are very fine and white, but the only furniture is a folding screen with some suggestions of landscape in Indian ink. I almost wish that the rooms were a little less exquisite, for I am in constant dread of spilling the ink, indenting the mats, or tearing the paper windows. Downstairs there is a room equally beautiful, and a large space where all the domestic avocations are carried on. There is a *kura*, or fire-proof storehouse, with a tiled roof, on the right of the house.

Kanaya leads the discords at the Shinto shrines; but his duties are few, and he is chiefly occupied in perpetually embellishing his house and garden. His mother, a venerable old lady, and his sister, the sweetest and most graceful Japanese woman but one that I have seen, live with him. She moves about the house like a floating fairy, and her voice has music in its tones. A half-witted servant-man and the sister's boy and girl complete the family. Kanaya is the chief man in the village, and is very intelligent and apparently well educated. He has divorced his wife, and his sister has practically divorced her husband. Of late, to help his income, he has let these charming rooms to foreigners who have brought letters to him, and he is very anxious to meet their views, while his good taste leads him to avoid Europeanizing his beautiful home.

Supper came up on a *zen*, or small table six inches high, of old gold lacquer, with the rice in a gold lacquer bowl, and the teapot and cup were fine Kaga porcelain. For my two rooms, with rice and tea, I pay two shillings a day. Itō forages for me, and can occasionally get chickens at ten pence each, and a dish of trout for six pence, and eggs are always to be had for one pence each. It is extremely interesting to live in a private house and to see the externalities, at least, of domestic life in a Japanese middle-class home.

45

The Beauties of Nikkō

I have been at Nikkō for nine days, and am therefore entitled to use the word *kekkō*!

Nikkō means "sunny splendor," and its beauties are celebrated in poetry and art all over Japan. Many are the attractions that surround the shrines of the two greatest *shōguns*: mountains for a great part of the year clothed or patched with snow, piled in great ranges round Mount Nantai, their monarch, worshipped as a god; forests of magnificent timber; ravines and passes scarcely explored; dark green lakes sleeping in endless serenity; the deep abyss of Kegon, into which the waters of Chūzenji plunge from a height of 250 feet; the bright beauty of the falls of Kirifuri, the loveliness of the gardens of Dainichidō; the sombre grandeur of the passes through which the Daiya River forces its way from the upper regions; a gorgeousness of azaleas and magnolias; and a luxuriousness of vegetation perhaps unequalled in Japan.

To a glorious resting place on the hill-slope of Hotoke Iwa, Hidetada, the second *shōgun* of the Tokugawa dynasty, conveyed the corpse of his father, Ieyasu, in 1617. The place has been sacred since 767, when a Buddhist saint, called Shōdō Shōnin, visited it, and declared the old Shinto deity of the mountain to be only a manifestation of Buddha It was a splendid burial. An imperial envoy, a priest of the emperor's family, court nobles from Kyoto, and hundreds of *daimyō*, captains, and nobles of inferior rank, took part in the ceremony. An army of priests in rich robes during three days intoned a sacred classic ten thousand times, and Ieyasu was deified by a decree of the emperor under a name signifying "light of the east, great incarnation of Buddha." The less important *shōguns* of the line of Tokugawa are buried

46

in Ueno and Shiba, in Tokyo. Since the restoration, and what may be called the disestablishment of Buddhism, the shrine of Ieyasu has been shorn of all its glories of ritual and its magnificent Buddhist paraphernalia. The two hundred priests who gave it splendor are scattered, and six Shinto priests alternately attend upon it as much for the purpose of selling tickets of admission as for any priestly duties.

All roads, bridges, and avenues here lead to these shrines, but the grand approach is by the Red Bridge, and up a broad road with steps at intervals and stone-faced embankments at each side, on the top of which are belts of cryptomeria. At the summit of this ascent is a fine granite *torii*, twenty-seven feet six inches high, with columns three feet six inches in diameter, offered by the *daimyō* of Chikuzen in 1618 from his own quarries. After this come 118 magnificent bronze lanterns on massive stone pedestals, each of which is inscribed with the posthumous title of Ieyasu, the name of the giver, and a legend of the offering—all the gifts of *daimyō*—a holy water cistern made of a solid block of granite, and covered by a roof resting on twenty square granite pillars, and a bronze bell, lantern, and candelabra of marvellous workmanship, offered by the kings of Korea and Ryūkyū. On the left is a five-storied pagoda, 104 feet high, richly carved in wood and as richly gilded and painted. The signs of the zodiac run round the lower story.

The grand entrance gate is at the top of a handsome flight of steps forty yards from the *torii*. A looped white curtain with the emperor's crest in black, hangs partially over the gateway, in which, beautiful as it is, one does not care to linger, to examine the gilded *amainu* in niches, or the spirited carvings of tigers under the eaves, for the view of the first court overwhelms one by its magnificence and beauty. The whole style of the buildings, the arrangements, the art of every kind, the thought which inspires the whole, are exclusively Japanese, and the glimpse from the *Niō* gate is a revelation of a previously undreamed-of beauty, both in form and color.

Round the neatly pebbled court, which is enclosed by a bright red timber wall, are three gorgeous buildings, which contain the treasures of the temple, a sumptuous stable for the three sacred white horses, which are kept for the use of the god, a magnificent granite cistern of holy water, fed from the Somendaki cascade, and a highly decorated building, in which a complete collection of Buddhist Scriptures is deposited. From this a flight of steps leads into a smaller court containing a bell tower of marvellous workmanship and ornamentation, a drum-tower, hardly less beautiful, a shrine, the candelabra, bell, and lantern mentioned before, and some very grand bronze lanterns.

From this court another flight of steps ascends to the Yomei gate, whose splendor I contemplated day after day with increasing astonishment. The white columns that support it have capitals formed of great red-throated heads of the mythical *kirin* (unicorn). Above the architrave is a projecting balcony which runs all round the gateway with a railing carried by dragons' heads. In the centre two white dragons fight eternally. Underneath, in high relief, there are groups of children playing, then a network of richly painted beams, and seven groups of Chinese sages. The high roof is supported by gilded dragons' heads with crimson throats. In the interior of the gateway there are side-niches painted white, which are lined with gracefully designed arabesques founded on the *botan* or peony. A piazza, whose outer walls of twenty-one compartments are enriched with magnificent carvings of birds, flowers, and trees, runs right and left, and encloses on three of its sides another court, the fourth side of which is a terminal stone wall built against the side of the hill. On the right are two decorated buildings, one of which contains a stage for the performance of the sacred dances, and the other an altar for the burning of cedar wood incense. On the left is a building for the reception of the three *mikoshi* that were used during festivals. To pass from court to court is to pass from splendor to splendor, One is almost glad to feel that this is the last, and that the strain on one's capacity for admiration is nearly over.

In the middle is the sacred enclosure, formed of gilded trelliswork with painted borders above and below, forming a square of which each side measures 150 feet, and which contains the *haiden* or chapel. Underneath the trellis work are groups of birds, with backgrounds of grass, very boldly carved in wood and richly gilded and painted. From the imposing entrance through a double avenue of cryptomeria, among courts, gates, temples, shrines, pagodas, colossal bells of bronze, and lanterns inlaid with gold, you pass through this final court bewildered by magnificence, through golden gates, into the dimness of a golden temple, and there is—simply a black lacquer table with a circular metal mirror upon it.

Within is a hall finely matted, forty-two feet wide by twenty-seven from front to back, with lofty apartments on each side, one for the *shōgun* and the other "for his Holiness the Abbot." Both, of course, are empty. The roof of the hall is panelled and richly frescoed. The *shōgun*'s room contains some very fine *fusuma*, on which *kirin* (fabulous monsters) are depicted on a dead gold ground, and four oak panels, eight feet by six, finely carved, with the phoenix in low relief variously treated. In the abbot's room there are similar panels adorned with hawks spiritedly executed. The only ecclesiastical ornament among the dim splendors of the chapel is the plain gold *gohei*. Steps at the back lead into a chapel paved with stone, with a fine panelled ceiling representing dragons on a dark blue ground. Beyond this some gilded doors lead into the principal chapel, containing four rooms which are not accessible. If they correspond with the outside, which is of highly polished black lacquer relieved by gold, they must be severely magnificent.

But not in any one of these gorgeous shrines did Ieyasu decree that his dust should rest. Re-entering the last court, it is necessary to leave the enclosures altogether by passing through a covered gateway in the eastern piazza into a stone gallery, green with mosses and hepaticae. Within, wealth and art have created a fairyland of gold and color. Without, nature, at her stateliest, has surrounded the great *shōgun*'s tomb with a pomp of mournful splendor. A staircase of 240 stone steps leads to the top of the hill, where, above and behind all the stateliness of the shrines raised in his honor, the dust of Ieyasu sleeps in an unadorned but Cyclopean tomb of stone and bronze, surmounted by a bronze urn. In front is a stone table decorated with a bronze incense burner, a vase with lotus blossoms and leaves in brass, and a bronze stork bearing a bronze candlestick in its mouth. A lofty stone wall, surmounted by a balustrade, surrounds the simple but stately enclosure, and cryptomeria of large size growing up the back of the hill create perpetual twilight round it. Slant rays of sunshine alone pass through them, no flower blooms or bird sings, only silence and mournfulness surround the grave of the ablest and greatest man that Japan has produced.

Impressed as I had been with the glorious workmanship in wood, bronze, and lacquer, I scarcely admired less the masonry of the vast retaining walls, the stone gallery, the staircase and its balustrade, all put together without mortar or cement, and so accurately fitted that the joints are scarcely affected by the rain, damp, and aggressive vegetation of 260 years. The steps of the staircase are fine monoliths, and the coping at the side, the massive balustrade, and the heavy rail at the top, are cut out of solid blocks of stone from ten to eighteen feet in length. Nor is the workmanship of the great granite cistern for holy water less remarkable. It is so carefully adjusted on its bed that the water brought from a neighboring cascade rises and pours over each edge in such carefully equalized columns that, as Satow says, "it seems to be a solid block of water rather than a piece of stone."

The temples of Iemitsu are close to those of Ieyasu, and though somewhat less magnificent are even more bewildering, as they are still in Buddhist hands, and are crowded with the gods of the Buddhist Pantheon and the splendid paraphernalia of Buddhist worship, in striking contrast to the simplicity of the lonely Shinto mirror in the midst of the blaze of gold and color. In the grand entrance gate are gigantic *Niō*, vermilion colored, and with draperies painted in imitation of flowered silk. A second pair, painted red and green, removed from Iemitsu's temple, are in niches within the gate. A flight of steps leads to another gate, in whose gorgeous niches stand hideous monsters, in human form, representing the gods of wind and thunder. Wind has crystal eyes and a half-jolly, half-demoniacal expression. He is painted green, and carries a wind-bag on his back, a long sack tied at each end, with the ends brought over his shoulders and held in his hands. The god of thunder is painted red, with purple hair on end, and stands on clouds holding thunderbolts in his hand. More steps, and another gate containing the Shitennō, or gods of the four quarters, boldly carved and in strong action, with long eyeteeth, and at last the principal temple is reached.

An old priest who took me over it on my first visit, on passing the gods of wind and thunder said, "We used to believe in these things, but we don't now," and his manner in speaking of the other deities was .rather contemptuous. He requested me to take off my hat as well as my shoes at the door of the temple. Within there was a gorgeous shrine, and when an acolyte drew aside the curtain of cloth of gold the interior was equally imposing, containing Buddha and two other figures of gilded brass, seated cross-legged on lotus-flowers, with rows of petals several times repeated, and with that look of eternal repose on their faces which is reproduced in the commonest roadside images. In front of the shrine several candles were burning, the offerings of some people who were having prayers said for them, and the whole was lighted by two lamps burning low. On a step of the altar a much-contorted devil was crouching uneasily, for he was subjugated and, by a grim irony, made to carry a massive incense-burner on his shoulders. In this temple there were more than a hundred idols standing in rows, many of them life-size, some of them trampling devils under their feet, but all hideous, partly from the bright greens, vermilions, and blues with which they are painted. Remarkable muscular development characterizes all, and the figures or faces are all in vigorous action of some kind, generally grossly exaggerated.

While we were crossing the court there were two shocks of earthquake. All the golden wind bells which fringe the roofs rang softly, and a number of priests ran into the temple and beat various kinds of drums for the space of half an hour. Iemitsu's tomb is reached by flights of steps on the right of the chapel. It is in the same style as Ieyasu's, but the gates in front are of bronze, and are inscribed with large Sanskrit characters in bright brass. One of the most beautiful of the many views is from the uppermost gate of the temple. The sun shone on my second visit and brightened the spring tints of the trees on Hotoke-iwa, which was vignetted by a frame of dark cryptomeria.

Some of the buildings are roofed with sheet-copper, but most of them are tiled. Tiling, however, has been raised almost to the dignity of a fine art in Japan. The tiles themselves are a coppery grey, with a suggestion of metallic lustre about it. They are slightly concave, and the joints are covered by others quite convex, which come down like massive tubes from the ridge pole, and terminate at the eaves with discs on which the Tokugawa crest is emblazoned in gold, as it is everywhere on these shrines where it would not be quite out of keeping. The roofs are so massive that they require all the strength of the heavy carved timbers below, and, like all else, they gleam with gold, or that which simulates it.

The shrines are the most wonderful work of their kind in Japan. In their stately setting of cryptomeria, few of which are less than twenty feet in girth at three feet from the ground, they take one prisoner by their beauty, in defiance of all rules of western art, and compel one to acknowledge the beauty of forms and combinations of color hitherto unknown, and that lacquered wood is capable of lending itself to the expression of a very high idea in art. Gold has been used in profusion, and black, dull red, and white, with a breadth and lavishness quite unique. The bronze fret-work alone is a study, and the wood-carving needs weeks of earnest work for the mastery of its ideas and details. One screen or railing only has sixty panels, each four feet long, carved with marvellous boldness and depth in open work, representing peacocks, pheasants, storks, lotuses, peonies, bamboos, and foliage. The fidelity to form and color in the birds, and the reproduction of the glory of motion, could not be excelled.

Yet the flowers please me even better. Truly the artist has revelled in his work, and has carved and painted with joy. The lotus leaf retains its dewy bloom, the peony its shades of creamy white, the bamboo leaf still trembles on its graceful stem, in contrast to the rigid needles of the pine, and countless corollas, in all the perfect coloring of passionate life, unfold themselves amidst the leafage of the gorgeous tracery. These carvings are from ten to fifteen inches deep, and single feathers in the tails of the pheasants stand out fully six inches in front of peonies nearly as deep.

The details fade from my memory daily as I leave the shrines. In their place are picturesque masses of black and red lacquer and gold, gilded doors opening without noise, halls laid with matting so soft that not a footfall sounds. Across their twilight, sunbeams fall aslant on richly arabesqued walls and panels carved with birds and flowers, and on ceilings panelled and wrought with elaborate art. I see visions of inner shrines of gold, and golden lilies six feet high, and curtains of gold brocade, and incense fumes, and colossal bells and golden ridge poles. I see images of the mythical fauna, *kirin*, dragon, and phoenix, of elephants, apes, and tigers, strangely mingled with flowers and trees, and golden tracery, and diaper work on a gold ground, and lacquer screens, and pagodas, and groves of bronze lanterns, and shaven priests in gold brocade, and Shinto attendants in black lacquer caps, and gleams of sunlit gold here and there, and simple monumental urns, and a mountainside covered with a cryptomeria forest, with rose azaleas lighting up its solemn shade.

Yadoya and Attendant

Yashimaya, Yumoto, Nikkō Mountains, June 22

Today I have made an experimental journey on horseback, have done fifteen miles in eight hours of continuous travelling, and have encountered for the first time the Japanese packhorse—an animal of which many unpleasing stories are told, and which has hitherto been as mythical to me as the *kirin*, or dragon. I have neither been kicked, bitten, nor pitched off, for mares are used exclusively in this district, gentle creatures about fourteen hands high, with weak hind-quarters, and heads nearly concealed by shaggy manes and forelocks. They are led by a rope round the nose, and go barefoot, except on stony ground, when the *mago*, or man who leads them, ties straw sandals on their feet.

The pack saddle is composed of two packs of straw eight inches thick, faced with red, and connected before and behind by strong oak arches gaily painted or lacquered. By way of girth, a rope is loosely tied under the body, and the security of the load depends on a crupper, usually a piece of bamboo attached to the saddle by ropes strung with wooden counters, and another rope round the neck, into which you put your foot as you scramble over the high front upon the top of the erection. The load must be carefully balanced or it comes to grief, and the *mago* handles it all over first, and, if an accurate division of weight is impossible, adds a stone to one side or the other. Women who wear enormous rain hats and gird their *kimono* over tight blue trousers, both load the horses and lead them.

I dropped upon my loaded horse from the top of a wall, the ridges, bars, tags, and knotted rigging of the saddle being smoothed over by a folded *futon*, or wadded cotton quilt, and I was then fourteen inches above the animal's back, with my feet hanging over his neck. You must balance yourself carefully, or you bring the whole erection over; but balancing soon becomes a matter of habit. If the horse does not stumble, the pack saddle is tolerable on level ground, but most severe on the spine in going uphill, and so intolerable in going down that I was relieved when I found that I had slid over the horse's head into a mud hole. You are quite helpless, as he does not understand a bridle, even if you had one, and blindly follows his leader, who trudges on six feet in front of him.

The hard day's journey ended in an exquisite *yadoya*, beautiful within and without, and more fit for fairies than for travel-soiled mortals. The *fusuma* are light planed wood with a sweet scent, the matting nearly white, the balconies polished pine. On entering, a smiling girl brought me some plum-flower tea with a delicate almond flavor, a sweetmeat made of beans and sugar, and a lacquer bowl of frozen snow. After making a difficult meal from a fowl of much experience, I spent the evening out of doors, as a Japanese watering place is an interesting novelty.

There is scarcely room between the lake and the mountains for the picturesque village with its trim neat houses, one above another, built of reddish cedar newly planed. The snow lies ten feet deep here in winter, and on October 10 the people wrap their beautiful dwellings up in coarse matting, not even leaving the roofs uncovered, and go to the low country till May 10, leaving one man in charge, who is relieved once a week. Were the houses mine I should be tempted to wrap them up on every rainy day! I did quite the wrong thing in riding here. It is proper to be carried up in a *kago*, or covered basket.

The village consists of two short streets, eight feet wide composed entirely of *yadoya* of various grades, with a picturesquely varied frontage of deep eaves, graceful balconies, rows of Chinese lanterns, and open lower fronts. The place is full of people, and the four bathing-sheds were crowded. Some energetic invalids bathe twelve times a day! Every one who was walking about carried a blue towel over his arm, and the rails of the balconies were covered with blue towels hanging to dry. There can be very little amusement. The mountains rise at once from the village, and are so covered with jungle that one can only walk in the short streets or along the track by which I came. There is one covered boat for excursions on the lake, and a few *geisha* were playing the *shamisen*. As gaming is illegal, and there is no place of public resort except the bathing-sheds, people must spend nearly all their time in bathing, sleeping, smoking, and eating. The great spring is beyond the village, in a square tank in a mound. It bubbles up with much strength, giving off fetid fumes. There are broad boards laid at intervals across it, and people crippled with rheumatism go and lie for hours upon them for the advantage of the sulphurous steam. The temperature of the spring is 130 degrees Fahrenheit. But after the water has travelled to the village along an open wooden pipe, it is only 84 degrees. Yumoto is over four thousand feet high, and very cold.

Urimichi

Before leaving Yumoto I saw the modus operandi of a squeeze. I asked for the bill, when, instead of giving it to me, the host ran upstairs and asked Itō how much it should be, the two dividing the overcharge. Your servant gets a squeeze on everything you buy, and on your hotel expenses, and, as it is managed very adroitly, and you cannot prevent it, it is best not to worry about it so long as it stays within reasonable limits.

A Juvenile Belle

My peacefully monotonous life here is nearly at an end. The people are so quiet and kindly, though almost too still, and I have learned to know something of the externals of village life, and have become quite fond of the place.

The village of Irimichi, which epitomizes for me at present the village life of Japan, consists of about three hundred houses built along three roads, across which steps in fours and threes are placed at intervals. Down the middle of each a rapid stream runs in a stone channel, and this gives endless amusement to the children, especially to the boys, who devise many ingenious models and mechanical toys, which are put in motion by water-wheels.

At 7 a.m. a drum beats to summon the children to a school whose buildings would not discredit any school-board at home. Too much Europeanized I thought it, and the children looked very uncomfortable sitting on high benches in front of desks, instead of squatting, native fashion. The school apparatus is very good, and there are fine maps on the walls. The teacher, a man about twenty-five, made very free use of the black-board, and questioned his pupils with much rapidity. The best answer moved its giver to the head of the class, as with us. Obedience is the foundation of the Japanese social order, and with children accustomed to unquestioning obedience at home the teacher has no trouble in securing quietness, attention, and docility.

There was almost a painful earnestness in the old-fashioned faces which pored over the schoolbooks; even such a rare event as the entrance of a foreigner failed to distract these childish students. The younger pupils were taught chiefly by object lessons, and the older were exercised in reading geographical and historical books aloud, a very high key being adopted, and a most disagreeable tone, both with the Chinese and Japanese pronunciation. Arithmetic and the elements of some of the branches of natural science are also taught. The children recited a verse of poetry which I understood contained the whole of the simple syllabary. It has been translated thus:

> Color and perfume vanish away.
> What can be lasting in this world?
> Today disappears in the abyss of nothingness;
> it is but the passing image of a dream,
> and causes only a slight trouble.

It is the echo of the wearied sensualist's cry, "Vanity of vanities, all is vanity," and indicates the singular Oriental distaste for life, but is a dismal ditty for young children to learn. The Chinese classics, formerly the basis of Japanese education, are now mainly taught as a vehicle for conveying a knowledge of Chinese characters, or *kanji*, in acquiring even a moderate acquaintance with which the children undergo a great deal of useless toil.

The penalties for bad conduct used to be a few blows with a switch on the front of the leg, or a slight burn with the moxa on the forefinger—still a common punishment in households. But I understood the teacher to say that detention in the schoolhouse is the only punishment now resorted to, and he expressed great disapprobation of our plan of imposing an added task. When twelve o'clock came the children marched in orderly fashion out of the school grounds, the boys in one division and the girls in another, after which they quietly dispersed.

On going home the children dine, and in the evening in nearly every house you hear the monotonous hum of the preparation of lessons. After dinner they are liberated for play, but the girls often hang about the house with babies on their backs the whole afternoon nursing dolls. One evening I met a procession of sixty boys and girls, all carrying white flags with black balls, except the leader, who carried a white flag with a gilded ball, and they sang, or rather howled, as they walked. The other amusements have been of a most sedentary kind. The mechanical toys, worked by water-wheels in the stream, are most fascinating.

Formal children's parties have been given in this house, for which formal invitations, in the name of the house-child, a girl of twelve, are sent out. About three p.m. the guests arrive, frequently attended by servants. This child, Haru, receives them at the top of the stone steps, and conducts each into the reception room, where they are arranged according to some well-understood rules of precedence. Haru's hair is drawn back, raised in front, and gathered into a double loop, in which some scarlet crepe is twisted. Her face and throat are much whitened, the paint terminating in three points at the back of the neck, from which all the short hair has been carefully extracted with pincers. Her lips are slightly touched with red paint, and her face looks like that of a cheap doll. She wears a blue, flowered silk *kimono*, with sleeves touching the ground, a blue girdle lined with scarlet, and a fold of scarlet crepe lies between her painted neck and her *kimono*. On her little feet she wears white *tabi*, socks of cotton cloth, with a separate place for the great toe, so as to allow the scarlet-covered thongs of the finely lacquered *geta*, which she puts on when she stands on the stone steps to receive her guests, to pass between it and the smaller toes. All the other little ladies were dressed in the same style, and all looked like ill-executed dolls. She met them with very formal but graceful bows.

When they were all assembled, she and her very graceful mother, squatting before each, presented tea and sweetmeats on lacquer trays, and then they played at very quiet and polite games till dusk. They addressed each other by their names with the honorific prefix *o*, only used in the case of women, and the respectful affix *san*. Thus Haru becomes o-Haru-*san*, which is equivalent to "Miss Haru." A mistress of a house is addressed as O-Kami-*san*, and O-Kusuma—something like "my lady"—is used to married ladies. Women have no surnames. Thus you do not speak of Mrs. Saguchi, but of the wife of Saguchi-*san*, and you would address her as o-Kusuma. Among the children's names were Haru (Spring), Yuki (Snow), Hana (Blossom), Kiku (Chrysanthemum), Gin (Silver).

One of their games was most amusing, and was played with some spirit and much dignity. It consisted in one child feigning sickness and another playing the doctor, and the pompousness and gravity of the latter, and the distress and weakness of the former, were most successfully imitated. Unfortunately the doctor killed his patient, who counterfeited the death-sleep very effectively with her whitened face. Then followed the funeral and the mourning. They dramatize thus weddings, dinner parties, and many other of the events of life. The dignity and self-possession of these children are wonderful. The fact is that their initiation into all that is required by the rules of Japanese etiquette begins as soon as they can speak, so that by the time they are ten years old they know exactly what to do and avoid under all possible circumstances. Before they went away tea and sweetmeats were again handed round, and, as it is neither etiquette to refuse them or to leave anything behind that you have once taken, several of the small ladies slipped the residue into their capacious sleeves. On departing the same formal courtesies were used as on arriving.

Yuki, Haru's mother, speaks, acts, and moves with a charming gracefulness. Except at night, and when friends drop in to afternoon tea, as they often do, she is always either at domestic avocations, such as cleaning, sewing, or cooking, or planting vegetables, or weeding them. All Japanese girls learn to sew and to make their own clothes, but there are none of the mysteries and difficulties which make the sewing lesson a thing of dread with us. The *kimono*, *haori*, and *obi*, and even the long hanging sleeves, have only parallel seams, and these are only tacked or basted, as the garments, when washed, are taken to pieces, and each piece, after being very slightly stiffened, is stretched upon a board to dry. There is no underclothing, with its bands, frills, gussets, and button-holes; the poorer women wear none, and those above them wear, like Yuki, an under-dress of a frothy-looking silk crepe, as simply made as the upper one. There are circulating libraries here, as in most villages, and in the evening both Yuki and Haru read love stories, or accounts of ancient heroes and heroines, dressed up to suit the popular taste, written in the easiest possible style. Itō has about ten volumes of novels in his room, and spends half the night in reading them.

Yuki's son, a lad of thirteen, often comes to my room to display his skill in writing Chinese characters. He is a very bright boy, and shows considerable talent for drawing. Indeed, it is only a short step from writing to drawing. Giotto's O hardly involved more breadth and vigor of touch than some of these characters. They are written with a camel's-hair brush dipped in Indian ink, instead of a pen, and this boy, with two or three vigorous touches, produces characters a foot long, such as are mounted and hung as tablets outside the different shops. Yuki plays the *shamisen*, which may be regarded as the national female instrument, and Haru goes to a teacher daily for lessons on the same.

The art of arranging flowers is taught in manuals, the study of which forms part of a girl's education, and there is scarcely a day in which my room is not newly decorated. It is an education to me; I am beginning to appreciate the extreme beauty of solitude in decoration. In the alcove hangs a *kakemono* of exquisite beauty, a single blossoming branch of the cherry. On one panel of a folding screen there is a single iris. The vases that hang so gracefully on the polished posts contain each a single peony, a single iris, a single azalea, stalk, leaves, and corolla—all displayed in their full beauty. Can anything be more grotesque and barbarous than our florists' bouquets, a series of concentric rings of flowers of divers colors, bordered by maidenhair and a piece of stiff lace paper, in which stems, leaves, and even petals are brutally crushed, and the grace and individuality of each flower systematically destroyed?

Kanaya is the chief man in this village, besides being the leader of the dissonant squeaks and discords which represent music at the Shinto festivals, and in some mysterious back region he compounds and sells drugs. Since I have been here the beautification of his garden has been his chief object, and he has made a very respectable waterfall, a rushing stream, a small lake, a rustic bamboo bridge, and several grass banks, and has transplanted several large trees. He kindly goes out with me a good deal, and, as he is very intelligent, and Itō is proving an excellent, and—I think—faithful interpreter, I find it very pleasant to be here.

They rise at daylight, fold up the wadded quilts or *futon* on and under which they have slept, and put them and the wooden pillows, much like stereoscopes in shape, with little rolls of paper or wadding on the top, into a press with a sliding door, sweep the mats carefully, dust all the woodwork and the verandahs, open the *amado*—wooden shutters which, by sliding in a groove along the edge of the verandah, box in the whole house at night, and retire into an ornamental projection in the day—and throw the paper windows back. Breakfast follows, then domestic avocations, dinner at one, and sewing, gardening, and visiting till six, when they take the evening meal.

Visitors usually arrive soon afterwards, and stay till eleven or twelve.

Japanese chess, storytelling, and the *shamisen* fill up the early part of the evening, but later, an agonizing performance, which they call singing, begins, which sounds like the very essence of heathenishness, and consists mainly in a prolonged vibrating "No." As soon as I hear it I feel as if I were among savages. *Sake*, or rice wine, is passed round before the visitors leave, in little cups with the gods of luck at the bottom of them. *Sake*, when heated, mounts readily to the head, and a single small cup excites the half-witted manservant to some very foolish musical performances. I am sorry to write it, but his master and mistress take great pleasure in seeing him make a fool of himself, and Itō, who is from policy a total abstainer, goes into convulsions of laughter.

One evening I was invited to join the family, and they entertained me by showing me picture and guide books. Most Japanese regions have their guidebooks, illustrated by woodcuts of the most striking objects, and giving itineraries, names of *yadoya*, and other local information. One volume of pictures, very finely executed on silk, was more than a century old. Old gold lacquer and china, and some pieces of antique embroidered silk, were also produced for my benefit, and some musical instruments of great beauty, said to be more than two centuries old. None of these treasures are kept in the house, but in the *kura*, or fireproof storehouse, close by. The rooms are not encumbered by ornaments. A single *kakemono*, or fine piece of lacquer or china, appears for a few days and then makes way for something else. So they have variety as well as simplicity, and each object is enjoyed in its turn without distraction.

Kanaya and his sister often pay me an evening visit, and, with Brunton's map on the floor, we project astonishing routes to Niigata, which are usually abruptly abandoned on finding a mountain chain in the way with never a road over it. The life of these people seems to pass easily enough, but Kanaya deplores the want of money. He would like to be rich, and intends to build a hotel for foreigners.

The only vestige of religion in his house is the *kamidana*, or "god shelf," on which stands a wooden shrine like a Shinto temple, which contains the memorial tablets to deceased relations. Each morning a sprig of evergreen and a little rice and *sake* are placed before it, and every evening a lighted lamp.

I don't wonder that the Japanese rise early, for their evenings are cheerless, owing to the dismal illumination. In this and other houses the lamp consists of a square or circular lacquer stand, with four uprights, two and a half feet high, and panes of white paper. A flatted iron dish is suspended in this full of oil, with the pith of a rush with a weight in the centre laid across it, and one of the projecting ends is lighted. This wretched apparatus is called an *andon*, and around its wretched darkness visible the family huddles—the children to play games and learn lessons, and the women to sew; for the Japanese daylight is short and the houses are dark. Almost more deplorable is a candlestick of the same height as the *andon*, with a spike at the top which fits into a hole at the bottom of a candle of vegetable wax, with a thick wick made of rolled paper, which requires constant snuffing, and, after giving for a short time a dim and jerky light, expires with a bad smell. Lamps, burning mineral oils, native and imported, are being manufactured on a large scale, but, apart from the peril connected with them, the carriage of oil into country districts is very expensive. No Japanese would think of sleeping without having an *andon* burning all night in his room.

These villages are full of shops. There is scarcely a house which does not sell something. Where the buyers come from, and how a profit can be made, is a mystery. Many of the things are edibles, such as dried fishes, one and a half inch long, impaled on sticks; cakes, sweetmeats composed of rice, flour, and very little sugar; circular lumps of rice dough, called *mochi*; roots boiled in brine; a white jelly made from beans. There are ropes, straw shoes for men and horses, straw cloaks, paper umbrellas, paper waterproofs, hair-pins, toothpicks, tobacco pipes, paper tissues, and numbers of other trifles made of bamboo, straw, grass, and wood. These goods are on stands, and in the room behind, open to the street, all the domestic avocations are going on, and the housewife is usually to be seen boiling water or sewing with a baby tucked into the back of her dress. A lucifer factory has recently been put up, and in many house fronts men are cutting up wood into lengths for matches. In others they are husking rice, a very laborious process, in which the grain is pounded in a mortar sunk in the floor by a flat-ended wooden pestle attached to a long horizontal lever, which is worked by the feet of a man, invariably naked, who stands at the other extremity.

In some houses women are weaving, in others spinning cotton. Usually there are three or four together—the mother, the eldest son's wife, and one or two unmarried girls. The girls marry at sixteen, and shortly these comely, rosy, wholesome-looking creatures pass into haggard, middle-aged women with vacant faces, owing to the blackening of the teeth and removal of the eyebrows, which, if they do not follow betrothal, are resorted to on the birth of the first child. In other houses women are at their toilet, blackening their teeth before circular metal mirrors placed in folding stands on the mats, or performing ablutions, unclothed to the waist.

Early the village is very silent, while the children are at school. Their return enlivens it a little, but they are quiet even at play. At sunset the men return, and things are a little livelier. You hear a good deal of splashing in baths, and after that they carry about and play with their younger children, while the older ones prepare lessons for the following day by reciting them in a high, monotonous twang. At dark the paper windows are drawn, the *amado*, or external wooden shutters, are closed, the lamp is lighted before the family shrine, supper is eaten, and the children play at quiet games round the *andon*. At about ten the quilts and wooden pillows are produced from the press, the *amado* are bolted, and the family lies down to sleep in one room. Small trays of food and the *tabakobon* are always within reach of adult sleepers, and one grows quite accustomed to hear the sound of ashes being knocked out of the pipe at intervals during the night. The children sit up as late as their parents, and are included in all their conversation.

I never saw people take so much delight in their offspring, carrying them about, or holding their hands in walking, watching and entering into their games, supplying them constantly with new toys, taking them to picnics and festivals, never being content to be without them, and treating other people's children also with a suitable measure of affection and attention. Both fathers and mothers take a pride in their children. It is most amusing about six every morning to see twelve or fourteen men sitting on a low wall, each with a child under two years in his arms, fondling and playing with it, and showing off its physique and intelligence. To judge from appearances, the children form the chief topic at this morning gathering. At night, after the houses are shut up, looking through the long fringe of rope or rattan which conceals the sliding door, you see the father, who wears nothing but a *fundoshi* in the company of his family, bending his kindly face over a gentle-looking baby, and the mother, who more often than not has dropped the *kimono* from her shoulders, enfolding two children destitute of clothing in her arms. For some reasons they prefer boys, but certainly girls are equally petted and loved. The children, though for our ideas too gentle and formal, are very prepossessing in looks and behavior. They are so perfectly docile and obedient, so ready to help their parents, so good to the little ones. In the many hours which I have spent in watching them at play, I have never heard an angry word or seen a sour look or act. But they are little men and women rather than children, and their old-fashioned appearance is greatly aided by their dress, which, as I have remarked before, is the same as that of adults.

There are various styles of dressing the hair of girls, by which you can form a pretty accurate estimate of any girl's age up to her marriage, when the coiffure undergoes a definite change. The boys all look top-heavy and their heads of an abnormal size, partly from a hideous practice of shaving the head altogether for the first three years. After this the hair is allowed to grow in three tufts, one over each ear, and the other at the back of the neck. As often, however, a tuft is grown at the top of the back of the head. At ten the crown alone is shaved and a forelock is worn, and at fifteen, when the boy assumes the responsibilities of manhood, his hair is allowed to grow like that of a man. The grave dignity of these boys, with the grotesque patterns on their big heads, is most amusing.

Would that these much-exposed skulls were always smooth and clean! It is painful to see the prevalence of such repulsive maladies as scabies, scald-head, ringworm, sore eyes, and unwholesome-looking eruptions, and fully thirty percent of the village people are badly seamed with smallpox.

I have had to do a little shopping in Hachiishi for my journey. The shop-fronts are all open, and at the height of the floor, about two feet from the ground, there is a broad ledge of polished wood on which you sit down. A woman everlastingly boiling water on a bronze *hibachi*, or brazier, shifting the embers about deftly with brass tongs like chopsticks, and with a baby looking calmly over her shoulders, is the shopwoman. She remains indifferent till she imagines that you have a definite purpose of buying, when she comes forward bowing to the ground, and I politely rise and bow too. Then I or Itō ask the price of a thing, and she names it, very likely asking four shillings for what ought to sell at six pence. You say three shillings, she laughs and says three shillings six pence; you say two shillings, she laughs again and says three shillings, offering you the *tabakobon*. Eventually the matter is compromised by your giving her one shilling, at which she appears quite delighted. With a profusion of bows and *sayōnara*s on each side, you go away with the pleasant feeling of having given an industrious woman twice as much as the thing was worth to her, and less than what it is worth to you!

There are several barbers' shops, and the evening seems a very busy time with them. This operation partakes of the general want of privacy of the life of the village, and is performed in the raised open front of the shop. Soap is not used, and the process is a painful one. The victims let their garments fall to their waists, and each holds in his left hand a lacquered tray to receive the croppings. The Japanese face at this time wears a most grotesque expression of stolid resignation as it is held and pulled about by the operator, who turns it in all directions, that he may judge of the effect that he is producing. The shaving the face till it is smooth and shiny, and the cutting, waxing, and tying of the queue with twine made of paper, are among the evening sights of Nikkō.

Lacquer and things curiously carved in wood are the great attractions of the shops, but they interest me far less than the objects of utility in Japanese daily life, with their ingenuity of contrivance and perfection of adaptation and workmanship. A seed shop, where seeds are truly idealized, attracts me daily. Thirty varieties are offered for sale, as various in form as they are in color, and arranged most artistically on stands, while some are put up in packages decorated with what one may call a facsimile of the root, leaves, and flower, in water-colors. A lad usually lies on the mat behind executing these very creditable pictures—for such they are—with a few bold and apparently careless strokes with his brush. He gladly sold me a peony as a scrap for a screen for three *sen*. My purchases, with this exception, were necessaries only—a paper waterproof cloak, a circular, black outside and yellow inside, made of square sheets of oiled paper cemented together, and some large sheets of the same for covering my baggage. I succeeded in getting Itō out of his obnoxious black wide-awake into a basin-shaped hat like mine, for, ugly as I think him, he has a large share of personal vanity, whitens his teeth, and powders his face carefully before a mirror, and is in great dread of sunburn. He powders his hands too, and polishes his nails, and never goes out without gloves.

Tomorrow I leave luxury behind and plunge into the interior, hoping to emerge somehow upon the Sea of Japan. No information can be got here except about the route to Niigata, which I have decided not to take. After much study of Brunton's map, I have fixed upon one place, and have said positively, "I go to Tajima." If I reach it I can get farther, but all I can learn is, "It's a very bad road, it's all among the mountains." Itō, who has a great regard for his own comforts, tries to dissuade me from going by saying that I shall lose mine, but, as these kind people have ingeniously repaired my bed by doubling the canvas and lacing it into holes in the side poles, and as I have lived for the last three days on rice, eggs, and coarse noodles about the thickness and color of earth-worms, this prospect does not appal me!

In Japan there is a Land Transport Company, called Rikuun Kaisha, with a head office in Tokyo, and branches in various towns and villages. It arranges for the transport of travellers and merchandise by packhorses and laborers at certain fixed rates, and gives receipts in due form. It hires the horses from the farmers, and makes a moderate profit on each transaction, but saves the traveller from difficulties, delays, and extortions. The prices vary considerably in different districts, and are regulated by the price of forage, the state of the roads, and the number of hireable horses. For a *ri*, nearly two and a half miles, they charge from six to ten *sen* for a horse and the man who leads it. For a *kuruma* with one man from four to nine *sen* for the same distance, and for baggage laborers about the same. The Rikuun Kaisha is admirably organized. I employed it in journeys of over twelve hundred miles, and always found it efficient and reliable. I intend to make use of it always, much against Itō's wishes, who reckoned on many a prospective squeeze in dealings with the farmers.

My journey will now be entirely over unbeaten tracks, and will lead through what may be called "old Japan." As it will be natural to use Japanese words for money and distances, for which there are no English terms, I give them here. A yen is a note representing a dollar, or about 3 shillings and seven pence. of our money; a *sen* is something less than a halfpenny; a *rin* is a thin round coin of iron or bronze, with a square hole in the middle, of which ten make a *sen*. Distances are measured by *ri*, *chō*, and *ken*. Six feet make one *ken*, sixty *ken* one *chō*, and thirty-six *chō* one *ri*, or nearly two and a half English miles. When I write of a road I mean a bridle path from four to eight feet wide, *kuruma* roads being specified as such.

Beauties of the Kinugawa

Fujihara, June 24

Itō's informants were right. Comfort was left behind at Nikkō!

A little woman brought two depressed-looking mares at six this morning. My saddle and bridle were put on one, and Itō and the baggage on the other. My hosts and I exchanged cordial good wishes and obeisances, and, with the women dragging my sorry mare by a rope round her nose, we left the glorious shrines and solemn cryptomeria groves of Nikkō behind, passed down its long, clean street, and where the In Memoriam avenue is densest and darkest turned off to the left by a path like the bed of a brook, which afterwards, as a most atrocious trail, wound about among the rough boulders of the Daiya River, which it crosses often on temporary bridges of timbers covered with branches and soil. After crossing one of the low spurs of the Nikkō mountains, we wound among ravines whose steep sides are clothed with maple, oak, magnolia, elm, pine, and cryptomeria, linked together by festoons of the redundant Chinese wisteria, and brightened by azalea and syringa clusters. Every vista was blocked by some grand mountain, waterfalls thundered, bright streams glanced through the trees, and in the glorious sunshine of June the country looked most beautiful.

We travelled less than a *ri* an hour, as it was a mere flounder either among rocks or in deep mud, the woman in her girt-up dress and straw sandals trudging bravely along, till she suddenly flung away the rope, cried out, and ran backwards, perfectly scared by a big grey snake, with red spots. The snake was much embarrassed by a large frog which he would not let go, though, like most of his kind, he was alarmed by human approach, and made desperate efforts to swallow his victim and wriggle into the bushes. After crawling for three hours we dismounted at the mountain farm of Kohiaku, on the edge of a rice valley. Here the woman counted her packages to see that they were all right, and without waiting for a gratuity turned homewards with her horses. I pitched my chair on the verandah of a house near a few poor dwellings inhabited by peasants with large families, the house being in the barnyard of a rich *sake* maker. I waited an hour, grew famished, got some weak tea and boiled barley. I waited another hour, and yet another, for all the horses were eating leaves on the mountains. There was a little stir. Men carried sheaves of barley home on their backs, and stacked them under the eaves. Children, with barely the rudiments of clothing, stood and watched me hour after hour, and adults were not ashamed to join the group, for they had never seen a foreign woman, a fork, or a spoon. Could there be a stranger sight one than a decent-looking middle-aged man lying on his chest on the verandah, raised on his elbows, and intently reading a book, clothed only in a pair of spectacles? Besides that curious piece of still life, women frequently drew water from a well by the primitive contrivance of a beam suspended across an upright, with the bucket at one end and a stone at the other.

When the horses arrived the men said they could not put on the bridle. After much talk, it was managed by two of them violently forcing open the jaws of the animal, while a third seized a propitious moment for slipping the bit into her mouth. At the next change a bridle was a thing unheard of, and when I suggested that the creature would open her mouth voluntarily if the bit were pressed close to her teeth, the standers-by mockingly said, "No horse ever opens his mouth except to eat or to bite," and were only convinced after I had put on the bridle myself. The new horses had a rocking gait like camels, and I was glad to dispense with them at Kisagoi, a small upland hamlet, a very poor place, with poverty-stricken houses, children very dirty and sorely afflicted by skin maladies, and women with complexions and features hardened by severe work and much wood smoke into positive ugliness, and with figures anything but statuesque.

I write the truth as I see it, and if my accounts conflict with those of tourists who write of the Tokaidō and Nakasendō, of Lake Biwa and Hakone, it does not follow that either is inaccurate. But truly this is a new Japan to me, of which no books have given me any idea, and it is not fairyland. The men may be said to wear nothing. Few of the women wear anything but a short petticoat wound tightly round them, or blue cotton trousers very tight in the legs and baggy at the top, with a blue cotton garment open to the waist tucked into the band, and a blue cotton handkerchief knotted round the head. From the dress no notion of the sex of the wearer could be gained, nor from the faces, if it were not for the shaven eyebrows and black teeth. The short petticoat is truly barbarous-looking, and when a woman has a nude baby on her back or in her arms, and stands staring vacantly at the foreigner, I can hardly believe myself in "civilized" Japan. A good-sized child, strong enough to hold up his head, sees the world right cheerfully looking over his mother's shoulders, but it is a constant distress to me to see small children of six and seven years old lugging on their backs gristly babies, whose shorn heads are frizzling in the sun and "wobbling" about as though they must drop off, their eyes, as nurses say, "looking over their heads."

A number of silkworms are kept in this region, and in the open barns groups of men in nature's costume, and women unclothed to their waists, were busy stripping mulberry branches. The houses were all poor, and the people dirty both in their clothing and persons. Some of the younger women might possibly have been comely, if soap and water had been plentifully applied to their faces. Soap is not used, and such washing as the garments get is only the rubbing them a little with sand in a running stream.

I heard many stories of the viciousness and aggressiveness of packhorses, and was told that they were muzzled to prevent them from pasturing upon the haunches of their companions and making vicious snatches at men. Now, I find that the muzzle is only to prevent them from eating as they travel. Mares are used exclusively in this region, and they are the gentlest of their race. If you have the weight of baggage reckoned at one horse-load, though it should turn out that the weight is too great for a weakly animal, and the transport agent distributes it among two or even three horses, you only pay for one. And though our cortege on leaving Kisagoi consisted of four small, shock-headed mares who could hardly see through their bushy forelocks, with three active foals, and one woman and three girls to lead them, I only paid for two horses at seven *sen* a ri.

My *mago*, with her toil-hardened, thoroughly good-natured face rendered hideous by black teeth, wore straw sandals, blue cotton trousers with a vest tucked into them, as poor and worn as they could be, and a blue cotton towel knotted round her head. As the sky looked threatening she carried a straw rain-cloak, a thatch of two connected capes, one fastening at the neck, the other at the waist, and a flat hat of flags, two and a half feet in diameter, hung at her back like a shield. Up and down, over rocks and through deep mud, she trudged with a steady stride, turning her kind, ugly face at intervals to see if the girls were following. I like the firm hardy gait which this unbecoming costume permits better than the painful shuffle imposed upon the more civilized women by their tight skirts and high *geta*.

From Kohiaku the road passed through an irregular grassy valley between densely-wooded hills, the valley itself timbered with park-like clumps of pine and Spanish chestnuts; but on leaving Kisagoi the scenery changed. A steep rocky tract brought us to the Kinu-*gawa*, a clear rushing river, which has cut its way deeply through colored rock, and is crossed at a considerable height by a bridge with an alarmingly steep curve, from which there is a fine view of high mountains, and among them Futara-*yama*, to which some of the most ancient Shinto legends are attached.

We rode for some time within hearing of the Kinu River, catching magnificent glimpses of it frequently—turbulent and locked in by walls of porphyry, or widening and calming and spreading its aquamarine waters over great slabs of pink and green rock, lighted fitfully by the sun, or spanned by rainbows, or pausing to rest in deep shady pools, but always beautiful. The mountains through which it forces its way on the other side are precipitous and wooded to their summits with coniferae, while the less abrupt side, along which the tract is carried, curves into green knolls in its lower slopes, sprinkled with grand Spanish chestnuts scarcely yet in blossom, with maples which have not yet lost the scarlet which they wear in spring as well as autumn. There are many flowering trees and shrubs which are new to me, and an undergrowth of red azaleas, syringa, blue hydrangea— the very blue of heaven—yellow raspberries, ferns, clematis, white and yellow lilies, blue irises, and fifty other trees and shrubs entangled and festooned by the wistaria, whose beautiful foliage is as common as is that of the bramble with us. The redundancy of the vegetation was truly tropical, and the brilliancy and variety of its living greens, dripping with recent rain, were enhanced by the slant rays of the afternoon sun.

The few hamlets we passed are of farm houses only, the deep-eaved roofs covering in one sweep dwelling house, barn, and stable. In every barn unclothed people were pursuing various industries. We met strings of pack-mares, tied head and tail, loaded with rice and *sake*, and men and women carrying large creels full of mulberry leaves. The ravine grew more and more beautiful, and an ascent through a dark wood of arrowy cryptomeria brought us to this village exquisitely situated, where a number of miniature ravines, industriously terraced for rice, come down upon the great chasm of the Kinu River. Eleven hours of travelling have brought me eighteen miles!

Ikari, June 25
Fujihara has forty-six farm houses and a *yadoya*— all dark, damp, dirty, and droughty, a combination of dwelling house, barn, and stable. The *yadoya* consisted of a *daidokoro*, or open kitchen, a stable below, and a small loft above, capable of division. I found on returning from a walk six Japanese in extreme deshabille occupying the part through which I had to pass. On this being remedied I sat down to write, but was soon driven upon the balcony, under the eaves, by myriads of fleas, which hopped out of the mats as sand hoppers do out of the sea sand, and even in the balcony, hopped over my letter. There were two outer walls of hairy mud with living creatures crawling in the cracks. Cobwebs hung from the uncovered rafters. The mats were brown with age and dirt, the rice was musty, and only partially cleaned, the eggs had seen better days, and the tea was musty.

I saw everything out of doors with Itō—the patient industry, the exquisitely situated village, the evening avocations, the quiet dulness—and then contemplated it all from my balcony and read the sentence (from a paper in the Transactions of the Asiatic Society) which had led me to devise this journey, "There is a most exquisitely picturesque, but difficult, route up the course of the Kinu-*gawa*, which seems almost as unknown to Japanese as to foreigners." There was a pure lemon-colored sky above, and slush a foot deep below. A road, at this time a quagmire, intersected by a rapid stream, crossed in many places by planks, runs through the village. This stream is at once "lavatory" and "drinking fountain." People come back from their work, sit on the planks, take off their muddy clothes and wring them out, and bathe their feet in the current. On either side are the dwellings, in front of which are much-decayed manure heaps, and the women were engaged in breaking them up and treading them into a pulp with their bare feet. All wear the vest and trousers at their work, but only the short petticoats in their houses, and I saw several respectable mothers of families cross the road and pay visits in this garment only, without any sense of impropriety. The younger children wear nothing but a string and an amulet. The persons, clothing, and houses are alive with vermin, and if the word squalor can be applied to independent and industrious people, they were squalid. Beetles, spiders, and wood-lice held a carnival in my room after dark, and the presence of horses in the same house brought a number of horseflies. I sprinkled my stretcher with insect powder, but my blanket had been on the floor for one minute, and fleas rendered sleep impossible.

The night was very long. The *andon* went out, leaving a strong smell of rancid oil. The primitive Japanese dog— a cream-colored wolfish-looking animal, the size of a collie, very noisy and aggressive, but as cowardly as bullies usually are—was in great force in Fujihara, and the barking, growling, and quarrelling of these useless curs continued at intervals until daylight. When they were not quarrelling, they were howling. Torrents of rain fell, obliging me to move my bed from place to place to get out of the drip.

At five Itō came and entreated me to leave, whimpering, "I've had no sleep; there are thousands and thousands of fleas!" He has travelled by another route to the Tsugaru Strait through the interior, and says that he would not have believed that there was such a place in Japan, and that people in Yokohama will not believe it when he tells them of it and of the costume of the women. He is "ashamed for a foreigner to see such a place," he says. His cleverness in travelling and his singular intelligence surprise me daily. He is very anxious to speak *good* English, as distinguished from *common* English, and to learn new words, with their correct pronunciation and spelling. Each day he puts down in his note-book all the words that I use that he does not quite understand, and in the evening brings them to me and puts down their meaning and spelling with their Japanese equivalents. He speaks English already far better than many professional interpreters, but would be more pleasing if he had not picked up some American vulgarisms and free-and-easy ways.

It is so important to me to have a good interpreter, or I should not have engaged so young and inexperienced a servant. But he is so clever that he is now able to be cook, laundryman, and general attendant, as well as courier and interpreter, and I think it is far easier for me than if he were an older man. I am trying to manage him, because I saw that he meant to manage me, especially in the matter of "squeezes." He is intensely Japanese, his patriotism has all the weakness and strength of personal vanity, and he thinks everything inferior that is foreign. Our manners, eyes, and modes of eating appear simply odious to him. He delights in retailing stories of the bad manners of Englishmen, describes them as "roaring out *ohayō* to every one on the road," frightening the teahouse nymphs, kicking or slapping their laborers, stamping over white mats in muddy boots, acting generally like ill-bred Satyrs, exciting an ill-concealed hatred in simple country districts, and bringing themselves and their country into contempt and ridicule.

He is very anxious about my good behavior, and as I am equally anxious to be courteous everywhere in Japanese fashion, and not to violate the general rules of Japanese etiquette, I take his suggestions as to what I ought to do and avoid in very good part, and my bows are growing more profound every day! The people are so kind and courteous, that it is truly brutal in foreigners not to be kind and courteous to them. I am entirely dependent on Itō, not only for travelling arrangements, but for making inquiries, gaining information, and even for companionship, such as it is. Our being mutually embarked on a hard and adventurous journey will, I hope, make us mutually kind and considerate. Nominally, he is a Shintoist, which means nothing. At Nikkō I read to him the earlier chapters of St. Luke, and when I came to the story of the Prodigal Son I was interrupted by a somewhat scornful laugh and the remark, "Why, all this is our Buddha over again!"

Today's journey, though very rough, has been rather pleasant. The rain moderated at noon, and I left Fujihara on foot, wearing my American "mountain dress" and Wellington boots—the only costume in which ladies can enjoy pedestrian or packhorse travelling in this country—with a light straw mat—the waterproof of the region—hanging over my shoulders. And so we plodded on with two baggage horses through the ankle-deep mud, till the rain cleared off, the mountains looked through the mist, the augmented Kinu-*gawa* thundered below, and enjoyment became possible, even in my half-fed condition.

Eventually I mounted a pack saddle, and we crossed a spur of Mount Takada at a height of 2100 feet on a well-devised series of zigzags, eight of which in one place could be seen one below another. The forest there is not so dense as usual, and the lower mountain slopes are sprinkled with noble Spanish chestnuts. The descent was steep and slippery, the horse had tender feet, and, after stumbling badly, eventually came down, and I went over his head, to the great distress of the kindly female *mago*. The straw shoes tied with wisps round the pasterns are a great nuisance. The "shoe strings" are always coming untied, and the shoes only wear about two *ri* on soft ground, and less than one on hard. They keep the feet so soft and spongy that the horses can't walk without them at all, and as soon as they get thin your horse begins to stumble, the *mago* gets uneasy, and presently you stop. Four shoes, which are hanging from the saddle, are soaked in water and are tied on with much coaxing, raising the animal fully an inch above the ground. Anything more temporary and clumsy could not be devised. The bridle paths are strewn with them, and the children collect them in heaps to decay for manure. They cost three or four *sen* the set, and in every village men spend their leisure time in making them.

At the next stage, called Takahara, we got one horse for the baggage, crossed the river and the ravine, and by a steep climb reached a solitary *yadoya* with the usual open front and *irori*, round which a number of people, old and young, were sitting. When I arrived a whole bevy of nice-looking girls took to flight, but were soon recalled by a word from Itō to their elders. Lady Parkes, on a side-saddle and in a riding-habit, has been taken for a man till the people saw her hair, and a young friend of mine, who is very pretty and has a beautiful complexion, when travelling lately with her husband, was supposed to be a man who had shaven off his beard. I wear a hat, which is a thing only worn by women in the fields as a protection from sun and rain, my eyebrows are unshaven, and my teeth are unblackened, so these girls supposed me to be a foreign man. Itō in explanation said, "They haven't seen any, but everybody brings them tales how rude foreigners are to girls, and they are awful scared."

There was nothing edible but rice and eggs, and I ate them under the concentrated stare of eighteen pairs of dark eyes. The hot springs, to which many people afflicted with sores resort, are by the river, at the bottom of a rude flight of steps, in an open shed, but I could not ascertain their temperature, as a number of men and women were sitting in the water. They bathe four times a day, and remain for an hour at a time.

We left for the five miles' walk to Ikari in a torrent of rain by a newly-made path completely shut in with the cascading Kinu-*gawa*, and carried along sometimes low, sometimes high, on props projecting over it from the face of the rock. I do not expect to see anything lovelier in Japan.

The river, always crystal-blue or crystal-green, largely increased in volume by the rains, forces itself through gates of brightly-colored rock, by which its progress is repeatedly arrested, and rarely lingers for rest in all its sparkling, rushing course. It is walled in by high mountains, gloriously wooded and cleft by dark ravines, down which torrents were tumbling in great drifts of foam, crashing and booming, boom and crash multiplied by many an echo, and every ravine afforded glimpses far back of more mountains, clefts, and waterfalls, and such over-abundant vegetation that I welcomed the sight of a gray cliff or bare face of rock. Along the path there were fascinating details, composed of the manifold greenery which revels in damp heat, ferns, mosses, confervae, fungi, trailers, shading tiny rills which dropped down into grottoes feathery with the exquisite bristle fern, or drooped over the rustic path and hung into the river, and overhead the finely incised and almost feathery foliage of several varieties of maple admitted the light only as a green mist. The spring tints have not yet darkened into the monotone of summer, rose azaleas still light the hillsides, and masses of cryptomeria give depth and shadow. Still, beautiful as it all is, one sighs for something which shall satisfy one's craving for startling individuality and grace of form, as in the coco-palm and banana of the tropics. The featheriness of the maple, and the arrowy straightness and pyramidal form of the cryptomeria, please me better than all else; but why criticize? Ten minutes of sunshine would transform the whole into fairyland.

There were no houses and no people. Leaving this beautiful river we crossed a spur of a hill, where all the trees were matted together by a very fragrant white honeysuckle, and came down upon an open valley where a quiet stream joins the loud-tongued Kinu-*gawa*, and another mile brought us to this beautifully-situated hamlet of twenty-five houses, surrounded by mountains, and close to a mountain stream called the Okawa. The names of Japanese rivers give one very little geographical information from their want of continuity. A river changes its name several times in a course of thirty or forty miles, according to the districts through which it passes. This is my old friend the Kinu-*gawa*, up which I have been travelling for two days. Want of space is a great aid to the picturesque. Ikari is crowded together on a hill slope, and its short, primitive-looking street, with its warm browns and grays, is quite attractive in "the clear shining after rain."

My halting-place is at the express office at the top of the hill—a place like a big barn, with horses at one end and a living-room at the other, and in the centre much produce awaiting transport, and a group of people stripping mulberry branches. The nearest *daimyō* used to halt here on his way to Tokyo, so there are two rooms for travellers, called *daimyō*'s rooms, fifteen feet high, handsomely ceiled in dark wood, the *shōji* of such fine work as to merit the name of fret-work, the *fusuma* artistically decorated, the mats clean and fine, and in the alcove a sword-rack of old gold lacquer. Mine is the inner room, and Itō and four travellers occupy the outer one. Though very dark, it is luxury after last night. The rest of the house is given up to the rearing of silkworms. The house masters here and at Fujihara are not used to passports, and Itō, who is posing as a town-bred youth, has explained and copied mine, all the village men assembling to hear it read aloud. He does not know the word used for "scientific investigation," but, in the idea of increasing his own importance by exaggerating mine, I hear him telling the people that I am a *gakusha*, i.e. learned! There is no police-station here, but every month policemen pay domiciliary visits to these outlying *yadoya* and examine the register of visitors.

This is a much neater place than the last, but the people look stupid and apathetic, and I wonder what they think of the men who have abolished the *daimyō* and the feudal regime, have raised the eta to citizenship, and are hurrying the empire forward on the tracks of western civilisation!

Since shingle has given place to thatch there is much to admire in the villages, with their steep roofs, deep eaves and balconies, the warm russet of roofs and walls, the quaint confusion of the farmhouses, the hedges of camellia and pomegranate, the bamboo clumps and persimmon orchards, and (in spite of dirt and bad smells) the generally satisfied look of the peasant proprietors.

No food can be got here except rice and eggs, and I am haunted by memories of the fowls and fish of Nikkō, to say nothing of the "flesh pots" of the legation.

The mercury falls to seventy degrees at night, and I generally awake from cold at 3 a.m., for my blankets are only summer ones, and I dare not supplement them with a quilt, either for sleeping on or under, because of the fleas which it contains. I usually retire about 7.30 p.m., for there is almost no twilight, and very little inducement for sitting up by the dimness of candle or *andon*. I have found these days of riding on slow, rolling, stumbling horses very severe. If I were anything of a walker, I should certainly prefer pedestrianism.

Amateur Doctoring

Kurumatoge, June 30

After the hard travelling of six days the rest of Sunday in a quiet place at a high elevation is truly delightful! Mountains and passes, valleys and rice swamps, forests and rice swamps, villages and rice swamps; poverty, industry, dirt, ruinous temples, prostrate Buddhas, strings of straw-shod packhorses; long, grey, featureless streets, and quiet, staring crowds, are all jumbled up fantastically in my memory. Fine weather accompanied me through beautiful scenery from Ikari to Yokokawa, where I ate my lunch in the street to avoid the innumerable fleas of the teahouse, with a circle round me of nearly all the inhabitants. At first the children, both old and young, were so frightened that they ran away, but by degrees they timidly came back, clinging to the skirts of their parents (skirts, in this case, being a metaphorical expression), running away again as often as I looked at them. The crowd was filthy and squalid beyond description.

Why should the quiver of poverty be so very full? one asks as one looks at the swarms of gentle, naked, children, born to a heritage of hard toil, to be, like their parents, devoured by vermin, and pressed hard for taxes. A horse kicked off my saddle before it was girthed, the crowd scattered right and left, and work, which had been suspended for two hours to stare at the foreigner, began again.

A long ascent took us to the top of a pass 2500 feet in height, a projecting spur not thirty feet wide, with a grand view of mountains and ravines, and a maze of involved streams, which unite in a vigorous torrent, whose course we followed for some hours, till it expanded into a quiet river, lounging lazily through a rice swamp of considerable extent. The map is blank in this region, but I judged, as I afterwards found rightly, that at that pass we had crossed the water-shed, and that the streams thenceforward no longer fall into the Pacific, but into the Sea of Japan. At Itōsawa the horses produced stumbled so intolerably that I walked the last stage, and reached Kayashima, a miserable village of fifty-seven houses, so exhausted that I could not go farther, and was obliged to put up with worse accommodation even than at Fujihara, with less strength for its hardships.

The *yadoya* was simply awful. The *daidokoro* had a large wood fire burning in a trench, filling the whole place with stinging smoke, from which my room, which was merely screened off by some dilapidated *shōji*, was not exempt. The rafters were black and shiny with soot and moisture. The house master, who knelt persistently on the floor of my room till he was dislodged by Itō, apologized for the dirt of his house, as well he might. Stifling, dark, and smoky, as my room was, I had to close the paper windows, owing to the crowd which assembled in the street. There was neither rice nor soy, and Itō, who values his own comfort, began to speak to the house master and servants loudly and roughly, and to throw my things about—a style of acting which I promptly terminated, for nothing could be more hurtful to a foreigner, or more unkind to the people, than for a servant to be rude and bullying. The man was most polite, and never approached me but on bended knees. When I gave him my passport, as the custom is, he touched his forehead with it, and then touched the earth with his forehead.

I found nothing that I could eat except black beans and boiled cucumbers. The room was dark, dirty, vile, noisy, and poisoned by sewage odors, as rooms unfortunately are very apt to be. At the end of the rice planting there is a holiday for two days, when many offerings are made to Inari Ōkami, the god of rice farmers. The holiday-makers kept up their revel all night, and drums, stationary and peripatetic, were constantly beaten in such a way as to prevent sleep.

A little boy, the house master's son, was suffering from a very bad cough, and a few drops of chlorodyne which I gave him allayed it so completely that the cure was noised abroad in the earliest hours of the next morning. By five o'clock nearly the whole population was assembled outside my room, with much whispering and shuffling of shoeless feet, and applications of eyes to the many holes in the paper windows. When I drew aside the *shōji* I was disconcerted by the painful sight which presented itself, for the people were pressing one upon another, fathers and mothers holding naked children covered with skin-disease, or with scald-head, or ringworm, daughters leading mothers nearly blind, men exhibiting painful sores, children blinking with eyes infested by flies and nearly closed with inflammation. All, sick and well, were in truly "vile raiment," lamentably dirty and swarming with vermin, the sick asking for medicine, and the well either bringing the sick or gratifying an apathetic curiosity.

Sadly I told them that I did not understand their manifold diseases and torments, and that, if I did, I had no stock of medicines, and that in my own country the constant washing of clothes, and the constant application of water to the skin, accompanied by friction with clean cloths, would be much relied upon by doctors for the cure and prevention of similar cutaneous diseases. To pacify them I made some ointment of animal fat and flowers of sulphur, extracted with difficulty from some man's hoard, and told them how to apply it to some of the worst cases. The horse, being unused to a girth, became fidgety as it was being saddled, creating a stampede among the crowd, and the *mago* would not touch it again. They are as much afraid of their gentle mares as if they were panthers. All the children followed me for a considerable distance, and a good many of the adults made an excuse for going in the same direction.

These people wear no linen, and their clothes, which are seldom washed, are constantly worn, night and day, as long as they will hold together. They seal up their houses as hermetically as they can at night, and herd together in numbers in one sleeping-room, with its atmosphere vitiated, to begin with, by charcoal and tobacco fumes, huddled up in their dirty garments in wadded quilts, which are kept during the day in close cupboards, and are seldom washed from one year's end to another. The *tatami*, beneath a tolerably fair exterior, swarm with insect life, and are receptacles of dust and organic matters. The hair, which is loaded with oil and bandoline, is dressed once a week, or less often in these districts, and it is unnecessary to enter into any details regarding the distressing results, and much besides may be left to the imagination. The persons of the people, especially of the children, are infested with vermin, and one fruitful source of skin sores is the irritation arising from this cause. The floors of houses, being concealed by mats, are laid down carelessly with gaps between the boards, and, as the damp earth is only eighteen inches or two feet below, emanations of all kinds enter the mats and pass into the rooms.

The houses in this region (and I believe everywhere) are hermetically sealed at night, both in summer and winter, the *amado*, which are made without ventilators, literally boxing them in, so that, unless they are falling to pieces, which is rarely the case, none of the air vitiated by the breathing of many persons, by the emanations from their bodies and clothing, by the miasmata produced by defective domestic arrangements, and by the fumes from charcoal *hibachi*, can ever be renewed. Exercise is seldom taken from choice, and, unless the women work in the fields, they hang over charcoal fumes the whole day for five months of the year, engaged in interminable processes of cooking, or in the attempt to get warm. Much of the food of the peasantry is raw or half-raw salted fish, and vegetables rendered indigestible by being coarsely pickled, all bolted with the most marvellous rapidity, as if the one object of life were to rush through a meal in the shortest possible time. The married women look as if they had never known youth, and their skin is apt to be like tanned leather. At Kayashima I asked the house master's wife, who looked about fifty, how old she was (a polite question in Japan), and she replied twenty-two—one of many similar surprises. Her boy was five years old, and was still unweaned.

We changed horses at Tajima, formerly a *daimyō*'s residence, and, for a Japanese town, rather picturesque. It makes and exports *geta*, coarse pottery, coarse lacquer, and coarse baskets.

After travelling through rice fields varying from thirty yards square to a quarter of an acre, with the tops of the dykes utilised by planting dwarf beans along them, we came to a large river, the Arakai, along whose affluents we had been tramping for two days. After passing through several filthy villages, thronged with filthy and industrious inhabitants, we crossed it in a scow. High forks planted securely in the bank on either side sustained a rope formed of several strands of the wistaria knotted together. One man hauled on this hand over hand, another poled at the stern, and the rapid current did the rest. In this fashion we have crossed many rivers subsequently. Tariffs of charges are posted at all ferries, as well as at all bridges where charges are made, and a man sits in an office to receive the money.

The country was really very beautiful. The views were wider and finer than on the previous days, taking in great sweeps of peaked mountains, wooded to their summits. From the top of the Sannō Pass the clustered peaks were glorified into unearthly beauty in a golden mist of evening sunshine. I slept at a house combining silk farm, post office, express office, and *daimyō*'s rooms, at the hamlet of Ouchi, prettily situated in a valley with mountainous surroundings, and, leaving early on the following morning, had a very grand ride, passing in a crateriform cavity the pretty little lake of Oyake, and then ascending the magnificent pass of Ichikawa.

We turned off what, by ironical courtesy, is called the main road, upon a villainous track, consisting of a series of lateral corrugations, about a foot broad, with depressions between them more than a foot deep, formed by the invariable treading of packhorses in each other's footsteps. Each hole was a quagmire of tenacious mud, the ascent of 2400 feet was very steep, and the *mago* adjured the animals the whole time with *Hai! Hai! Hai!* which is supposed to suggest to them that extreme caution is requisite. Their shoes were always coming untied, and they wore out two sets in four miles.

The top of the pass, like that of a great many others, is a narrow ridge, on the farther side of which the track dips abruptly into a tremendous ravine, along whose side we descended for a mile or so in company with a river whose reverberating thunder drowned all attempts at speech. A glorious view it was, looking down between the wooded precipices to a rolling wooded plain, lying in depths of indigo shadow, bounded by ranges of wooded mountains, and overtopped by heights heavily splotched with snow!

The vegetation was significant of a milder climate. The magnolia and bamboo re-appeared, and tropical ferns mingled with the beautiful blue hydrangea, the yellow Japan lily, and the great blue campanula. There was an ocean of trees entangled with a beautiful trailer (*matatabi*) with a profusion of white leaves, which, at a distance, look like great clusters of white blossoms. But the rank undergrowth of the forests of this region is not attractive. Many of its component parts deserve the name of weeds, being gawky, ragged umbels, coarse docks, rank nettles, and many other things which I don't know, and never wish to see again.

Near the end of this descent my mare took the bit between her teeth and carried me at an ungainly gallop into the beautifully situated, precipitous village of Ichikawa, which is absolutely saturated with moisture by the spray of a fine waterfall which tumbles through the middle of it, and its trees and roadside are green with algae. The transport agent there was a woman. Women keep *yadoya* and shops, and cultivate farms as freely as men. Boards giving the number of inhabitants, male and female, and the number of horses and bullocks, are put up in each village, and I noticed in Ichikawa, as everywhere hitherto, that men preponderate.

Swallowing a Fishbone

Kurumatoge, June 30

A short ride took us from Ichikawa to a plain about eleven miles broad by eighteen long. The large town of Wakamatsu stands near its southern end, and it is sprinkled with towns and villages. The great lake of Inawashirō is not far off. The plain is rich and fertile. In the distance the steep roofs of its villages, with their groves, look very picturesque. As usual not a fence or gate is to be seen, or any other hedge than the tall one used as a screen for the dwellings of the richer farmers.

Bad roads and bad horses detracted from my enjoyment. One hour of a good horse would have carried me across the plain. As it was, seven weary hours were expended upon it. The day degenerated, and closed in still, hot rain. The air was stifling and electric, the saddle slipped constantly from being too big, the shoes were more than usually troublesome, the horseflies tormented, and the men and horses crawled. The rice fields were undergoing a second process of puddling, and many of the men engaged in it wore only a hat, and a fan attached to the *obi*.

An avenue of cryptomeria and two handsome and somewhat gilded Buddhist temples denoted the approach to a place of some importance. And such Takata is, as being a large town with a considerable trade in silk, and the residence of one of the higher officials of the prefecture. The street is a mile long, and every house is a shop. The general aspect is mean and forlorn. In these little-travelled districts, as soon as one reaches the margin of a town, the first man one meets turns and flies down the street, calling out the Japanese equivalent of "Here's a foreigner!" and soon blind and seeing, old and young, clothed and naked, gather together. At the *yadoya* the crowd assembled in such force that the house master removed me to some pretty rooms in a garden. But then the adults climbed on the house roofs which overlooked it, and the children on a palisade at the end, which broke down under their weight, and admitted the whole inundation. I had to close the *shōji*, with the fatiguing consciousness during the whole time of nominal rest of a multitude surging outside. Then five policemen in black alpaca frock-coats and white trousers invaded my precarious privacy, desiring to see my passport—a demand never made before except where I halted for the night. In their European clothes they cannot bow with Japanese punctiliousness, but they were very polite, and expressed great annoyance at the crowd, and dispersed it. They had hardly disappeared when it gathered again. When I went out I found fully a thousand people. These Japanese crowds are quiet and gentle, and never press rudely upon one. I could not find it in my heart to complain of them. Four of the policemen returned, and escorted me to the outskirts of the town. The noise made by such great crowds shuffling along in *geta* is like the clatter of a hail-storm.

After this there was a dismal tramp of five hours through rice fields. The moist climate and the fatigue of this manner of travelling are deteriorating my health, and the pain in my spine, which has been daily increasing, was so severe that I could neither ride nor walk for more than twenty minutes at a time; and the pace was so slow that it was six when we reached Bange, a commercial town of five thousand people, literally in the rice swamp, mean, filthy, damp, and decaying, and full of an overpowering stench from black, slimy ditches. The mercury was eighty-four degrees, and hot rain fell fast through the motionless air. We dismounted in a shed full of bales of dried fish, which gave off an overpowering odor, and wet and dirty people crowded in to stare at the foreigner till the air seemed unbreathable.

But there were signs of progress. A three days' congress of schoolmasters was being held; candidates for vacant situations were being examined; there were lengthy educational discussions going on, especially on the value of the Chinese classics as a part of education; and every inn was crowded.

Bange was malarious: there was so much malarious fever that the government had sent additional medical assistance. The hills were only a *ri* off, and it seemed essential to go on. But not a horse could be got till ten p.m. The road was worse than the one I had travelled. The pain became more acute, and I more exhausted, and I was obliged to remain. Then followed a weary hour, in which the express agent's five emissaries were searching for a room, and considerably after dark I found myself in a rambling old overcrowded *yadoya*, where my room was mainly built on piles above stagnant water, and the mosquitoes were in such swarms as to make the air dense, and after a feverish and miserable night I was glad to get up early and depart.

Fully two thousand people had assembled. After I was mounted I was on the point of removing my telescope from the case, which hung on the saddle horn, when a regular stampede occurred, old and young running as fast as they possibly could, children being knocked down in the haste of their elders. Itō said that they thought I was taking out a pistol to frighten them, and I made him explain what the object really was, for they are a gentle, harmless people, whom one would not annoy without sincere regret. In many European countries, and certainly in some parts of our own, a solitary lady- traveller in a foreign dress would be exposed to rudeness, insult, and extortion, if not to actual danger. But I have not met with a single instance of incivility or real overcharge, and there is no rudeness even about the crowding. The *mago* are anxious that I should not get wet or be frightened, and very scrupulous in seeing that all straps and loose things are safe at the end of the journey. Instead of hanging about asking for gratuities, or stopping to drink and gossip, they quickly unload the horses, get a paper from the transport agent, and go home. Only yesterday a strap was missing, and, though it was after dark, the man went back a *ri* for it, and refused to take some *sen* which I wished to give him, saying he was responsible for delivering everything right at the journey's end. They are so kind and courteous to each other, which is very pleasing. Itō is not pleasing or polite in his manner to me, but when he speaks to his own people he cannot free himself from the shackles of etiquette, and bows as profoundly and uses as many polite phrases as anybody else.

In an hour the malarious plain was crossed, and we have been among the mountains ever since. The infamous road was so slippery that my horse fell several times, and the baggage horse, with Itō upon him, rolled head over heels, sending his miscellaneous pack in all directions. Good roads are really the most pressing need of Japan. It would be far better if the government were to enrich the country by such a remunerative outlay as making passable roads for the transport of goods through the interior, than to impoverish it by buying ironclads in England, and indulging in expensive western vanities.

That so horrible a road should have so good a bridge as that by which we crossed the broad Agano River is surprising. It consists of twelve large scows, each one secured to a strong cable of plaited wistaria, which crosses the river at a great height, so as to allow of the scows and the plank bridge which they carry rising and falling with the twelve feet variation of the water.

Itō's disaster kept him back for an hour, and I sat meanwhile on a rice sack in the hamlet of Katakado, a collection of steep-roofed houses huddled together in a height above the Agano. It was one mob of packhorses, over 200 of them, biting, squealing, and kicking. Before I could dismount, one vicious creature struck at me violently, but only hit the great wooden stirrup. I could hardly find any place out of the range of hoofs or teeth. My baggage horse showed great fury after he was unloaded. He attacked people right and left with his teeth, struck out savagely with his fore feet, lashed out with his hind ones, and tried to pin his master up against a wall.

Leaving this fractious scene we struck again through the mountains. Their ranges were interminable, and every view from every fresh ridge grander than the last, for we were now near the lofty range of the Aizu Mountains, and the double-peaked Bandai-*san*, the abrupt precipices of Itōya-*san*, and the grand mass of Mount Myōjintake in the south-west, with their vast snow-fields and snow-filled ravines, were all visible at once. These summits of naked rock or dazzling snow, rising above the smothering greenery of the lower ranges into a heaven of delicious blue, gave exactly that individuality and emphasis which, to my thinking, Japanese scenery usually lacks. Riding on first, I arrived alone at the little town of Nozawa, to encounter the curiosity of a crowd. After a rest, we had a very pleasant walk of three miles along the side of a ridge above a rapid river with fine grey cliffs on its farther side, with a grand view of the Aizu giants, violet colored in a golden sunset.

At dusk we came upon the picturesque village of Nojiri, on the margin of a rice valley. I shrank from spending Sunday in a hole, and, having spied a solitary house on the very brow of a hill fifteen hundred feet higher, I dragged out the information that it was a teahouse, and came up to it. It took three-quarters of an hour to climb the series of precipitous zigzags by which this remarkable pass is surmounted. Darkness came on, accompanied by thunder and lightning, and just as we arrived a tremendous zigzag of blue flame lit up the house and its interior, showing a large group sitting round a wood fire, and then all was thick darkness again. It had a most startling effect. This house is magnificently situated, almost hanging over the edge of the knife-like ridge of the Kuruma Pass, on which it is situated. It is the only *yadoya* I have been at from which there has been any view. The villages are nearly always in the valleys, and the best rooms are at the back, and have their prospects limited by the paling of the conventional garden. If it were not for the fleas, which are here in legions, I should stay longer, for the view of the Aizu snow is delicious, and, as there are only two other houses, one can ramble without being mobbed.

In one a child two and a half years old swallowed a fish-bone last night, and has been suffering and crying all day, and the grief of the mother so won Itō's sympathy that he took me to see her. She had walked up and down with it for eighteen hours, but never thought of looking into its throat, and was very unwilling that I should do so. The bone was visible, and easily removed with a crochet needle. An hour later the mother sent a tray with a quantity of cakes and coarse confectionery upon it as a present, with the piece of dried seaweed which always accompanies a gift. Before night seven people with sore legs applied for "advice." The sores were all superficial and all alike, and their owners said that they had been produced by the incessant rubbing of the bites of ants.

On this summer day the country looks as prosperous as it is beautiful, and one would not think that acute poverty could exist in the steep-roofed village of Nojiri, which nestles at the foot of the hill. But two hemp ropes dangling from a cryptomeria just below tell the sad tale of an elderly man who hanged himself two days ago, because he was too poor to provide for a large family. The house-mistress and Itō tell me that when a man who has a young family gets too old or feeble for work he often destroys himself.

My hostess is a widow with a family, a good-natured, bustling woman, with a great love of talk. All day her house is open all round, having literally no walls. The roof and solitary upper room are supported on posts, and my ladder almost touches the kitchen fire. During the daytime the large matted area under the roof has no divisions, and groups of travellers and *mago* lie about, for every one who has toiled up either side of the Kuruma Pass takes a cup of tea with eating, and the house mistress is busy the whole day. A big well is near the fire. Of course there is no furniture; but a shelf runs under the roof, on which there is a Buddhist shrine, with two black idols in it, one of them being that much-worshipped divinity, Daikoku, the god of wealth. Besides a rack for kitchen utensils, there is only a stand on which are six large brown dishes with food for sale—salt shell-fish, in a black liquid, dried trout impaled on sticks, sea slugs in soy, a paste made of pounded roots, and green cakes made of the slimy river confervae, pressed and dried—all ill-favored and unsavory viands. This afternoon a man without clothes was treading flour paste on a mat, a traveller in a blue silk robe was lying on the floor smoking, and five women in loose attire, with elaborate chignons and blackened teeth, were squatting round the fire.

At the house-mistress's request I wrote a eulogistic description of the view from her house, and read it in English, Itō translating it, to the very great satisfaction of the assemblage. Then I was asked to write on four fans. The woman has never heard of England. It is not a name to conjure with in these wilds. Neither has she heard of America. She knows of Russia as a great power, and, of course, of China, but there her knowledge ends, though she has been to Tokyo and Kyoto.

July 1

I was just falling asleep last night, in spite of mosquitoes and fleas, when I was roused by much talking and loud outcries of poultry. Itō, carrying a screaming, refractory hen, and a man and woman whom he had with difficulty bribed to part with it, appeared by my bed. I feebly said I would have it boiled for breakfast, but when Itō called me this morning he told me with a most rueful face that just as he was going to kill it it had escaped to the woods! In order to understand my feelings, one must have experienced what it is not to have tasted fish, flesh, or fowl, for ten days! The alternative was eggs and some of the paste which the man was treading yesterday on the mat cut into strips and boiled! It was coarse flour and buckwheat, so I have learned not to be particular!

The Tsugawa Yadoya

Yesterday's journey was one of the most severe I have yet had, for in ten hours of hard travelling I only accomplished fifteen miles. The road from Kuruma Pass westwards is so infamous that the stages are sometimes little more than a mile. Yet it is by it, so far at least as the Tsugawa River, that the produce and manufactures of the rich plain of Aizu, with its numerous towns, and a very large interior district, must find an outlet at Niigata. In defiance of all modern ideas, it goes straight up and straight downhill, at a gradient that I should be afraid to hazard a guess at, and at present it is a perfect quagmire, into which great stones have been thrown, some of which have subsided edgewise, and others have disappeared altogether. It is the very worst road I ever rode over, and that is saying a good deal!

The Kuruma Pass was the last of seventeen mountain passes, over two thousand feet high, which I have crossed since leaving Nikkō. Between it and Tsugawa the scenery, though on a smaller scale, is of much the same character as hitherto—hills wooded to their tops, cleft by ravines which open out occasionally to divulge more distant ranges, all smothered in greenery, which, when I am ill-pleased, I am inclined to call "rank vegetation." Oh that an abrupt scaur, or a strip of flaming desert, or something salient and brilliant, would break in, however discordantly, upon this monotony of green!

The villages of the district must, I think, have reached the lowest abyss of filthiness in Hozawa and Saikaiyama. Fowls, dogs, horses, and people herded together in sheds black with wood smoke, and manure heaps drained into the wells. No young boy wore any clothing. Few of the men wore anything but the *fundoshi*, the women were unclothed to their waists and such clothing as they had was very dirty, and held together by mere force of habit. The adults were covered with inflamed bites of insects, and the children with skin disease. Their houses were dirty, and, as they squatted on their heels, or lay face downwards, they looked little better than savages. Their appearance and the want of delicacy of their habits are simply abominable, and in the latter respect they contrast to great disadvantage with several savage peoples that I have been among. If I had kept to Nikkō, Hakone, Miyanoshita, and similar places visited by foreigners with less time, I should have formed a very different impression. Is their spiritual condition, I often wonder, much higher than their physical one? They are courteous, kindly, industrious, and free from gross crimes. But from the conversations that I have had with Japanese, and from much that I see, I judge that their standard of foundational morality is very low, and that life is neither truthful nor pure.

I put up here at a crowded *yadoya*, where they have given me two cheerful rooms in the garden, away from the crowd. Itō's great desire on arriving at any place is to shut me up in my room and keep me a close prisoner till the start the next morning. But here I emancipated myself, and enjoyed myself very much sitting in the *daidokoro*. The house master is of the samurai, or two-sworded class, now, as such, extinct. His face is longer, his lips thinner, and his nose straighter and more prominent than those of the lower class, and there is a difference in his manner and bearing. I have had a great deal of interesting conversation with him.

In the same open space his clerk was writing at a lacquer desk of the stereotyped form—a low bench with the ends rolled over—a woman was tailoring, laborers were washing their feet on the *itama*, and several more were squatting round the *irori* smoking and drinking tea. A laborer servant washed some rice for my dinner, but before doing so took off his clothes, and the woman who cooked it let her *kimono* fall to her waist before she began to work, as is customary among respectable women. The house master's wife and Itō talked about me unguardedly. I asked what they were saying. "She says," said he, "that you are very polite—for a foreigner," he added. I asked what she meant, and found that it was because I took off my boots before I stepped on the matting, and bowed when they handed me the *tabakobon*.

We walked through the town to find something edible for tomorrow's river journey, but only succeeded in getting wafers made of white of egg and sugar, balls made of sugar and barley flour, and beans coated with sugar. Thatch, with its picturesqueness, has disappeared, and the Tsugawa roofs are of strips of bark weighted with large stones. As the houses turn their gable ends to the street, and there is a promenade the whole way under the eaves, and the street turns twice at right angles and terminates in temple grounds on a bank above the river, it is less monotonous than most Japanese towns. It is a place of three thousand people, and a good deal of produce is shipped to Niigata by the river. today it is thronged with packhorses. I was much mobbed, and one child formed the solitary exception to the general rule of politeness by calling me a *gaijin* (alien), but he was severely chidden, and a policeman has just called with an apology. A slice of fresh salmon has been produced, and I think I never tasted anything so delicious. I have finished the first part of my land journey, and leave for Niigata by boat tomorrow morning.

Running the Rapids

The boat for Niigata was to leave at eight, but at five Itō roused me by saying they were going at once, as it was full, and we left in haste, the house master running to the river with one of my large baskets on his back to speed the parting guest. Two rivers unite to form a stream over whose beauty I would gladly have lingered, and the morning, singularly rich and tender in its coloring, ripened into a glorious day of light without glare, and heat without oppressiveness.

The boat was stoutly-built, forty-five feet long by six feet broad, propelled by one man sculling at the stern, and another pulling a short broad-bladed oar, which worked in a wistaria loop at the bow. It had a croquet mallet handle about eighteen inches long, to which the man gave a wriggling turn at each stroke. Both rower and sculler stood the whole time, clad in umbrella hats. The fore part and centre carried bags of rice and crates of pottery, and the hinder part had a thatched roof which, when we started, sheltered twenty-five Japanese, but we dropped them at hamlets on the river, and reached Niigata with only three. I had my chair on the top of the cargo, and found the voyage a delightful change from the fatiguing crawl through quagmires at the rate of from fifteen to eighteen miles a day.

This trip is called "running the rapids of the Tsugawa," because for about twelve miles the river, hemmed in by lofty cliffs, studded with visible and sunken rocks, making several abrupt turns and shallowing in many places, hurries a boat swiftly downwards. It is said that it requires long practice, skill, and coolness on the part of the boatmen to prevent grave and frequent accidents. But if they are rapids, they are on a small scale, and look anything but formidable. With the river at its present height the boats run down forty-five miles in eight hours, charging only thirty *sen*, but it takes from five to seven days to get up, and much hard work in poling and towing.

The boat had a thoroughly native look, with its bronzed crew, thatched roof, and the umbrella hats of all its passengers hanging on the mast. I enjoyed every hour of the day. It was luxury to drop quietly down the stream, the air was delicious. Having heard nothing of it, the beauty of the Tsugawa came upon me as a pleasant surprise, besides that every mile brought me nearer the hoped-for home letters. Almost as soon as we left Tsugawa the downward passage was barred by fantastic mountains, which just opened their rocky gates wide enough to let us through, and then closed again. Pinnacles and needles of bare, flushed rock rose out of luxuriant vegetation—Quiraing without its bareness, the Rhine without its ruins, and more beautiful than both. There were mountains connected by ridges no broader than a horse's back, others with great gray buttresses, deep chasms cleft by streams, temples with pagoda roofs on heights, sunny villages with deep-thatched roofs hidden away among blossoming trees, and through rifts in the nearer ranges glimpses of snowy mountains.

After a rapid run of twelve miles through this enchanting scenery, the remaining course of the Tsugawa is that of a broad, full stream winding marvellously through a wooded and tolerably level country, partially surrounded by snowy mountains. The river life was very pretty. Canoes abounded, some loaded with vegetables, some with wheat, others with boys and girls returning from school. *Bezaisen* with their white puckered sails in flotillas of a dozen at a time crawled up the deep water, or were towed through the shallows by crews frolicking and shouting. Then the scene changed to a broad and deep river, with a peculiar alluvial smell from the quantity of vegetable matter held in suspension, flowing calmly between densely wooded, bamboo-fringed banks, just high enough to conceal the surrounding country.

No houses, or nearly none, are to be seen, but signs of a continuity of population abound. Every hundred yards almost there is a narrow path to the river through the jungle, with a canoe moored at its foot. Erections like gallows, with a swinging bamboo, with a bucket at one end and a stone at the other, occurring continually, show the vicinity of households dependent upon the river for their water supply. Wherever the banks allowed, horses were being washed by having water poured over their backs with a dipper, naked children were rolling in the mud, and cackling of poultry, human voices, and sounds of industry, were ever floating towards us from the dense greenery of the shores, making one feel without seeing that the margin was very populous.

Except the boatmen and myself, no one was awake during the hot, silent afternoon—it was dreamy and delicious. Occasionally, as we floated down, vineyards were visible with the vines trained on horizontal trellises, or bamboo rails, often forty feet long, nailed horizontally on cryptomeria to a height of twenty feet, on which small sheaves of barley were placed astride to dry till the frame was full

More forest, more dreams, then the forest and the abundant vegetation altogether disappeared, the river opened out among low lands and banks of shingle and sand, and by three we were on the outskirts of Niigata, whose low houses, with rows of stones upon their roofs, spread over a stretch of sand, beyond which is a sandy roll with some clumps of firs. Tea-houses with many balconies studded the riverside, and pleasure parties were enjoying themselves with *geisha* and *sake*. On the whole, the waterside streets are shabby and tumble down, and the landward side of the great city of western Japan is certainly disappointing. It was difficult to believe it a treaty port, for the sea was not in sight, and there were no consular flags flying. We poled along one of the numerous canals, which are the carriage-ways for produce and goods, among hundreds of loaded boats, landed in the heart of the city. As the result of repeated inquiries, eventually reached the church mission house, an unshaded wooden building without verandahs, close to the government buildings, where I was most kindly welcomed by the Fysons.[1]

---

1 Philip Kemball Fyson (1846–1928) began missionary work with the Church Missionary Society in Japan in 1874 at Yokohama, and would go on to be consecrated (in 1897) as Anglican bishop of the Diocese of Hokkaido, in the Nippon Sei Kōkai, the province of the Anglican Communion in Japan.

Niigata Gardens

I have spent over a week in Niigata, and leave it regretfully tomorrow, rather for the sake of the friends I have made than for its own interests. I never experienced a week of more abominable weather. The sun has been seen just once, the mountains, which are thirty miles off, not at all. The clouds are a brownish grey, the air moist and motionless, and the mercury has varied from eighty-two degrees in the day to eighty degrees at night. The household is afflicted with lassitude and loss of appetite. Evening does not bring coolness, but myriads of flying, creeping, jumping, running creatures, all with power to hurt, which replace the day mosquitoes, villains with spotted legs, which bite and poison one without the warning hum. The night mosquitoes are legion. There are no walks except in the streets and the public gardens, for Niigata is built on a sand spit, hot and bare. Neither can you get a view of it without climbing to the top of a wooden look-out.

Niigata is a treaty port without foreign trade, and almost without foreign residents. Not a foreign ship visited the port either last year or this. There are only two foreign firms, and these are German, and only eighteen foreigners, of which number, except the missionaries, nearly all are in government employment. Its river, the Shinano, is the largest in Japan, and it and its affluents bring down a prodigious volume of water. But Japanese rivers are much choked with sand and shingle washed down from the mountains. In all that I have seen, except those which are physically limited by walls of hard rock, a riverbed is a waste of sand, boulders, and shingle, through the middle of which, among sandbanks and shallows, the river takes its devious course. In the freshets, which occur to a greater or lesser extent every year, enormous volumes of water pour over these wastes, carrying sand and detritus down to the mouths, which are all obstructed by bars. Of these rivers the Shinano, being the biggest, is the most refractory, and has piled up a bar at its entrance through which there is only a passage seven feet deep, which is perpetually shallowing. The minds of engineers are much exercised upon the Shinano, and the government is most anxious to deepen the channel and give western Japan what it has not—a harbour. But the expense of the necessary operation is enormous, and in the meantime a limited ocean traffic is carried on by *bezaisen* and by a few small Japanese steamers which call outside. There is a British vice-consulate, but, except as a step, few would accept such a dreary post or outpost.

But Niigata is a handsome, prosperous city of fifty thousand inhabitants, the capital of the wealthy eponymous prefecture, with a population of one and a half millions, and is the seat of the prefectural governor, of the chief law courts, of fine schools, a hospital, and barracks. It is curious to find in such an excluded town a school deserving the designation of a college, as it includes intermediate, primary, and normal schools, an English school with one hundred and fifty pupils, organized by English and American teachers. There is also an engineering school, a geological museum, splendidly equipped laboratories, and the newest and most approved scientific and educational apparatus. The government buildings, which are grouped near the Fysons, are of painted white wood, and are imposing from their size and their innumerable glass windows.

There is a large hospital arranged by a European doctor, with a medical school attached. This hospital is large and well ventilated, but has not as yet succeeded in attracting many in-patients. Out-patients, especially sufferers from inflammation of the eye, are very numerous. The Japanese chief physician regards the great prevalence of the malady in this neighborhood as the result of damp, the reflection of the sun's rays from sand and snow, inadequate ventilation and charcoal fumes.

The prefectural government office, the court house, the schools, the barracks, and a large bank, which is rivalling them all, have a go-ahead, Europeanized look, bold, staring, and tasteless. There are large public gardens, very well laid out, and with finely gravelled walks. There are three hundred street lamps, which burn the mineral oil of the district.

Because the riotous Shinano persistently bars it out from the sea, its natural highway, the capital of one of the richest prefectures of Japan is left out in the cold. The prefecture, which yields not only rice, silk, tea, hemp, and indigo, in large quantities, but also gold, copper, coal, and petroleum, has to send most of its produce to Tokyo across ranges of mountains, on the backs of packhorses, by roads scarcely less infamous than the one by which I came.

Niigata is the neatest, cleanest, and most comfortable-looking town I have yet seen, and altogether free from the jostlement of a foreign settlement. It is renowned for the beautiful teahouses, which attract visitors from distant places, and for the excellence of the theatres, and is the centre of the recreation and pleasure of a large district. It is so beautifully clean that, as at Nikkō, I should feel reluctant to walk upon its well-swept streets in muddy boots. It would afford a good lesson to the Edinburgh authorities, for every vagrant bit of straw, stick, or paper, is at once pounced upon and removed, and no rubbish may stand for an instant in its streets except in a covered box or bucket.

The town is correctly laid out in square divisions, formed by five streets over a mile long, crossed by very numerous short ones, and is intersected by canals, which are its real roadways. I have not seen a packhorse in the streets; everything comes in by boat, and there are few houses in the city which cannot have their goods delivered by canal very near to their doors. These water-ways are busy all day, but in the early morning, when the boats come in loaded with the vegetables, without which the people could not exist for a day, the bustle is indescribable. The cucumber boats just now are the great sight. The canals are usually in the middle of the streets, and have fairly broad roadways on both sides. They are much below the street level, and their nearly perpendicular banks are neatly faced with wood, broken at intervals by flights of stairs. They are bordered by trees, among which are many weeping willows. As the river water runs through them, keeping them quite sweet, and they are crossed at short intervals by light bridges, they form a very attractive feature of Niigata.

The houses have very steep roofs of shingle, weighted with stones. As they are of very irregular heights, and all turn the steep gables of the upper stories streetwards, the town has a picturesqueness very unusual in Japan. The deep verandahs are connected all along the streets, so as to form a sheltered promenade when the snow lies deep in winter. With its canals with their avenues of trees, its fine public gardens, and clean, picturesque streets, it is a really attractive town. Its improvements are recent, and were only lately completed by Masakata Kusumoto, now governor of Tokyo. There is no appearance of poverty in any part of the town, but if there be wealth, it is carefully concealed. One marked feature of the city is the number of streets of dwelling houses with projecting windows of wooden slats, through which the people can see without being seen, though at night, when the *andon* are lit, we saw, as we walked from Dr. Palm's,[1] that in most cases families were sitting round the *hibachi* in a deshabille of the scantiest kind.

The fronts are very narrow, and the houses extend backwards to an amazing length, with gardens in which flowers, and shrubs are grown, and bridges are several times repeated, so as to give the effect of fairyland as you look through from the street. The principal apartments in all Japanese houses are at the back, looking out on these miniature landscapes, for a landscape is skilfully dwarfed into a space often not more than thirty feet square. A lake, a rock-work, a bridge, a stone lantern, and a deformed pine, are indispensable. Whenever circumstances and means allow, quaintnesses of all kinds are introduced. Small pavilions, retreats for tea-making, reading, sleeping in quiet and coolness, fishing under cover, and drinking *sake*; bronze pagodas, cascades falling from the mouths of bronze dragons; rock caves, with gold and silver fish darting in and out; lakes with rocky islands, streams crossed by green bridges, just high enough to allow a rat or frog to pass under; lawns, and slabs of stone for crossing them in wet weather; grottoes, hills, valleys, groves of miniature palms, cycas, and bamboo; and dwarfed trees of many kinds, of purplish and dull green hues, are cut into startling likenesses of beasts and creeping things, or stretch distorted arms over tiny lakes.

I have walked about a great deal in Niigata, and when with Mrs. Fyson, who is the only European lady here at present, and her little Ruth, a pretty child of three years old, we have been followed by an immense crowd, as

---

1 Theobald A. Palm, of the Edinburgh Medical Missionary Society, came to Niigata on April 15, 1875, after studying the Japanese language in Tokyo and went on to found a hospital, where he would treat more than forty-thousand patients.

the sight of this fair creature, with golden curls falling over her shoulders, is most fascinating. Both men and women have gentle, winning ways with infants, and Ruth, instead of being afraid of the crowds, smiles upon them, bows in Japanese fashion, speaks to them in Japanese, and seems a little disposed to leave her own people altogether. It is most difficult to make her keep with us, and two or three times, on missing her and looking back, we have seen her seated, native fashion, in a ring in a crowd of several hundred people, receiving a homage and admiration from which she was most unwillingly torn. The Japanese have a perfect passion for children, but it is not good for European children to be much with them, as they corrupt their morals, and teach them to tell lies.

The climate of Niigata and of most of this great prefecture contrasts unpleasantly with the region on the other side of the mountains, warmed by the gulf-stream of the North Pacific, in which the autumn and winter, with their still atmosphere, bracing temperature, and blue and sunny skies, are the most delightful seasons of the year. Thirty-two days of snowfall occur on an average. The canals and rivers freeze, and even the rapid Shinano sometimes bears a horse. In January and February the snow lies three or four feet deep, a veil of clouds obscures the sky, people inhabit their upper rooms to get any daylight, packhorse traffic is suspended, pedestrians go about with difficulty in rough snow-shoes, and for nearly six months the coast is unsuitable for navigation, owing to the prevalence of strong, cold, north-west winds. In this city people in wadded clothes, with only their eyes exposed, creep about under the verandahs. The population huddles round *hibachi* and shivers, for the mercury, which rises to ninety-two degrees in summer, falls to fifteen degrees in winter. And all this is in latitude 37 degrees 55'—three degrees south of Naples!

A Noisy Matsuri

Two foreign ladies, two fair-haired foreign infants, a long-haired foreign dog, and a foreign gentleman, who, without these accompaniments, might have escaped notice, attracted a large but kindly crowd to the canal side when I left Niigata. The natives bore away the children on their shoulders, the Fysons walked to the extremity of the canal to bid me good-bye, the sampan shot out upon the broad, swirling flood of the Shinano, and an awful sense of loneliness fell upon me.

We crossed the Shinano, poled up the narrow, embanked Shinkawa, had a desperate struggle with the flooded Aganokawa, were much impeded by strings of nauseous manure boats on the narrow, discolored Kajikawa, wondered at the interminable melon and cucumber fields, and at the odd river life, and, after hard poling for six hours, reached Kisaki, having accomplished exactly ten miles. Then three *kuruma* with trotting runners took us twenty miles at the low rate of four and a half *sen* per *ri*. In one place a board closed the road, but, on representing to the chief man of the village that the traveller was a foreigner, he courteously allowed me to pass, the express agent having accompanied me thus far to see that I got through.

The road was tolerably populous throughout the day's journey, and the farming villages which extended much of the way—Tsuiji, Kasayanage, Mono, and Mari—were neat, and many of the farms had bamboo fences to screen them from the road. It was, on the whole, a pleasant country, and the people, though little clothed, did not look either poor or very dirty. The soil was very light and sandy. There were, in fact, "pine barrens," sandy ridges with nothing on them but spindly firs and fir scrub. The sandy levels between them, being heavily manured and cultivated like gardens, bore splendid crops of cucumbers trained like peas, melons, vegetable marrow, *taro*, sweet potatoes, maize, tea, tiger-lilies, beans, and onions. Extensive orchards with apples and pears trained laterally on trelliswork eight feet high, were a novelty in the landscape.

Though we were all day drawing nearer to mountains wooded to their summits on the east, the amount of vegetation was not burdensome, the rice swamps were few, and the air felt drier and less relaxing. As my runners were trotting merrily over one of the pine barrens, I met Dr. Palm returning from one of his medico-religious expeditions, with a tandem of two naked *kurumaya*. They were going over the ground at a great pace, and I wished that some of the most staid directors of the Edinburgh Medical Missionary Society could have the shock of seeing him! I shall not see a European again for some weeks. From Tsuiji, a very neat village, where we changed *kuruma*, we were jolted along over a shingly road to Nakajo, a considerable town just within treaty limits. The Japanese doctors there, as in some other places, are Dr. Palm's cordial helpers, and five or six of them, whom he regards as possessing the rare virtues of candor, earnestness, and single-mindedness, and who have studied English medical works, have clubbed together to establish a dispensary. Under Dr. Palm's instructions, they are even carrying out the antiseptic treatment successfully, after some ludicrous failures!

We dashed through Nakajo as *kurumaya* always dash through towns and villages, got out of it in a drizzle upon an avenue of firs, three or four deep, which extends from Nakajo to Kurokawa, and for some miles beyond were jolted over a damp valley on which tea and rice alternated, crossed two branches of the shingly Kuro River on precarious bridges, rattled into the town of Kurokawa, much decorated with flags and lanterns, where the people were all congregated at a shrine where there was much drumming. A few girls, much painted and bedizened, were dancing or posturing on a raised and covered platform, in honor of the god of the place, whose *matsuri* or festival it was. Then we were out again, to be mercilessly jolted under the firs in the twilight to a solitary house where the owner made some difficulty about receiving us, as his licence did not begin till the next day. Eventually he succumbed, and gave me his one upstairs room, exactly five feet high, which hardly allowed of my standing upright with my hat on. He then rendered it suffocating by closing the *amado*, for the reason often given, that if he left them open and the house was robbed, the police would not only blame him severely, but would not take any trouble to recover his property. He had no rice, so I indulged in a feast of delicious cucumbers. I never saw so many eaten as in that district. Children gnaw them all day long, and even babies on their mothers' backs suck them with avidity. Just now they are sold for a *sen* a dozen.

It is a mistake to arrive at a *yadoya* after dark. Even if the best rooms are not full it takes fully an hour to get my food and the room ready. Meanwhile I cannot employ my time usefully because of the mosquitoes. There was heavy rain all night, accompanied by the first wind that I have heard since landing. The fitful creaking of the pines and the drumming from the shrine made me glad to get up at sunrise, or rather at daylight, for there has not been a sunrise since I came, or a sunset either. That day we travelled by Sekki to Kawaguchi by *kuruma*. We were sometimes bumped over stones, sometimes deposited on the edge of a quagmire, and asked to get out. Sometimes we were compelled to walk for two or three miles at a time along the infamous bridle-track above the Arai River, up which two men could hardly push and haul an empty vehicle. As they often had to lift them bodily and carry them for some distance, I was really glad when we reached the village of Kawaguchi to find that they could go no farther. Yet, as we could only get one horse, I had to walk the last stage in a torrent of rain, poorly protected by my paper waterproof cloak.

We are now in the midst of the great central chain of the Japanese Alps, which extends almost without a break for nine hundred miles, and is from forty to a hundred miles in width, broken up into interminable ranges traversable only by steep passes from one to five thousand feet in height, with innumerable rivers, ravines, and valleys. The heights and ravines are heavily timbered, the rivers impetuous and liable to freshets, and the valleys invariably terraced for rice. It is in the valleys that the villages are found, and regions more isolated I have never seen, shut out by bad roads from the rest of Japan. The houses are very poor, the summer costume of the men consists of the *fundoshi* only, and that of the women of trousers with an open shirt. When we reached Kurosawa last night it had dwindled to trousers only. There is little traffic, and very few horses are kept, one, two, or three constituting the live stock of a large village. The shops, such as they are, contain the barest necessaries of life. Millet and buckwheat rather than rice, with the universal daikon, are the staples of diet The climate is wet in summer and bitterly cold in winter. Even now it is comfortless enough for the people to come in wet, just to warm the tips of their fingers at the *irori*, stifled the while with the stinging smoke, while the damp wind flaps the torn paper of the windows about, and damp droughts sweep the ashes over the *tatami* until the house is hermetically sealed at night. These people never know anything of what we regard as comfort. In the long winter, when the wretched bridle-tracks are blocked by snow and the freezing wind blows strong, and the families huddle round the smoky fire by the doleful glimmer of the *andon*, without work, books, or play, to shiver through the long evenings in chilly dreariness, and herd together for warmth at night like animals, their condition must be as miserable as anything short of grinding poverty can make it.

I saw things at their worst that night as I tramped into the hamlet of Numa, down whose sloping street a swollen stream was running, which the people were banking out of their houses. I was wet and tired, and the woman at the one wretched *yadoya* met me, saying, "I'm sorry it's very dirty and quite unfit for so honorable a guest." She was right, for the one room was up a ladder, the windows were in tatters, there was no charcoal for a *hibachi*, no eggs, and the rice was so dirty and so full of a small black seed as to be unfit to eat. Worse than all, there was no transport office, the hamlet did not possess a horse. It was only by sending to a farmer five miles off, and by much bargaining, that I got on the next morning. In estimating the number of people in a given number of houses in Japan, it is usual to multiply the houses by five. I had the curiosity to walk through Numa and get Itō to translate the tallies which hang outside all Japanese houses with the names, number, and sexes of their inmates, and in twenty-four houses there were only three hundred and seven people! In some there were four families—the grand-parents, the parents, the eldest son with his wife and family, and a daughter or two with their husbands and children. The eldest son, who inherits the house and land, almost invariably brings his wife to his father's house, where she often becomes little better than a slave to her mother-in-law. By rigid custom she literally forsakes her own kindred, and her filial duty is transferred to her husband's mother, who often takes a dislike to her, and instigates her son to divorce her if she has no children. My hostess had induced her son to divorce his wife, and she could give no better reason for it than that she was lazy.

The Numa people, she said, had never seen a foreigner, so, though the rain still fell heavily, they were astir in the early morning. They wanted to hear me speak, so I gave my orders to Itō in public. Yesterday was a most toilsome day, mainly spent in stumbling up and sliding down the great passes of Futai, Takanasu, and Enoiki, all among forest-covered mountains, deeply cleft by forest-choked ravines, with now and then one of the snowy peaks of Aizu breaking the monotony of the ocean of green. The horses' shoes were tied and untied every few minutes, and we made just a mile an hour!

At last we were deposited in a most unpromising place in the hamlet of Tamagawa, and were told that a rice merchant, after waiting for three days, had got every horse in the country. At the end of two hours' chaffering one baggage carrier was produced, some of the things were put on the rice horses. A steed with a pack saddle was produced for me in the shape of a plump and pretty little cow, which carried me safely over the magnificent pass of Ori and down to the town of Okimi, among rice fields, where, in a drowning rain, I was glad to get shelter with a number of laborers by a wood-fire till another pack-cow was produced. We walked on through the rice fields and up into the hills again to Kurosawa. There I had intended to remain, but there was no inn. The farm house where they did take in travellers, besides being on the edge of a malarious pond and being dark and full of stinging smoke, was so awfully dirty and full of living creatures, that, exhausted as I was, I was obliged to go on. It was growing dark, there was no transport office, and for the first time the people were very slightly extortionate, and drove Itō nearly to his wits' end. The peasants do not like to be out after dark, for they are afraid of ghosts and all sorts of devilments, and it was difficult to induce them to start so late in the evening.

There was not a house clean enough to rest in, so I sat on a stone and thought about the people for over an hour. Children with scald-head, scabies, and sore eyes swarmed. Every woman carried a baby on her back, and every child who could stagger under one carried one too. Not one woman wore anything but cotton trousers. One woman reeled about drunk and disorderly. Itō sat on a stone hiding his face in his hands, and when I asked him if he were ill, he replied in a most lamentable voice, "I don't know what I am to do, I'm so ashamed for you to see such things!" The boy is only eighteen, and I pitied him. I asked him if women were often drunk, and he said they were in Yokohama, but they usually kept in their houses. He says that when their husbands give them money to pay bills at the end of a month, they often spend it in *sake*, and that they sometimes get *sake* in shops and have it put down as rice or tea. The old, old story! I looked at the dirt and barbarism, and asked if this were the Japan of which I had read. Yet a woman in this unseemly costume firmly refused to take the two or three *sen* which it is usual to leave at a place where you rest, because she said that I had had water and not tea, and after I had forced it on her, she returned it to Itō, and this redeeming incident sent me away much comforted.

From Numa the distance here is only one and a half *ri*, but it is over the steep pass of Honoki, which is ascended and descended by hundreds of rude stone steps, not pleasant in the dark. On this pass I saw birches for the first time. At its foot we entered Yamagata prefecture by a good bridge, and shortly reached this village, in which an unpromising-looking farm house is the only accommodation. Though all the rooms but two are taken up with silkworms, those two are very good and look upon a miniature lake and rockery. The one objection to my room is that to get either in or out of it I must pass through the other, which is occupied by five tobacco merchants who are waiting for transport and while away the time by strumming on that instrument of dismay, the *shamisen*.

No horses or cows can be got for me, so I am spending the day quietly here, rather glad to rest, for I am much exhausted. When I am suffering much from my spine Itō always gets into a fright and thinks I am going to die, as he tells me when I am better, but shows his anxiety by a short, surly manner, which is most disagreeable. He thinks we shall never get through the interior! Brunton's excellent map fails in this region, so it is only by fixing on the well-known city of Yamagata and devising routes to it that we get on. Half the evening is spent in consulting Japanese maps, if we can get them, and in questioning the house master and transport agent, and any chance travellers. The people know nothing beyond the distance of a few *ri*, and the agents seldom tell one anything beyond the next stage. When

I inquire about the unbeaten tracks that I wish to take, the answers are, "It's an awful road through mountains," or "There are many bad rivers to cross," or "There are none but farmers' houses to stop at." No encouragement is ever given, but we get on, and shall get on, I doubt not, though the hardships are not what I would desire in my present state of health.

Very few horses are kept here. Cows and laborers carry much of the merchandise, and women as well as men carry heavy loads. A baggage carrier carries about fifty pounds, but here merchants carrying their own goods from Yamagata actually carry from ninety to one hundred and forty pounds, and even more. It is sickening to meet these poor fellows struggling over the mountain-passes in evident distress. Last night five of them were resting on the summit ridge of a pass gasping violently. Their eyes were starting out. All their muscles, rendered painfully visible by their leanness, were quivering. Rills of blood from the bite of insects, which they cannot drive away, were literally running all over their naked bodies, washed away here and there by copious perspiration. Truly in the sweat of their brows they were eating bread and earning an honest living for their families!

Suffering and hard-worked as they were, they were quite independent. I have not seen a beggar or beggary in this strange country. The women were carrying seventy pounds. These burden-bearers have their backs covered by a thick pad of plaited straw. On this rests a ladder, curved up at the lower end like the runners of a sleigh. On this the load is carefully packed till it extends from below the man's waist to a considerable height above his head. It is covered with waterproof paper, securely roped, and thatched with straw, and is supported by a broad padded band just below the collar bones. Of course, as the man walks nearly bent double, and the position is a very painful one, he requires to stop and straighten himself frequently, and unless he meets with a bank of convenient height, he rests the bottom of his burden on a short, stout pole with an L-shaped top, carried for this purpose. The carrying of enormous loads is quite a feature of this region, and so, I am sorry to say, are red stinging ants and the small gadflies which molest the laborers.

Yesterday's journey was eighteen miles in twelve hours! Ichinono is a nice, industrious hamlet, given up, like all others, to rearing silkworms, and the pure white and sulphur yellow cocoons are drying on mats in the sun everywhere.

A Vicious Horse

A severe day of mountain travelling brought us into another region. We left Ichinono early on a fine morning, with three pack-cows, one of which I rode (and their calves), very comely kine, with small noses, short horns, straight spines, and deep bodies. I thought that I might get some fresh milk, but the idea of anything but a calf milking a cow was so new to the people that there was a universal laugh, and Itō told me that they thought it "most disgusting," and that the Japanese think it "most disgusting" in foreigners to put anything "with such a strong smell and taste" into their tea! All the cows had cotton cloths, printed with blue dragons, suspended under their bodies to keep them from mud and insects, and they wear straw shoes and cords through the cartilages of their noses. The day being fine, a great deal of rice and *sake* was on the move, and we met hundreds of pack-cows, all of the same comely breed, in strings of four.

We crossed the Sakura Pass, from which the view is beautiful, got horses at the mountain village of Shirakasawa, crossed more passes, and in the afternoon reached the village of Tenoko. There, as usual, I sat under the verandah of the transport office, and waited for the one horse that was available. It was a large shop, but contained not a single article of European make. In the one room a group of women and children sat round the fire, and the agent sat as usual with a number of ledgers at a table a foot high, on which his grandchild was lying on a cushion. Here Itō dined on seven dishes of horrors, and they brought me *sake*, tea, rice, and black beans. The last are very good. We had some talk about the country, and the man asked me to write his name in English characters, and to write my own in a book. Meanwhile a crowd assembled, and the front row sat on the ground that the others might see over their heads. They were dirty and pressed very close, and when the women of the house saw that I felt the heat they gracefully produced fans and fanned me for a whole hour. On asking the charge they refused to make any, and would not receive anything. They had not seen a foreigner before, they said, they would despise themselves for taking anything, they had my "honorable name" in their book. Not only that, but they put up a parcel of sweetmeats, and the man wrote his name on a fan and insisted on my accepting it. I was grieved to have nothing to give them but some English pins, but they had never seen such before, and soon circulated them among the crowd. I told them truly that I should remember them as long as I remember Japan, and went on, much touched by their kindness.

The lofty Utsu Pass, which is ascended and descended by a number of stone slabs, is the last of the passes of these choked-up ranges. From its summit in the welcome sunlight I joyfully looked down upon the noble plain of Yonezawa, about thirty miles long and from ten to eighteen broad, one of the gardens of Japan, wooded and watered, covered with prosperous towns and villages, surrounded by magnificent mountains not altogether timbered, and bounded at its southern extremity by ranges white with snow even in the middle of July.

In the long street of the farming village of Matsuhara a man amazed me by running in front of me and speaking to me, and on Itō coming up, he assailed him vociferously, and it turned out that he took me for an Ainu, one of the subjugated aborigines of Ezo. I have before now been taken for a Chinese!

Throughout the prefecture of Niigata I have occasionally seen a piece of cotton cloth suspended by its four corners from four bamboo poles just above a quiet stream. Behind it there is usually a long narrow tablet, notched at the top, similar to those seen in cemeteries, with characters upon it. Sometimes bouquets of flowers are placed in the hollow top of each bamboo, and usually there are characters on the cloth itself. Within it always lies a wooden dipper. In coming down from Tenoko I passed one of these close to the road, and a Buddhist priest was at the time pouring a dipper full of water into it, which strained slowly through. As he was going our way we joined him, and he explained its meaning.

According to him the tablet bears on it the *kaimyō*, or posthumous name, of a woman. The flowers have the same significance as those which loving hands place on the graves of kindred. If there are characters on the cloth, they represent the well-known invocation of the Nichiren sect, *Namu myōhō rengekyō*. The pouring of the water into the cloth, often accompanied by telling the beads on a rosary, is a prayer. The whole is called "The Flowing Invocation." I have seldom seen anything more plaintively affecting, for it denotes that a mother in the first joy of maternity has passed away to suffer (according to popular belief) in the Lake of Blood, one of the Buddhist hells, for a sin committed in a former state of being, and it appeals to every passer-by to shorten the penalties of a woman in anguish, for in that lake she must remain until the cloth is so utterly worn out that the water falls through it at once.

Where the mountains touch the plain of Yonezawa there are several raised banks, and you can take one step from the hillside to a dead level. The soil is dry and gravelly at the junction, ridges of pines appeared, and the look of the houses suggested increased cleanliness and comfort. A walk of six miles took us from Tenoko to Komatsu, a beautifully situated town of three thousand people, with a large trade in cotton goods, silk, and *sake*.

As I entered Komatsu the first man whom I met turned back hastily, called into the first house the words which mean "Quick, here's a foreigner." The three carpenters who were at work there flung down their tools and, without waiting to put on their *kimono*, sped down the street calling out the news, so that by the time I reached the *yadoya* a large crowd was pressing upon me. The front was mean and unpromising-looking, but, on reaching the back by a stone bridge over a stream which ran through the house, I found a room forty feet long by fifteen high, entirely open along one side to a garden with a large fish-pond with goldfish, a pagoda, dwarf trees, and all the usual miniature adornments. *Fusuma* of wrinkled blue paper splashed with gold turned this "gallery" into two rooms. There was no privacy, for the crowds climbed upon the roofs at the back, and sat there patiently until night.

These were *daimyō*'s rooms. The posts and ceilings were ebony and gold, the mats very fine, the polished alcoves decorated with inlaid writing-tables and sword-racks. Spears nine feet long, with handles of lacquer inlaid with Venus' ear, hung in the verandah. The washing bowl was fine inlaid black lacquer, and the rice-bowls and their covers were gold lacquer.

In this, as in many other *yadoya*, there were *kakemono* with large Chinese characters representing the names of the prime minister, prefectural governor, or distinguished general, who had honored it by halting there, and lines of poetry were hung up, as is usual, in the same fashion. I have several times been asked to write something to be thus displayed. I spent Sunday at Komatsu, but not restfully, owing to the nocturnal croaking of the frogs in the pond. As in most towns, there were shops which sell nothing but white, frothy-looking cakes, which are used for the goldfish which are so much prized, and three times daily the women and children of the household came into the garden to feed them.

When I left Komatsu there were fully sixty people inside the house and fifteen hundred outside—walls, verandahs, and even roofs being packed. From Nikkō to Komatsu mares had been exclusively used, but there I encountered for the first time the terrible Japanese packhorse. Two horridly fierce-looking creatures were at the door, with their heads tied down till their necks were completely arched. When I mounted the crowd followed, gathering as it went, frightening the horse with the clatter of *geta* and the sound of a multitude, till he broke his head-rope. The frightened *mago* letting him go, he proceeded down the street mainly on his hind feet, squealing, and striking savagely with his fore feet, the crowd scattering to the right and left, till, as it surged past the police station, four policemen came out and arrested it. Then it gathered again, for there was a longer street, down which my horse proceeded in the same fashion, and, looking round, I saw Itō's horse on his hind legs and Itō on the ground. My beast jumped over all ditches, attacked all foot-passengers with his teeth, and behaved so like a wild animal that not all my previous acquaintance with the idiosyncrasies of horses enabled me to cope with him. On reaching Akayu we found a horse fair. As all the horses had their heads tightly tied down to posts, they could only squeal and lash out with their hind feet, which so provoked our animals that the baggage horse, by a series of jerks and rearings, divested himself of Itō and most of the baggage. When I dismounted from mine, he stood upright, and my foot catching I fell on the ground, when he made several vicious dashes at me with his teeth and fore feet, which were happily frustrated by the dexterity of some *mago*. These beasts forcibly remind me of the words, "Whose mouth must be held with bit and bridle, lest they turn and fall upon thee."

It was a lovely summer day, though very hot, and the snowy peaks of Aizu scarcely looked cool as they glittered in the sunlight. The plain of Yonezawa, with the prosperous town of Yonezawa in the south, and the frequented watering place of Akayu in the north, is a perfect garden of Eden, growing in rich profusion rice, cotton, maize, tobacco, hemp, indigo, beans, egg-plants, walnuts, melons, cucumbers, persimmons, apricots, and pomegranates. It is a smiling and plenteous land, an Asiatic Arcadia, prosperous and independent, all its bounteous acres belonging to those who cultivate them, who live under their vines, figs, and pomegranates, free from oppression—a remarkable spectacle under an Asiatic despotism. Daikoku is the chief deity, and material good is the one object of desire.

It is an enchanting region of beauty, industry, and comfort, mountain girdled, and watered by the bright Matsuka River. Everywhere there are prosperous and beautiful farming villages, with large houses with carved beams and ponderous tiled roofs. Each stands in its own grounds, buried among persimmons and pomegranates, with flower-gardens under trellised vines. Privacy is secured by high, closely-clipped screens of pomegranate and cryptomeria. Besides the villages of Yoshida, Semoshima, Kurokawa, Takayama, and Takataki, through or near which we passed, I counted over fifty on the plain with their brown, sweeping barn roofs looking out from the woodland. I cannot see any differences in the style of cultivation. Yoshida is rich and prosperous-looking, Numa poor and wretched-looking. But the scanty acres of Numa, rescued from the mountainsides, are as exquisitely trim and neat, as perfectly cultivated, and yield as abundantly of the crops which suit the climate, as the broad acres of the sunny plain of Yonezawa, and this is the case everywhere.

We rode for four hours through these beautiful villages on a road four feet wide, and then, to my surprise, after ferrying a river, emerged at Tsukuno upon what appears on the map as a secondary road, but which is in reality a main road twenty-five feet wide, well kept, trenched on both sides, and with a line of telegraph poles along it. It was a new world at once. The road for many miles was thronged with well-dressed foot-passengers, *kuruma*, packhorses, and waggons either with solid wheels, or wheels with spokes but no tires. It is a mail carriage-road, but without carriages. In such civilized circumstances it was curious to see two or four brown skinned men pulling the carts, and quite often a man and his wife— the man unclothed, and the woman unclothed to her waist— doing the same. Also it struck me as incongruous to see telegraph wires above, and below, men whose only clothing consisted of a sunhat and fan. Children with books and slates were returning from school, conning their lessons.

At Akayu, a town of hot sulphur springs, I hoped to sleep, but it was one of the noisiest places I have seen. In the most crowded part, where four streets meet, there are bathing sheds, which were full of people of both sexes, splashing loudly. The *yadoya* close to it had about forty rooms, in nearly all of which several rheumatic people were lying on the mats, *shamisen* were twanging, and *koto* screeching. The hubbub was so unbearable that I came on here, ten miles farther, by a fine new road, up an uninteresting strath of rice fields and low hills, which opens out upon a small plain surrounded by elevated gravelly hills. On one of their slopes, Kaminoyama, a watering place of over three thousand people, is pleasantly situated. It is keeping festival; there are lanterns and flags on every house, and crowds are thronging the temple grounds, of which there are several on the hills above. It is a clean, dry place, with beautiful *yadoya* on the heights, and pleasant houses with gardens, and plenty of walks over the hills. The people say that it is one of the driest places in Japan. If it were within reach of for-eigners, they would find it a wholesome health resort, with picturesque excursions in many directions.

This is one of the great routes of Japanese travel, and it is interesting to see watering places with their habits, amusements, and civilisation quite complete, borrowing nothing from Europe. The hot springs here contain iron, and are strongly impregnated with sulphuretted hydrogen. I tried the temperature of three, and found them 100 degrees, 105 degrees, and 107 degrees. They are supposed to be very valuable in rheumatism, and they attract visitors from great distances. The police, who are my frequent informants, tell me that there are nearly six hundred people now staying here for the benefit of the baths, of which six daily are usually taken. I think that in rheumatism, as in some other maladies, the old-fashioned Japanese doctors pay little attention to diet and habits, and much to drugs and external applications. The benefit of these and other medicinal waters would be much increased if vigorous friction replaced the dabbing with soft towels.

This is a large *yadoya*, very full of strangers, and the house mistress, a buxom and most prepossessing widow, has a truly exquisite hotel for bathers higher up the hill. She has eleven children, two or three of whom are tall, handsome, and graceful girls. One blushed deeply at my evident admiration, but was not displeased, and took me up the hill to see the temples, baths, and *yadoya* of this very attractive place. I am much delighted with her grace and savoir faire. I asked the widow how long she had kept the inn, and she proudly answered, "Three hundred years," not an uncommon instance of the heredity of occupations.

My accommodation is unique—a *kura*, in a large conventional garden. These *kura*, or fire-proof storehouses, are one of the most marked features of Japanese towns, both because they are white where all else is grey, and because they are solid where all else is perishable. This one contains a bathhouse that receives a hot spring at a temperature of 105 degrees, in which I luxuriate. Last night the mosquitoes were awful. If the widow and her handsome girls had not fanned me perseveringly for an hour, I should not have been able to write a line. My new mosquito net succeeds admirably, and, when I am once within it, I rather enjoy the disappointment of the hundreds of drumming blood-thirsty wretches outside. The widow tells me that house masters pay two yen once for all for the sign, and an annual tax of two yen on a first-class *yadoya*, one yen for a second, and fifty cents for a third, with five yen for the license to sell *sake*.

I am lodged in the lower part, but the iron doors are open, and in their place at night is a paper screen. A few things are kept in my room. Two handsome shrines from which the unemotional faces of two Buddhas looked out all night, a fine figure of the goddess Kannon, and a venerable one of the god of longevity, suggested curious dreams.

A New Bridge

Three days of travelling on the same excellent road have brought me nearly sixty miles. The prefecture of Yamagata impresses me as being singularly prosperous, progressive, and go-ahead. The plain of Yamagata, which I entered soon after leaving Kaminoyama, is populous and highly cultivated, and the broad road, with its enormous traffic, looks wealthy and civilized. It is being improved by convicts in dull red *kimono* printed with Chinese characters, who correspond with our ticket-of-leave men, as they are working for wages in the employment of contractors and farmers, and are under no other restriction than that of always wearing the prison dress.

At the Sakamoki River I was delighted to come upon the only thoroughly solid piece of modern Japanese work that I have met with: a remarkably handsome stone bridge nearly finished—the first I have seen. I introduced myself to the engineer, Okuno Chiuzo, a very gentlemanly, agreeable Japanese, who showed me the plans, took a great deal of trouble to explain them, and courteously gave me tea and sweetmeats.

Yamagata, a thriving town of 21,000 people and the capital of the prefecture, is well situated on a slight eminence, and this and the dominant position of the governor's office at the top of the main street give it an emphasis unusual in Japanese towns. The outskirts of all the cities are very mean, and the appearance of the lofty white buildings of the new governor's offices above the low grey houses was much of a surprise. The streets of Yamagata are broad and clean, and it has good shops, among which are long rows selling nothing but ornamental iron kettles and ornamental brasswork.

So far in the interior I was annoyed to find several shops almost exclusively for the sale of villainous forgeries of European edibles and drinkables, especially the latter. The Japanese, from the emperor downwards, have acquired a love of foreign intoxicants, which would be hurtful enough to them if the intoxicants were genuine, but is far worse when they are compounds of vitriol, fusel oil, bad vinegar, and I know not what. I saw two shops in Yamagata that sold champagne of the best brands, Martel's cognac, Bass' ale, Medoc, St. Julian, and Scotch whisky, at about one-fifth of their cost price—all poisonous compounds, the sale of which ought to be interdicted.

The government buildings, though in the usual confectionery style, are improved by the addition of verandahs; and the governor's offices, the court house, the normal school with advanced schools attached, and the police buildings, are all in keeping with the good road and obvious prosperity. A large two-storied hospital, with a cupola, which will accommodate one hundred and fifty patients, and is to be a medical school, is nearly finished. It is very well arranged and ventilated. I cannot say as much for the present hospital, which I went over. At the court house I saw twenty officials doing nothing, and as many policemen, all in European dress, to which they had added an imitation of European manners, the total result being unmitigated vulgarity. They demanded my passport before they would tell me the population of the prefecture and city. Once or twice I have found fault with Itō's manners, and he has asked me twice since if I think them like the manners of the policemen at Yamagata!

North of Yamagata the plain widens, and fine longitudinal ranges capped with snow mountains on the one side, and broken ranges with lateral spurs on the other, enclose as cheerful and pleasant a region as one would wish to see, with many pleasant villages on the lower slopes of the hills. The mercury was only seventy degrees, and the wind north, so it was an especially pleasant journey, though I had to go three and a half *ri* beyond Tendo, a town of five thousand people, where I had intended to halt, because the only inns at Tendo that were not houses of ill repute were occupied with silkworms that they could not receive me.

The next day's journey was still along the same fine road, through a succession of farming villages and towns of fifteen hundred to two thousand people, such as Tochiida and Obanasawa, were frequent. From both these there was a glorious view of Chōkai-*san*, a grand, snow-covered dome, said to be eight thousand feet high, which rises in an altogether unexpected manner from comparatively level country. As the great snowfields of Udono-*san* are in sight at the same time, with most picturesque curtain ranges below, it may be considered one of the grandest views of Japan. After leaving Obanasawa the road passes along a valley watered by one of the affluents of the Mogami River, and, after crossing it by a fine wooden bridge, ascends a pass from which the view is most magnificent. After a long ascent through a region of light, peaty soil, wooded with pine, cryptomeria, and scrub oak, a long descent and a fine avenue terminate in Shinjo, a wretched town of over five thousand people, situated in a plain of rice fields.

The day's journey, of over twenty-three miles, was through villages of farms without *yadoya*, and in many cases without even teahouses. The style of building has quite changed. Wood has disappeared, and all the houses are now built with heavy beams and walls of laths and brown mud mixed with chopped straw, and very neat. Nearly all are great oblong barns, turned endwise to the road, fifty, sixty, and even a hundred feet long, with the end nearest the road the dwelling house. These farm houses have no paper windows, only *amado*, with a few panes of paper at the top. These are drawn back in the daytime, and, in the better class of houses, blinds, formed of reeds or split bamboo, are let down over the opening. There are no ceilings, and in many cases an unmolested rat snake lives in the rafters, who, when he is much gorged, occasionally falls down upon a mosquito net.

Again I write that Shinjo is a wretched place. It is a *daimyō*'s town. And every *daimyō*'s town that I have seen has an air of decay, partly owing to the fact that the castle is either pulled down, or has been allowed to fall into decay. Shinjo has a large trade in rice, silk, and hemp, and ought not to be as poor as it looks. The mosquitoes were in thousands, and I had to go to bed, so as to be out of their reach, before I had finished my wretched meal of sago and condensed milk. There was a hot rain all night, my wretched room was dirty and stifling, and rats gnawed my boots and ran away with my cucumbers.

today the temperature is high and the sky murky. The good road has come to an end, and the old hardships have begun again. After leaving Shinjo this morning we crossed over a steep ridge into a singular basin of great beauty, with a semicircle of pyramidal hills, rendered more striking by being covered to their summits with pyramidal cryptomeria, and apparently blocking all northward progress. At their feet lies Kanayama in a romantic situation, and, though I arrived as early as noon, I am staying for a day or two, for my room at the transport office is cheerful and pleasant, the agent is most polite, a very rough region lies before me, and Itō has secured a chicken for the first time since leaving Nikkō!

I find it impossible in this damp climate, and in my present poor health, to travel with any comfort for more than two or three days at a time, and it is difficult to find pretty, quiet, and wholesome places for a halt of two nights. Freedom from fleas and mosquitoes one can never hope for, though the last vary in number, and I have found a way of dodging the first by laying down a piece of oiled paper six feet square upon the mat, dusting along its edges a band of Persian insect powder, and setting my chair in the middle. I am then insulated, and, though myriads of fleas jump on the paper, the powder stupefies them, and they are easily killed. I have been obliged to rest here at any rate, because I have been stung on my left hand both by a hornet and a gadfly, and it is badly inflamed. In some places the hornets are in hundreds, and make the horses wild. I am also suffering from inflammation produced by the bites of horse ants, which attack one in walking. The Japanese suffer very much from these, and a neglected bite often produces an intractable ulcer. Besides these, there is a fly, as harmless in appearance as our house-fly, which bites as badly as a mosquito. These are some of the drawbacks of Japanese travelling in summer, but worse than these is the lack of such food as one can eat when one finishes a hard day's journey without appetite, in an exhausting atmosphere.

July 18
I have had so much pain and fever from stings and bites that last night I was glad to consult a Japanese doctor from Shinjo. Itō, who looks twice as big as usual when he has to do any "grand" interpreting, and always puts on silk *hakama* in honor of it, came in with a middle-aged man dressed entirely in silk, who prostrated himself three times on the ground, and then sat down on his heels. Itō in many words explained my calamities, and Dr. Nosoki

then asked to see my "honorable hand," which he examined carefully, and then my "honorable foot." He felt my pulse and looked at my eyes with a magnifying glass, and with much sucking in of his breath—a sign of good breeding and politeness—informed me that I had much fever, which I knew before. He told me I must rest, which I also knew. Then he lighted his pipe and contemplated me. Then he felt my pulse and looked at my eyes again, then felt the swelling from the hornet bite, and said it was much inflamed, of which I was painfully aware, and then clapped his hands three times. At this signal a carrier appeared, carrying a handsome black lacquer chest with the same crest in gold upon it as Dr. Nosoki wore in white on his *haori*. This contained a medicine chest of fine gold lacquer, fitted up with shelves, drawers, bottles, etc. He compounded a lotion first, with which he bandaged my hand and arm rather skilfully, telling me to pour the lotion over the bandage at intervals till the pain abated. The whole was covered with oiled paper, which answers the purpose of oiled silk. He then compounded a febrifuge, which, as it is purely vegetable, I have not hesitated to take, and told me to drink it in hot water, and to avoid *sake* for a day or two!

I asked him what his fee was, and, after many bows and much spluttering and sucking in of his breath, he asked if I should think half a yen too much. When I presented him with a yen, and told him with a good deal of profound bowing on my part that I was exceedingly glad to obtain his services, his gratitude quite abashed me by its immensity.

Dr. Nosoki is one of the old-fashioned practitioners, whose medical knowledge has been handed down from father to son, and who holds out, as probably most of his patients do, against European methods and drugs. A strong prejudice against surgical operations, especially amputations, exists throughout Japan. With regard to the latter, people think that, as they came into the world complete, so they are bound to go out of it, and in many places a surgeon would hardly be able to buy at any price the privilege of cutting off an arm.

Except from books these older men know nothing of the mechanism of the human body, as dissection is unknown to native science. Dr. Nosoki told me that he relies mainly on the application of the moxa and on acupuncture in the treatment of acute diseases, and in chronic maladies on friction, medicinal baths, certain animal and vegetable medicines, and certain kinds of food. The use of leeches and blisters is unknown to him, and he regards mineral drugs with obvious suspicion. He has heard of chloroform, but has never seen it used, and considers that in maternity it must necessarily be fatal either to mother or child. He asked me (and I have twice before been asked the same question) whether it is not by its use that we endeavour to keep down our redundant population! He has great faith in ginseng, and in rhinoceros horn, and in the powdered liver of some animal, which, from the description, I understood to be a tiger—all specifics of the Chinese school of medicines. Dr. Nosoki showed me a small box of "unicorn's" horn, which he said was worth more than its weight in gold! As my arm improved coincidently with the application of his lotion, I am bound to give him the credit of the cure.

I invited him to dinner, and two tables were produced covered with different dishes, of which he ate heartily, showing most singular dexterity with his chopsticks in removing the flesh of small, bony fish. It is proper to show appreciation of a repast by noisy gulpings, and much gurgling and drawing in of the breath. Etiquette rigidly prescribes these performances, which are most distressing to a European, and my guest nearly upset my gravity by them.

The host and the chief man of the village paid me a formal visit in the evening, and Itō, *en grande tenue*, exerted himself immensely on the occasion. They were much surprised at my not smoking, and supposed me to be under a vow! They asked me many questions about our customs and government, but frequently reverted to tobacco.

The Fatal Close

Shingoji, July 21

Very early in the morning, after my long talk with the village chief of Kanayama, Itō wakened me by saying, "You'll be able for a long day's journey today, as you had a chicken yesterday," and under this chicken's marvellous influence we got away at 6.45, only to verify the proverb, "The more haste the worse speed." Unsolicited by me the chief sent round the village to forbid the people from assembling, so I got away in peace with a packhorse and one runner. It was a terrible road, with two severe mountain passes to cross, and I not only had to walk nearly the whole way, but to help the man with the *kuruma* up some of the steepest places. Halting at the exquisitely situated village of Nosoki, we got one horse, and walked by a mountain road along the head-waters of the Omono to Innai. I wish I could convey the beauty and wildness of that mountain route, the surprises on the way, the views, the violent deluges of rain which turned rivulets into torrents, the hardships and difficulties of the day, the scanty fare of sun-dried rice dough and sour yellow rasps, and the depth of the mire through which we waded. We crossed the Shione and Sakatsu passes, and in twelve hours accomplished fifteen miles! Everywhere we were told that we should never get through the country by the way we are going.

The women still wear trousers, but with a long garment tucked into them instead of a short one, and the men wear a cotton combination of breastplate and apron, either without anything else, or over their *kimono*. The descent to Innai under an avenue of cryptomeria, and the village itself, shut in with the rushing Omono, are very beautiful.

The *yadoya* at Innai was a remarkably cheerful one, but my room was entirely *fusuma* and *shōji*, and people were peeping in the whole time. It is not only a foreigner and his strange ways which attract attention in these remote districts, but, in my case, my india-rubber bath, air-pillow, and, above all, my white mosquito net. Their nets are all of a heavy green canvas, and they admire mine so much, that I can give no more acceptable present on leaving than a piece of it to twist in with the hair. There were six engineers in the next room who are surveying the passes which I had crossed, in order to see if they could be tunnelled, in which case *kuruma* might go all the way from Tokyo to Kubota on the Sea of Japan, and, with a small additional outlay, carts also.

In the two villages of Upper and Lower Innai there has been an outbreak of a malady much dreaded by the Japanese, called *kakke* (beriberi), which, in the last seven months, has carried off a hundred persons out of a population of about fifteen hundred, and the local doctors have been aided by two sent from the medical school at Kubota. Its first symptoms are a loss of strength in the legs, "looseness in the knees," cramps in the calves, swelling, and numbness. This, Dr. Anderson, who has studied *kakke* in more than 1100 cases in Tokyo, calls the sub-acute form. The chronic is a slow, numbing, and wasting malady, which, if unchecked, results in death from paralysis and exhaustion in from six months to three years. The third, or acute form, Dr. Anderson describes thus. After remarking that the grave symptoms set in quite unexpectedly, and go on rapidly increasing, he says:

The patient now can lie down no longer; he sits up in bed and tosses restlessly from one position to another, and, with wrinkled brow, staring and anxious eyes, dusky skin, blue, parted lips, dilated nostrils, throbbing neck, and laboring chest, presents a picture of the most terrible distress that the worst of diseases can inflict. There is no inter-mission even for a moment, and the physician, here almost powerless, can do little more than note the failing pulse and falling temperature, and wait for the moment when the brain, paralysed by the carbonized blood, becomes insensible, and allow the dying patient to pass his or her last moments in merciful unconsciousness.

The next morning, after riding nine miles through a quagmire, under grand avenues of cryptomeria, and noticing with regret that the telegraph poles ceased, we reached Yuzawa, a town of seven thousand people, in which, had it not been for provoking delays, I should have slept instead of at Innai, and found that a fire a few hours previously had destroyed seventy houses, including the *yadoya* at which I should have lodged. We had to wait two hours for horses, as all were engaged in moving property and people. The ground where the houses had stood was absolutely bare of everything but fine black ash, among which the *kura* stood blackened, and, in some instances, slightly cracked, but in all unharmed. Already skeletons of new houses were rising. No life had been lost except that of a tipsy man, but I should probably have lost everything but my money.

Yuzawa is a specially objectionable-looking place. I took my lunch—a wretched meal of a tasteless white curd made from beans, with some condensed milk added to it—in a yard, and the people crowded in hundreds to the gate, and those behind, being unable to see me, got ladders and climbed on the adjacent roofs, where they remained till one of the roofs gave way with a loud crash, and precipitated about fifty men, women, and children into the room below, which fortunately was vacant. Nobody screamed—a noteworthy fact—and the casualties were only a few bruises. Four policemen then appeared and demanded my passport, as if I were responsible for the accident, and failing, like all others, to read a particular word upon it, they asked me what I was travelling for, and on being told "to learn about the country," they asked if I was making a map!

Having satisfied their curiosity they disappeared, and the crowd surged up again in fuller force. The transport agent begged them to go away, but they said they might never see such a sight again! One old peasant said he would go away if he were told whether "the sight" were a man or a woman, and, on the agent asking if that were any business of his, he said he should like to tell at home what he had seen, which awoke my sympathy at once, and I told Itō to tell them that a Japanese horse galloping night and day without ceasing would take five and a half weeks to reach my county—a statement which he is using lavishly as I go along. These are such queer crowds, so silent and gaping, and they remain motionless for hours, the wide-awake babies on the mothers' backs and in the fathers' arms never crying. I should be glad to hear a hearty aggregate laugh, even if I were its object. The great melancholy stare is depressing.

The road for ten miles was thronged with country people going in to see the fire. It was a good road and very pleasant country, with numerous roadside shrines and figures of the goddess of mercy. I had a wicked horse, thoroughly vicious. His head was doubly chained to the saddle-girth, but he never met man, woman, or child, without laying back his ears and running at them to bite them. I was so tired and in so much spinal pain that I got off and walked several times, and it was most difficult to get on again, for as soon as I put my hand on the saddle he swung his hind legs round to kick me, and it required some agility to avoid being hurt. Nor was this all. The evil beast made dashes with his tethered head at flies, threatening to twist or demolish my foot at each, flung his hind legs upwards, attempted to dislodge flies on his nose with his hind hoof, executed capers which involved a total disappearance of everything in front of the saddle, squealed, stumbled, kicked his old shoes off, and resented the feeble attempts which the *mago* made to replace them, and finally walked in to Yokote and down its long and dismal street mainly on his hind legs, shaking the rope out of his timid leader's hand, and shaking me into a sort of aching jelly! I used to think that horses were made vicious either by being teased or by violence in breaking, but this does not account for the malignity of the Japanese horses. The people are so much afraid of them that they treat them with great respect. They are not beaten or kicked, are spoken to in soothing tones, and, on the whole, live better than their masters. Perhaps this is the secret of their villainy.

Yokote, a town of ten thousand people, in which the best *yadoya* are all non-respectable, is an ill-favored, ill-smelling, forlorn, dirty, damp, miserable place, with a large trade in cottons. As I rode through on my temporary biped the people rushed out from the baths to see me, men and women alike without a particle of clothing. The house master was very polite, but I had a dark and dirty room, up a bamboo ladder, and it swarmed with fleas and mosquitoes to an exasperating extent. On the way I heard that a bullock was killed every Thursday in Yokote, and had decided on having a broiled steak for supper and taking another with me, but when I arrived it was all sold, there were no eggs, and I made a miserable meal of rice and bean curd, feeling somewhat starved, as the condensed milk I bought at Yamagata had to be thrown away. I was somewhat wretched from fatigue and inflamed ant bites. In the early morning, hot and misty as all the mornings have been, I went to see a Shinto temple and, though I went alone, escaped a throng.

The entrance into the temple court was, as usual, by a *torii*, which consisted of two large posts twenty feet high, surmounted with cross beams, the upper one of which projects beyond the posts and frequently curves upwards at both ends. The whole, as is often the case, was painted a dull red. This *torii*, or "birds' rest," is said to be so called because the fowls, which were formerly offered but not sacrificed, were accustomed to perch upon it. A straw rope (*shimenawa*), with straw tassels and strips of paper (*shide*) hanging from it, the special emblem of Shinto, hung across the gateway. In the paved court there were several handsome granite lanterns on fine granite pedestals, such as are the nearly universal accompaniments of both Shinto and Buddhist temples.

After leaving Yokote we passed through very pretty country with mountain views and occasional glimpses of the snowy dome of Chōkai-*san*, crossed the Omono River (which has burst its banks and destroyed its bridges) by two troublesome ferries, and arrived at Rokugo, a town of five thousand people, with fine temples, exceptionally mean houses, and the most aggressive crowd by which I have yet been asphyxiated.

Through the good offices of the police, I was enabled to attend a Buddhist funeral of a merchant of some wealth. It interested me very much from its solemnity and decorum, and Itō's explanations of what went before were remarkably distinctly given. I went in a Japanese woman's dress, borrowed at the teahouse, with a blue hood over my head, and thus escaped all notice, but I found the restraint of the scanty "tied forward" *kimono* very tiresome. Itō gave me many injunctions as to what I was to do and avoid, which I carried out faithfully, being nervously anxious to avoid jarring on the sensibilities of those who had kindly permitted a foreigner to be present.

The illness was a short one, and there had been no time either for prayers or pilgrimages on the sick man's behalf. When death occurs the body is laid with its head to the north (a position that the living Japanese scrupulously avoid), near a folding screen, between which and it a new *zen* is placed, on which are a saucer of oil with a lighted rush, cakes of uncooked rice dough, and a saucer of incense sticks. The priests directly after death choose the *kaimyō*, or posthumous name, write it on a tablet of white wood, and seat themselves by the corpse. His *zen*, bowls, cups, etc., are filled with vegetable food and are placed by his side, the chopsticks being put on the wrong, i.e. the left, side of the *zen*. At the end of forty-eight hours the corpse is arranged for the coffin by being washed with warm water, and the priest, while saying certain prayers, shaves the head. In all cases, rich or poor, the dress is of the usual make, but of pure white linen or cotton.

At Omagori large earthenware jars are manufactured, which are much used for interment by the wealthy. In this case there were two square boxes, the outer one being of finely planed wood of the cypress. The poor use what is called the "quick-tub," a covered tub of pine hooped with bamboo. Women are dressed for burial in the silk robe worn on the marriage day, *tabi* are placed beside them or on their feet, and their hair usually flows loosely behind them. The wealthiest people fill the coffin with vermilion and the poorest use chaff. In this case I heard that only the mouth, nose, and ears were filled with vermilion, and that the coffin was filled up with coarse incense. The body is placed within the tub or box in the usual squatting position. It is impossible to understand how a human body, many hours after death, can be pressed into the limited space afforded by even the outermost of the boxes. It has been said that the rigidity of a corpse is overcome by the use of a powder called *dōsha*, which is sold by the priests.

Bannerets of small size and ornamental staves were outside the house door. Two men in blue dresses, with pale blue over-garments resembling wings received each person, two more presented a lacquered bowl of water and a white silk crepe towel, and then we passed into a large room, round which were arranged a number of very handsome folding screens, on which lotuses, storks, and peonies were realistically painted on a dead gold ground. Near the end of the room the coffin, under a canopy of white silk, upon which there was a very beautiful arrangement of artificial white lotuses, rested upon trestles, the face of the corpse being turned towards the north. Six priests, very magnificently dressed, sat on each side of the coffin, and two more knelt in front of a small temporary altar.

The widow, an extremely pretty woman, squatted near the deceased, below the father and mother. After her came the children, relatives, and friends, who sat in rows, dressed in winged garments of blue and white. The widow was painted white. Her lips were reddened with vermilion; her hair was elaborately dressed and ornamented with carved shell pins. She wore a beautiful dress of sky-blue silk, with a *haori* of fine white crepe and a scarlet crepe *obi* embroidered in gold, and looked like a bride on her marriage day rather than a widow. Indeed, owing to the beauty of the dresses and the amount of blue and white silk, the room had a festal rather than a funereal look. When all the guests had arrived, tea and sweetmeats were passed round. Incense was burned profusely. Litanies were mumbled, and the bustle of moving to the grave began, during which I secured a place near the gate of the temple grounds.

The procession did not contain the father or mother of the deceased, but I understood that the mourners who composed it were all relatives. The oblong tablet with the "dead name" of the deceased was carried first by a priest, then the lotus blossom by another priest. Ten priests followed, two and two, chanting litanies from books. Then came the coffin on a platform borne by four men and covered with white drapery, then the widow, and then the other relatives. The coffin was carried into the temple and laid upon trestles, while incense was burned and prayers were said. It was then carried to a shallow grave lined with cement, and prayers were said by the priests until the earth was raised to the proper level, when all dispersed, and the widow, in her gay attire, walked home unattended. There were no hired mourners or any signs of grief, but nothing could be more solemn, reverent, and decorous than the whole service. I have since seen many funerals, chiefly of the poor, and, though shorn of much of the ceremony, and with only one officiating priest, the decorum was always most remarkable. The fees to the priests are from two up to forty or fifty yen.

The graveyard, which surrounds the temple, was extremely beautiful, and the cryptomeria especially fine. It was very full of stone gravestones, and, like all Japanese cemeteries, exquisitely kept. As soon as the grave was filled in, a life-size pink lotus plant was placed upon it, and a lacquer tray, on which were lacquer bowls containing tea or *sake*, beans, and sweetmeats.

The temple at Rokugo was very beautiful, and, except that its ornaments were superior in solidity and good taste, differed little from a Romish church. The low altar, on which were lilies and lighted candles, was draped in blue and silver, and on the high altar, draped in crimson and cloth of gold, there was nothing but a closed shrine, an incense-burner, and a vase of lotuses.

At a wayside teahouse, soon after leaving Rokugo in a *kuruma*, I met the same courteous and agreeable young doctor who was stationed at Innai during the prevalence of *kakke*, and he invited me to visit the hospital at Kubota, of which he is junior physician, and told Itō of a restaurant at which "foreign food" can be obtained—a pleasant prospect, of which he is always reminding me.

Travelling along a very narrow road, I as usual first, we met a man leading a prisoner by a rope, followed by a policeman. As soon as my runner saw the latter he fell down on his face so suddenly in the shafts as nearly to throw me out, at the same time trying to wriggle into a garment which he had carried on the crossbar, while the young men who were drawing the two *kuruma* behind, crouching behind my vehicle, tried to scuttle into their clothes. I never saw such a picture of abjectness as my man presented. He trembled from head to foot and literally grovelled in the dust. With every sentence that the policeman spoke he raised his head a little, to bow it yet more deeply than before. It was all because he had no clothes on. I interceded for him as the day was very hot, and the policeman said he would not arrest him, as he should otherwise have done, because of the inconvenience that it would cause to a foreigner. He was quite an elderly man, and never recovered his spirits, but, as soon as a turn of the road took us out of the policeman's sight, the two younger men threw their clothes into the air and gambolled in the shafts, shrieking with laughter!

On reaching Shingoji, being too tired to go farther, I was dismayed to find nothing but a low, dark, foul-smelling room, enclosed only by dirty *shōji*, in which to spend Sunday. One side looked into a little mildewed court, with a slimy growth of algae, and into which the people of another house constantly came to stare. The other side opened on the earthen passage into the street, where travellers wash their feet, the third into the kitchen, and the fourth into the front room. Even before dark it was alive with mosquitoes, and the fleas hopped on the mats like sand flies. There were no eggs, nothing but rice and cucumbers. At five on Sunday morning I saw three faces pressed against the outer lattice, and before evening the *shōji* were riddled with finger-holes, at each of which a dark eye appeared. There was a still, fine rain all day, with the mercury at eighty-two degrees, and the heat, darkness, and smells were difficult to endure. In the afternoon a small procession passed the house, consisting of a decorated palanquin, carried and followed by priests, with capes and stoles over crimson chasubles and white cassocks. This ark, they said, contained papers inscribed with the names of people and the evils they feared, and the priests were carrying the papers to throw them into the river.

I went to bed early as a refuge from mosquitoes, with the *andon*, as usual, dimly lighting the room, and shut my eyes. About nine I heard a good deal of whispering and shuffling, which continued for some time, and, on looking up, saw opposite to me about forty men, women, and children (Itō says a hundred), all staring at me, with the light upon their faces. They had silently removed three of the *shōji* next to the passage! I called Itō loudly, and clapped my hands, but they did not stir till he came, and then fled like a flock of sheep. I have patiently, even smilingly, borne all out-of-doors crowding and curiosity, but this kind of intrusion is unbearable. I sent Itō to the police station, much against his will, to beg the police to keep the people out of the house, as the house master was unable to do so. This morning, as I was finishing dressing, a policeman appeared in my room, ostensibly to apologize for the behavior of the people, but in reality to have a privileged stare at me, and, above all, at my stretcher and mosquito net, from which he hardly took his eyes. Itō says he could make a yen a day by showing them! The policeman said that the people had never seen a foreigner.

The Kubota Hospital

I arrived here on Monday afternoon by the Omono River, what would have been two long days' journey by land having been easily accomplished in nine hours by water. This was an instance of forming a plan wisely, and adhering to it resolutely! Firmness in travelling is nowhere more necessary than in Japan. I decided some time ago, from Brunton's map, that the Omono must be navigable from Shingoji, and a week ago told Itō to inquire about it, but at each place difficulties have been started: there was too much water, there was too little; there were bad rapids, there were shallows; it was too late in the year; all the boats which had started lately were lying aground. But at one of the ferries I saw in the distance a merchandise boat going down. I told Itō I should go that way and no other.

On arriving at Shingoji they said it was not on the Omono at all, but on a stream with some very bad rapids, in which boats are broken to pieces. Lastly, they said there was no boat, but on my saying that I would send ten miles for one, a small, flat-bottomed scow was produced by the transport agent, into which Itō, the luggage, and myself accurately fitted. Itō sententiously observed, "Not one thing has been told us on our journey which has turned out true!" This is not an exaggeration.

The usual crowd did not assemble round the door, but preceded me to the river, where it covered the banks and clustered in the trees. Four policemen escorted me down. The voyage of forty-two miles was delightful. The rapids were a mere ripple, the current was strong, one boatman almost slept upon his paddle, the other only woke to bale the boat when it was half-full of water. The shores were silent and pretty, and almost without population till we reached the large town of Araya, which straggles along a high bank for a considerable distance. After nine peaceful hours we turned off from the main stream of the Omono River just at the outskirts of Kubota, and poled up a narrow, green river. It was fringed by dilapidated backs of houses, boat-building yards, and rafts of timber on one side, and dwelling houses, gardens, and damp greenery on the other. This stream is crossed by very numerous bridges.

I got a cheerful upstairs room at a most friendly *yadoya*, and my three days here have been fully occupied and very pleasant. "Foreign food"—a good beefsteak, an excellent curry, cucumbers, and foreign salt and mustard, were at once obtained, and I felt my eyes lightened after partaking of them.

Kubota is a very attractive and purely Japanese town of thirty-six thousand people, the capital of Akita prefecture. A fine mountain, called Taihei-*san*, rises above its fertile valley, and the Omono falls into the Sea of Japan close to it. It has a number of *kuruma*, but, owing to heavy sand and the badness of the roads, they can only go three miles in any direction. It is a town of activity and brisk trade, and manufactures a silk fabric in stripes of blue and black, and yellow and black, much used for making *hakama* and *kimono*, a species of white silk crepe with a raised woof, which brings a high price in Tokyo shops, as well as *fusuma* and *geta*. Though it is a castle town, it is free from the usual "deadly-lively" look, and has an air of prosperity and comfort. Though it has few streets of shops, it covers a great extent of ground with streets and lanes of pretty, isolated dwelling houses, surrounded by trees, gardens, and well-trimmed hedges, each garden entered by a substantial gateway. The existence of something like a middle class with home privacy and home life is suggested by these miles of comfortable suburban residences. Foreign influence is hardly at all felt, there is not a single foreigner in government or any other employment, and even the hospital was organized from the beginning by Japanese doctors.

This fact made me greatly desire to see it, but, on going there at the proper hour for visitors, I was met by the director with courteous but vexatious denial. No foreigner could see it, he said, without sending his passport to the governor and getting a written order. So I complied with these preliminaries, and 8 a.m. of the next day was fixed for my visit. Itō, who is lazy about interpreting for the lower orders, but exerts himself to the utmost on such an occasion as this, went with me, handsomely clothed in silk, as befitted an interpreter, and surpassed all his former efforts.

The director and the staff of six physicians, all handsomely dressed in silk, met me at the top of the stairs, and conducted me to the management room, where six clerks were writing. Here there was a table, solemnly covered with a white cloth, and four chairs, on which the director, the chief physician, Itō, and I sat, and pipes, tea, and sweetmeats, were produced. After this, accompanied by fifty medical students, whose intelligent looks promise well for their success, we went round the hospital, which is a large two- storied building in semi-European style, but with deep verandahs all round. The upper floor is used for classrooms, and the lower accommodates a hundred patients, besides a number of resident students. Ten is the largest number treated in any one room, and severe cases are treated in separate rooms. Gangrene has prevailed, and the chief physician, who is at this time remodelling the hospital, has closed some of the wards in consequence. There is a lock hospital under the same roof. About fifty important operations are annually performed under chloroform, but the people of Akita prefecture are very conservative, and object to part with their limbs and to foreign drugs. This conservatism diminishes the number of patients.

The odor of carbolic acid pervaded the whole hospital, and there were spray producers enough to satisfy Mr. Lister![1] At the request of doctor Kayabashi I saw the dressing of some very severe wounds carefully performed with carbolized gauze, under spray of carbolic acid, the fingers of the surgeon and the instruments used being all carefully bathed in the disinfectant. doctor Kayabashi said it was difficult to teach the students the extreme carefulness with regard to minor details which is required in the antiseptic treatment, which he regards as one of the greatest discoveries of this century. I was very much impressed with the fortitude shown by the surgical patients, who went through very severe pain without a wince or a moan. Eye cases are unfortunately very numerous. Doctor Kayabashi attributes their extreme prevalence to overcrowding, defective ventilation, poor living, and bad light.

---

1 Joseph Lister, a British surgeon and a pioneer of antiseptic surgery, who successfully introduced carbolic acid (now known as phenol) to sterilise surgical instruments and to clean wounds.

After our round we returned to the management room to find a meal laid out in English style—coffee in cups with handles and saucers, and plates with spoons. After this pipes were again produced, and the director and medical staff escorted me to the entrance, where we all bowed profoundly. I was delighted to see that doctor Kayabashi, a man under thirty, and fresh from Tokyo, and all the staff and students were in the national dress, with the *hakama* of rich silk. It is a beautiful dress, and assists dignity as much as the ill-fitting European costume detracts from it. This was a very interesting visit, in spite of the difficulty of communication through an interpreter.

The public buildings, with their fine gardens, and the broad road near which they stand, with its stone-faced embankments, are very striking in such a far-off prefecture. Among the finest of the buildings is the normal school, where I shortly afterwards presented myself, but I was not admitted till I had shown my passport and explained my objects in travelling. These preliminaries being settled, Tomatsu Aoki, the chief director, and Shude Kane Nigishi, the principal teacher, lionized me.

The first was most trying, for he persisted in attempting to speak English, of which he knows about as much as I know of Japanese, but the last, after some grotesque attempts, accepted Itō's services. The school is a commodious Europeanized building, three stories high, and from its upper balcony the view of the city, with its gray roofs and abundant greenery, and surrounding mountains and valleys, is very fine. The equipments of the different classrooms surprised me, especially the laboratory of the chemical classroom, and the truly magnificent illustrative apparatus in the natural science classroom. Ganot's *Physics* is the text book of that department.

A Silk Factory

My next visit was to a factory of handloom silk weavers, where one hundred and eighty hands, half of them women, are employed. These new industrial openings for respectable employment for women and girls are very important, and tend in the direction of a much-needed social reform. The striped silk fabrics produced are entirely for home consumption.

Afterwards I went into the principal street. After a long search through the shops, bought some condensed milk with the "Eagle" brand and the label all right, but, on opening it, found it to contain small pellets of a brownish, dried curd, with an unpleasant taste! As I was sitting in the shop, half stifled by the crowd, the people suddenly fell back to a respectful distance, leaving me breathing space, and a message came from the chief of police to say that he was very sorry for the crowding, and had ordered two policemen to attend upon me for the remainder of my visit. The black and yellow uniforms were most truly welcome, and since then I have escaped all annoyance. On my return I found the card of the chief of police, who had left a message with the house master apologizing for the crowd by saying that foreigners very rarely visited Kubota, and he thought that the people had never seen a foreign woman.

I went afterwards to the central police station to inquire about an inland route to Aomori, and received much courtesy, but no information. The police everywhere are very gentle to the people—a few quiet words or a wave of the hand are sufficient, when they do not resist them. They belong to the samurai class, and, doubtless, their naturally superior position weighs with the commoners. Their faces and a certain hauteur of manner show the indelible class distinction. The entire police force of Japan numbers 23,300 educated men in the prime of life, and if thirty percent of them do wear spectacles, it does not detract from their usefulness. 5600 of them are stationed at Tokyo (as from thence they can be easily sent wherever they are wanted), 1004 at Kyoto, and 815 at Osaka, and the remaining 10,000 are spread over the country. The police force costs something over 400,000 pounds annually, and certainly is very efficient in preserving good order. The pay of ordinary constables ranges from six to ten yen a month.

An enormous quantity of superfluous writing is done by all officialdom in Japan, and one usually sees policemen writing. What comes of it I don't know. They are mostly intelligent and gentlemanly-looking young men, and foreigners in the interior are really much indebted to them. If I am at any time in difficulties I apply to them, and, though they are disposed to be somewhat condescending, they are sure to help one, except about routes, of which they always profess ignorance.

On the whole, I like Kubota better than any other Japanese town, perhaps because it is so completely Japanese and has no air of having seen better days. I no longer care to meet Europeans— indeed I should go far out of my way to avoid them. I have become quite used to Japanese life, and think that I learn more about it in travelling in this solitary way than I should otherwise.

Itō's Diary

Kubota, July 24

I am here still, not altogether because the town is fascinating, but because the rain is so ceaseless as to be truly a plague of immoderate rain and waters. Travellers keep coming in with stories of the impassability of the roads and the carrying away of bridges. Itō amuses me very much by his remarks. He thinks that my visit to the school and hospital must have raised Japan in my estimation, and he is talking rather big. He asked me if I noticed that all the students kept their mouths shut like educated men and residents of Tokyo, and that all country people keep theirs open. I have said little about him for some time, but I daily feel more dependent on him, not only for all information, but actually for getting on. At night he has my watch, passport, and half my money, and I often wonder what would become of me if he absconded before morning. He is not a good boy. He has no moral sense, according to our notions: he dislikes foreigners; his manner is often very disagreeable; and yet I doubt whether I could have obtained a more valuable servant and interpreter. When we left Tokyo he spoke fairly good English, but by practice and industrious study he now speaks better than any official interpreter I have seen, and his vocabulary is daily increasing. He never uses a word inaccurately when he has once got hold of its meaning, and his memory never fails. He keeps a diary both in English and Japanese, and it shows much painstaking observation. He reads it to me sometimes, and it is interesting to hear what a young man who has travelled as much as he has regards as novel in this northern region. He has made a hotel book and a transport book, in which all the bills and receipts are written, and he daily transliterates the names of all places into English letters, and puts down the distances and the sums paid for transport and hotels on each bill.

He inquires the number of houses in each place from the police or transport agent, and the special trade of each town, and notes them down for me. He takes great pains to be accurate, and occasionally remarks about some piece of information that he is not quite certain about, "If it's not true, it's not worth having." He is never late, never dawdles, never goes out in the evening except on errands for me, never touches *sake*, is never disobedient, never requires to be told the same thing twice, is always within hearing, has a good deal of tact as to what he repeats, and all with an undisguised view to his own interest. He sends most of his wages to his mother, who is a widow—"It's the custom of the country"— and seems to spend the remainder on sweetmeats, tobacco, and the luxury of frequent shampooing.

That he would tell a lie if it served his purpose, and would squeeze up to the limits of extortion, if he could do it unobserved, I have not the slightest doubt. He seems to have but little heart, or any idea of any but vicious pleasures. He has no religion of any kind; he has been too much with foreigners for that. His frankness is something startling. He has no idea of reticence on any subject; but probably I learn more about things as they really are from this very defect. In virtue in man or woman, except in that of his former master, he has little, if any belief. He thinks that Japan is right in availing herself of the discoveries made by foreigners, that they have as much to learn from her, and that she will outstrip them in the race, because she takes all that is worth having, and rejects the incubus of Christianity. Patriotism is, I think, his strongest feeling, and I never met with such a boastful display of it, except in a Scotchman or an American. He despises the uneducated, as he can read and write both the syllabaries. For foreign rank or position he has not an atom of reverence or value, but a great deal of both for Japanese officialdom. He despises the intellects of women, but flirts in a town-bred fashion with the simple teahouse girls.

He is anxious to speak the very best English, and to say that a word is slangy or common interdicts its use. Sometimes, when the weather is fine and things go smoothly, he is in an excellent and communicative humor, and talks a good deal as we travel. A few days ago I remarked, "What a beautiful day this is!" and soon after, note-book in hand, he said, "You say 'a beautiful day.' Is that better English than 'a devilish fine day,' which most foreigners say?" I replied that it was "common," and "beautiful" has been brought out frequently since. Again, "When you ask a question you never say, 'What the devil is it?' as other foreigners do. Is it proper for men to say it and not for women?" I told him it was proper for neither, it was a very "common" word, and I saw that he erased it from his note-book. At first he always used fellows for men, as, "Will you have one or two *fellows* for your *kuruma*?" "*Fellows* and women." At last he called the chief physician of the hospital here a *fellow*, on which I told him that it was slightly slangy, and at least "colloquial," and for two days he has scrupulously spoken of man and men. today he brought a boy with very sore eyes to see me, on which I exclaimed, "Poor little fellow!" and this evening he said, "You called that boy a fellow, I thought it was a bad word!" The habits of many of the Yokohama foreigners have helped to obliterate any distinctions between right and wrong, if he ever made any. If he wishes to tell me that he has seen a very tipsy man, he always says he has seen "a fellow as drunk as an Englishman." At Nikkō I asked him how many legal wives a man could have in Japan, and he replied, "Only one lawful one, but as many others (*mekake*) as he can support, just as Englishmen have." He never forgets a correction. Till I told him it was slangy he always spoke of inebriated people as "tight," and when I gave him the words "tipsy," "drunk," "intoxicated," he asked me which one would use in writing good English, and since then he has always spoken of people as "intoxicated."

He naturally likes large towns, and tries to deter me from taking the unbeaten tracks, which I prefer—but when he finds me immovable, always concludes his arguments with the same formula, "Well, of course you can do as you like; it's all the same to me." I do not think he cheats me to any extent. Board, lodging, and travelling expenses for us both are about six shillings six pence a day, and about two shillings six pence when we are stationary, and this includes all gratuities and extras. True, the board and lodging consist of tea, rice, and eggs, a copper basin of water, an *andon* and an empty room. Though there are plenty of chickens in all the villages, the people won't be bribed to sell them for slaughter, though they would gladly part with them if they were to be kept to lay eggs. Itō amuses me nearly every night with stories of his unsuccessful attempts to provide me with meat.

The travelling is the nearest approach to "a ride on a rail" that I have ever made. I have now ridden, or rather sat, upon seventy-six horses, all horrible. They all stumble. The loins of some are higher than their shoulders, so that one slips forwards, and the back-bones of all are ridgy. Their hind feet grow into points which turn up, and their hind legs all turn outwards, like those of a cat, from carrying heavy burdens at an early age. The same thing gives them a roll in their gait, which is increased by their awkward shoes. In summer they feed chiefly on leaves, supplemented with mashes of bruised beans, and instead of straw they sleep on beds of leaves. In their stalls their heads are tied where their tails should be, and their fodder is placed not in a manger, but in a swinging bucket. Those used in this part of Japan are worth from fifteen to thirty yen. I have not seen any overloading or ill-treatment; they are neither kicked, nor beaten, nor threatened in rough tones, and when they die they are decently buried, and have stones placed over their graves. It might be well if the end of a worn-out horse were somewhat accelerated, but this is mainly a Buddhist region, and the aversion to taking animal life is very strong.

A Marriage Ceremony

Kubota, July 25

The weather at last gives a hope of improvement, and I think I shall leave tomorrow. I had written this sentence when Itō came in to say that the man in the next house would like to see my stretcher and mosquito net, and had sent me a bag of cakes with the usual bit of seaweed attached, to show that it was a present. The Japanese believe themselves to be descended from a race of fishermen. They are proud of it, and Ebisu, the god of fishermen, is one of the most popular of the household divinities. The piece of seaweed sent with a present to any ordinary person, and the piece of dried fish skin which accompanies a present to the emperor, record the origin of the race, and at the same time typify the dignity of simple industry.

Of course I consented to receive the visitor, and with the mercury at eighty-four degrees, five men, two boys, and five women entered my small, low room, and after bowing to the earth three times, sat down on the floor. They had evidently come to spend the afternoon. Trays of tea and sweetmeats were handed round, and a *tabakobon* was brought in, and they all smoked, as I had told Itō that all usual courtesies were to be punctiliously performed. They expressed their gratification at seeing so "honorable" a traveller. I expressed mine at seeing so much of their "honorable" country, and we all bowed profoundly.

Then I laid Brunton's map on the floor and showed them my route, showed them the Asiatic Society's Transactions, and how we read from left to right, instead of from top to bottom, showed them my knitting, which amazed them, and my Berlin work, and then had nothing left. Then they began to entertain me, and I found that the real object of their visit was to exhibit an infant prodigy, a boy of four, with a head shaven all but a tuft on the top, a face of preternatural thoughtfulness and gravity, and the self-possessed and dignified demeanor of an elderly man. He was dressed in scarlet silk *hakama*, and a dark, striped, blue silk *kimono*, and fanned himself gracefully, looking at everything as intelligently and courteously as the others. To talk child's talk to him, or show him toys, or try to amuse him, would have been an insult. He has taught himself to read and write, and has composed poetry. His father says that he never plays, and understands everything just like a grown person. The intention was that I should ask him to write, and I did so.

It was a solemn performance. A red blanket was laid in the middle of the floor, with a lacquer writing-box upon it. He rubbed the ink with water on the inkstone, unrolled four rolls of paper, five feet long, and inscribed them with Chinese characters, nine inches long, of the most complicated kind, with firm and graceful curves of his brush, and with the ease and certainty of Giotto in turning his O. He sealed them with his seal in vermilion, bowed three times, and the performance was ended. People get him to write *kakemono* and signboards for them, and he had earned ten yen, or about two pounds, that day. His father is going to travel to Kyoto with him, to see if anyone under fourteen can write as well. I never saw such an exaggerated instance of child worship. Father, mother, friends, and servants, treated him as if he were a prince.

The house master, who is a most polite man, procured me an invitation to the marriage of his niece, and I have just returned from it. He has three wives himself. One keeps a *yadoya* in Kyoto, another in Morioka, and the third and youngest is with him here. From her limitless stores of apparel she chose what she considered a suitable dress for me—an under-dress of sage green silk crepe, a *kimono* of soft, green, striped silk of a darker shade, with a fold of white crepe, spangled with gold at the neck, and a *obi* of sage green corded silk, with the family crest here and there upon it in gold. I went with the house master, Itō, to his disgust, not being invited, and his absence was like the loss of one of my senses, as I could not get any explanations till afterwards.

The ceremony did not correspond with the rules laid down for marriages in the books of etiquette that I have seen, but this is accounted for by the fact that they were for persons of the samurai class, while this bride and bridegroom, though the children of well-to-do merchants, belong to the commoners. In this case the trousseau and furniture were conveyed to the bridegroom's house in the early morning, and I was allowed to go to see them. There were several *obi* of silk embroidered with gold, several pieces of brocaded silk for *kimono*, several pieces of silk crepe, a large number of made-up garments, a piece of white silk, six barrels of wine or *sake*, and seven sorts of condiments. Jewellery is not worn by women in Japan.

The furniture consisted of two wooden pillows, finely lacquered, one of them containing a drawer for ornamental hairpins, some cotton *futon*, two very handsome silk ones, a few silk cushions, a lacquer workbox, a spinning-wheel, a lacquer rice bucket and ladle, two ornamental iron kettles, various kitchen utensils, three bronze *hibachi*, two *tabakobon*, some lacquer trays, and *zen*, china kettles, teapots, and cups, some lacquer rice bowls, two copper basins, a few towels, some bamboo switches, and an inlaid lacquer etagere. As the things are all very handsome the parents must be well off. The *sake* is sent in accordance with rigid etiquette.

The bridegroom is twenty-two, the bride seventeen, and very comely, so far as I could see through the paint with which she was profusely disfigured. Towards evening she was carried in a *kago*, accompanied by her parents and friends, to the bridegroom's house, each member of the procession carrying a lantern. When the house master and I arrived the wedding party was assembled in a large room, the parents and friends of the bridegroom being seated on one side, and those of the bride on the other. Two young girls, very beautifully dressed, brought in the bride, a very pleasing-looking creature dressed entirely in white silk, with a veil of white silk covering her from head to foot. The bridegroom, who was already seated in the middle of the room near its upper part, did not rise to receive her, and kept his eyes fixed on the ground, and she sat opposite to him, but never looked up. A low table was placed in front, on which there was a two-spouted kettle full of *sake*, some *sake* bottles, and some cups, and on another there were some small figures representing a fir tree, a plum tree in blossom, and a stork standing on a tortoise, the last representing length of days, and the former the beauty of women and the strength of men. Shortly a *zen*, loaded with edibles, was placed before each person, and the feast began, accompanied by the noises which signify gastronomic gratification.

After this, which was only a preliminary, the two girls who brought in the bride handed round a tray with three cups containing *sake*, which each person was expected to drain till he came to the god of luck at the bottom.

The bride and bridegroom then retired, but shortly reappeared in other dresses of ceremony, but the bride still wore her white silk veil, which one day will be her shroud. An old gold lacquer tray was produced, with three *sake* cups, which were filled by the two bridesmaids, and placed before the parents-in-law and the bride. The father-in-law drank three cups, and handed the cup to the bride, who, after drinking two cups, received from her father-in- law a present in a box, drank the third cup, and then returned the cup to the father-in-law, who again drank three cups. Rice and fish were next brought in, after which the bridegroom's mother took the second cup, and filled and emptied it three times, after which she passed it to the bride, who drank two cups, received a present from her mother-in-law in a lacquer box, drank a third cup, and gave the cup to the elder lady, who again drank three cups. Soup was then served, and then the bride drank once from the third cup, and handed it to her husband's father, who drank three more cups, the bride took it again, and drank two, and lastly the mother-in-law drank three more cups. Thus each of the three had imbibed nine cups of some generous liquor! I failed to learn what the liquor was that was drunk so freely, but as no unseemly effects followed its use, I think it must either have been light wine, or light *sake*.

After this the two bridesmaids raised the two-spouted kettle and presented it to the lips of the married pair, who drank from it alternately, till they had exhausted its contents. This concluding ceremony is said to be emblematic of the tasting together of the joys and sorrows of life. And so they became man and wife till death or divorce parted them.

This drinking of *sake* or wine, according to prescribed usage, appeared to constitute the marriage service, to which none but relations were bidden. Immediately afterwards the wedding guests arrived, and the evening was spent in feasting and *sake* drinking. The fare is simple, and intoxication is happily out of place at a marriage feast. Every detail is a matter of etiquette, and has been handed down for centuries. Except for the interest of the ceremony, in that light it was a very dull and tedious affair, conducted in melancholy silence, and the young bride, with her whitened face and painted lips, looked and moved like an automaton.

Gods and Demons

Three miles of good road thronged with half the people of Kubota on foot
and by *kuruma*, red vans drawn by horses, pairs of policemen in *kuruma*,
hundreds of children being carried, hundreds more on foot, little girls,
formal and precocious looking, with hair dressed with scarlet crepe and
flowers, hobbling toilsomely along on high *geta*, groups of men and women,
never intermixing, stalls driving a roaring trade in cakes and sweetmeats,
women making *mochi* as fast as the buyers ate it, broad rice fields rolling
like a green sea on the right, an ocean of liquid turquoise on the left, the
grey roofs of Kubota looking out from their green surroundings, Taihei-
san in deepest indigo blocking the view to the south, a glorious day, and
a summer sun streaming over all, made up the cheeriest and most festal
scene that I have seen in Japan; men, women, and children, vans and
kuruma, policemen and horsemen, all on their way to the port of Kubota,
which was holding a *matsuri*. Towering above the low grey houses there
were objects which at first looked like five enormous black fingers, then
like trees with their branches wrapped in black, and then—comparisons
ceased; they were a mystery.

Dismissing the *kuruma*, which could go no farther, we dived into the crowd,
which was wedged along a mean street, nearly a mile long—a miserable
street of poor teahouses and poor shopfronts. You could hardly see the street
for the people. Paper lanterns were hung close together along its whole
length. There were rude scaffoldings supporting matted and covered
platforms, on which people were drinking tea and *sake* and enjoying the

crowd below. There were monkey theatres and dog theatres, two mangy sheep and a lean pig attracting wondering crowds, for neither of these animals is known in this region of Japan. There was a booth in which a woman was having her head cut off every half-hour for two *sen* a spectator. There were floats (*dashi*) with roofs like temples, on which, with forty men at the ropes, dancing children of the highest class were being borne in procession. There was a theatre with an open front, on the boards of which two men in antique dresses, with sleeves touching the ground, were performing with tedious slowness a classic dance of tedious posturings, which consisted mainly in dexterous movements of the aforesaid sleeves, and occasional emphatic stampings, and utterances of the word "*no*" in a hoarse howl. Needless to say, a foreign lady was not the least of the attractions of the fair. The cultus of children was in full force, all sorts of masks, dolls, sugar figures, toys, and sweetmeats were exposed for sale on mats on the ground, and found their way into the hands and sleeves of the children, for no Japanese parent would ever attend a *matsuri* without making an offering to his child.

The police told me that there were 22,000 strangers in Minato, yet for 32,000 holiday-makers a force of twenty-five policemen was sufficient. I did not see one person under the influence of *sake* up to three p.m., when I left, nor a solitary instance of rude or improper behavior, nor was I in any way rudely crowded upon. Even where the crowd was densest, the people of their own accord formed a ring and left me breathing space.

We went to the place where the throng was greatest, round the two great floats, whose colossal erections we had seen far off. These were structures of heavy beams, thirty feet long, with eight huge, solid wheels. Upon them there were several scaffoldings with projections, like flat surfaces of cedar branches, and two special peaks of unequal height at the top, the whole being nearly fifty feet from the ground. All these projections were covered with black cotton cloth, from which branches of pines protruded. In the middle three small wheels, one above another, over which striped white cotton was rolling perpetually, represented a waterfall. At the bottom another arrangement of white cotton represented a river, and an arrangement of blue cotton, fitfully agitated by a pair of bellows below, represented the sea. The whole is intended to represent a mountain on which the Shinto gods slew some devils, but anything more rude and barbarous could scarcely be seen. On the fronts of each car, under a canopy, were thirty performers on thirty diabolical instruments, which rent the air with a truly infernal discord, and suggested devils rather than their conquerors.

High up on the flat projections there were groups of monstrous figures. On one a giant in brass armour, much like the *Niō* of temple gates, was killing a revolting-looking demon. On another a *daimyō*'s daughter, in robes of cloth of gold with satin sleeves richly flowered, was playing on the *shamisen*. On another a hunter, thrice the size of life, was killing a wild horse equally magnified, whose hide was represented by the hairy wrappings of the leaves of a palm. On others highly-colored gods, and devils equally hideous, were grouped miscellaneously. These two cars were being drawn up and down the street at the rate of a mile in three hours by two hundred men each, numbers of men with levers assisting the heavy wheels out of the mud holes. This *matsuri*, which, like an English fair, feast, or revel, has lost its original religious significance, goes on for three days and nights, and this was its third and greatest day.

We left on mild-tempered horses, quite unlike the fierce fellows of Yamagata prefecture. Between Minato and Kado there is a very curious lagoon on the left, about seventeen miles long by sixteen broad, connected with the sea by a narrow channel, guarded by two high hills called Shin-zan and Hon-zan. Two Dutch engineers are now engaged in reporting on its capacities, and if its outlet could be deepened without enormous cost it would give north-western Japan the harbour it so greatly needs. Extensive rice fields and many villages lie along the road, which is an avenue of deep sand and ancient pines much contorted and gnarled. Down the pine avenue hundreds of people on horseback and on foot were trooping into Minato from all the farming villages, glad in the glorious sunshine which succeeded four days of rain. There were hundreds of horses, wonderful-looking animals in bravery of scarlet cloth and lacquer and fringed nets of leather, and many straw wisps and ropes, with saddles like Gothic roofs, and dependent panniers on each side, carrying two grave and stately-looking children in each, and sometimes a father or a fifth child on the top of the pack saddle.

I was so far from well that I was obliged to sleep at the wretched village of Abukawa, in a loft alive with fleas, where the rice was too dirty to be eaten, and where the house master's wife, who sat for an hour on my floor, was sorely afflicted with skin disease. The clay houses have disappeared and the villages are now built of wood, but Abukawa is an antiquated, ramshackle place, propped up with posts and slanting beams projecting into the roadway for the entanglement of unwary passengers.

The village smith was opposite, but he was not a man of ponderous strength, nor were there those wondrous flights and scintillations of sparks which were the joy of our childhood in the Tattenhall forge. A fire of powdered charcoal on the floor, always being trimmed and replenished by a lean and grimy satellite, a man still leaner and grimier, clothed in goggles and a girdle, always sitting in front of it, heating and hammering iron bars with his hands, with a clink which went on late into the night, and blowing his bellows with his toes. Bars and pieces of rusty iron pinned on the smoky walls, and a group of idle men watching his skilful manipulation, were the sights of the Abukawa smithy, and kept me enthralled in the balcony, though the whole clothesless population stood for the whole evening in front of the house with a silent, open-mouthed stare.

Early in the morning the same melancholy crowd appeared in the dismal drizzle, which turned into a tremendous torrent, which has lasted for sixteen hours. Low hills, broad rice valleys in which people are puddling the rice a second time to kill the weeds, bad roads, pretty villages, much indigo, few passengers, were the features of the day's journey. At Morioka and several other villages in this region I noticed that if you see one large, high, well-built house, standing in enclosed grounds, with a look of wealth about it, it is always that of the *sake* brewer. A bush denotes the manufacture as well as the sale of *sake*, and these are of all sorts, from the mangy bit of fir which has seen long service to the vigorous truss of pine constantly renewed. It is curious that this should formerly have been the sign of the sale of wine in England.

The wind and rain were something fearful all that afternoon. I could not ride, so I tramped on foot for some miles under an avenue of pines, through water a foot deep. With my paper waterproof soaked through, I reached Toyoka half drowned and very cold, to shiver over a *hibachi* in a clean loft, hung with my dripping clothes, which had to be put on wet the next day.

By 5 a.m. all Toyoka assembled, and while I took my breakfast I was not only the "cynosure" of the eyes of all the people outside, but of those of about forty more who were standing in the *doma*, looking up the ladder. When asked to depart by the house master, they said, "It's neither fair nor neighborly in you to keep this great sight to yourself, seeing that our lives may pass without again looking on a foreign woman;" so they were allowed to remain!

A Boatman Drowned

I have been suffering so much from my spine that I have been unable to travel more than seven or eight miles daily for several days, and even that with great difficulty. I try my own saddle, then a pack saddle, then walk through the mud, but I only get on because getting on is a necessity, and as soon as I reach the night's halting place I am obliged to lie down at once. Only strong people should travel in northern Japan. The inevitable fatigue is much increased by the state of the weather, and doubtless my impressions of the country are affected by it also, as a hamlet in a quagmire in a gray mist or a soaking rain is a far less delectable object than the same hamlet under bright sunshine. There has not been such a season for thirty years. The rains have been tremendous. I have lived in soaked clothes, in spite of my rain cloak, and have slept on a soaked stretcher in spite of all waterproof wrappings for several days, and still the weather shows no signs of improvement. The rivers are so high on the northern road that I am storm-bound as well as pain-bound here. Itō shows his sympathy for me by intense surliness, though he did say very sensibly, "I'm very sorry for you, but it's no use saying so over and over again, as I can do nothing for you. You'd better send for the blind man!"

In Japanese towns and villages you hear every evening men making a low peculiar whistle as they walks along, and in large towns the noise is quite a nuisance. It is made by blind men. A blind beggar is never seen throughout Japan, and the blind are an independent, respected, and well-to-do class, carrying on the occupations of shampooing, money-lending, and music.

We have had a very severe journey from Toyoka. That day the rain was ceaseless, and in the driving mists one could see little but low hills looming on the horizon, pine barrens, scrub, and flooded rice fields. Villages stood along roads that were quagmires a foot deep, and where the people's clothing was especially ragged and dirty. Hinokiyama, a village of samurai, on a beautiful slope, was an exception, with its fine detached houses, pretty gardens, deep-roofed gateways, grass and stone-faced terraces, and look of refined, quiet comfort. Everywhere there was a quantity of indigo, as is necessary, for nearly all the clothing of the lower classes is blue. Near a large village we were riding on a causeway through the rice fields, Itō on the packhorse in front, when we met a number of children returning from school, who, on getting near us, turned, ran away, and even jumped into the ditches, screaming as they ran. The *mago* ran after them, caught the hindmost boy, and dragged him back—the boy scared and struggling, the man laughing. The boy said that they thought that Itō was a monkey-player, i.e. the keeper of a monkey theatre, I a big ape, and the poles of my bed the scaffolding of the stage!

Splashing through mire and water we found that the people of Tobine wished to detain us, saying that all the ferries were stopped in consequence of the rise in the rivers. But I had been so often misled by false reports that I took fresh horses and went on by a track along a very pretty hillside, overlooking the Yonetsuru River, a large and swollen river, which nearer the sea had spread itself over the whole country. Torrents of rain were still falling, and all out-of-doors industries were suspended. Straw rain-cloaks hanging to dry dripped under all the eaves, our paper cloaks were sodden, our dripping horses steamed, and thus we slid down a steep descent into the hamlet of Kiriishi, thirty-one houses clustered under persimmon trees under a wooded hillside, all standing in a quagmire, and so abject and filthy that one could not ask for five minutes' shelter in any one of them. Sure enough, on the bank of the river, which was fully four hundred yards wide, and swirling like a mill-stream with a suppressed roar, there was an official order prohibiting the crossing of man or beast, and before I had time to think the *mago* had deposited the baggage on an islet in the mire and was over the crest of the hill. I wished that the government was a little less paternal.

Just in the nick of time we discerned a punt drifting down the river on the opposite side, where it brought up, and landed a man. Itō and two others yelled, howled, and waved so lustily as to attract its notice. To my joy an answering yell came across the roar and rush of the river. The torrent was so strong that the boatmen had to pole up on that side for half a mile, and in about three-quarters of an hour they reached our side. They were returning to Kotsunagi—the very place I wished to reach. Though only two and a half miles off, the distance took nearly four hours of the hardest work I ever saw done by men. Every moment I expected to see them rupture blood vessels or tendons. All their muscles quivered. It is a mighty river, and was from eight to twelve feet deep, and whirling down in muddy eddies. Often with their utmost efforts in poling, when it seemed as if poles or backs must break, the boat hung trembling and stationary for three or four minutes at a time. After the slow and eventless tramp of the last few days this was an exciting transit. Higher up there was a flooded wood, and, getting into this, the men aided themselves considerably by hauling by the trees. When we got out of this, another river joined the Yonetsuru-*gawa*, which with added strength rushed and roared more wildly.

I had long been watching a large houseboat far above us on the other side, which was being poled by desperate efforts by ten men. At that point she must have been half a mile off, when the stream overpowered the crew and in no time she swung round and came drifting wildly down and across the river, broadside on to us. We could not stir against the current, and had large trees on our immediate left, and for a moment it was a question whether she would not smash us to atoms. Itō was livid with fear. His white, appalled face struck me as ludicrous. I had no other thought than the imminent peril of the large boat with her freight of helpless families, when, just as she was within two feet of us, she struck a stem and glanced off. Then her crew grappled a headless trunk and got their hawser round it, and eight of them, one behind the other, hung on to it, when it suddenly snapped, seven fell backwards, and the forward one went overboard to be no more seen. Some house that night was desolate. Reeling downwards, the big mast and spar of the ungainly craft caught in a tree, giving her such a check that they were able to make her fast. It was a saddening incident. I asked Itō what he felt when we seemed

153

in peril, and he replied, "I thought I'd been good to my mother, and honest, and I hoped I should go to a good place."

The fashion of boats varies much on different rivers. On this one there are two sizes. Ours was a small one, flat-bottomed, twenty-five feet long by two and a half broad, drawing six inches, very low in the water, and with sides slightly curved inwards. The prow forms a gradual long curve from the body of the boat, and is very high.

The mists rolled away as dusk came on, and revealed a lovely country with much picturesqueness of form. Near Kotsunagi the river disappears into a narrow gorge with steep, sentinel hills, dark with pine and cryptomeria. To cross the river we had to go fully a mile above the point aimed at. A few minutes of express speed brought us to a landing in a deep, tough quagmire in a dark wood, through which we groped our lamentable way to the *yadoya*. A heavy mist came on, and the rain returned in torrents. The *doma* was ankle deep in black slush. The *daidokoro* was open to the roof, roof and rafters were black with smoke, and a great fire of damp wood was smoking lustily. Round some live embers in the *irori* fifteen men, women, and children were lying, doing nothing, by the dim light of an *andon*. It was decidedly picturesque, and I was well disposed to be content when the production of some handsome *fusuma* created *daimyō*'s rooms out of the farthest part of the dim and wandering space, opening upon a damp garden, into which the rain splashed all night.

The solitary spoil of the day's journey was a glorious lily, which I presented to the house master, and in the morning it was blooming on the *kamidana* in a small vase of priceless old Satsuma china. I was woken from a sound sleep by Itō coming in with a rumor, brought by some travellers, that the prime minister had been assassinated, and fifty policemen killed! This was probably a distorted version of the partial mutiny of the Imperial Guard, which I learned on landing in Ezo. Very wild political rumors are in the air in these outlandish regions, and it is not very wonderful that the peasantry lack confidence in the existing order of things after the changes of the last ten years, and the recent assassination of the home minister. I did not believe the rumor, for fanaticism, even in its wildest moods, usually owes some allegiance to common sense. But it was disturbing, as I have naturally come to feel a deep interest in Japanese affairs.[1]

154

A few hours later Itō again presented himself with a bleeding cut on his temple. In lighting his pipe—an odious nocturnal practice of the Japanese— he had fallen over the edge of the fire-pot. I always sleep in a *yukata* to be ready for emergencies, and soon bound up his head, and slept again, to be woken early by another deluge.

We made an early start, but got over very little ground, owing to bad roads and long delays. All day the rain came down in even torrents, the tracks were nearly impassable, my horse fell five times, I suffered severely from pain and exhaustion, and almost fell into despair about ever reaching the sea. In these wild regions there are no *kago* to be had, and a packhorse is the only conveyance. Yesterday, having abandoned my own saddle, I had the bad luck to get a pack saddle with specially angular and uncompromising peaks, with a soaked and extremely unwashed *futon* on the top, spars, tackle, ridges, and furrows of the most exasperating description, and two nooses of rope to hold on by as the animal slid downhill on his haunches, or let me almost slide over his tail as he scrambled and plunged uphill.

It was pretty country, even in the downpour, when white mists parted and fir-crowned heights looked out for a moment, or we slid down into a deep glen with mossy boulders, lichen-covered stumps, ferny carpet, and the damp, balsamy smell of cryptomeria, and a tawny torrent dashing through it in gusts of passion. Then there were low hills, much scrub, immense rice fields, and violent inundations. But it is not pleasant, even in the prettiest country, to cling on to a pack saddle with a saturated quilt below you and the water slowly soaking down through your wet clothes into your boots, knowing all the time that when you halt you must sleep on a wet bed, and change into damp clothes, and put on the wet ones again the next morning. The villages were poor, and most of the houses were of boards rudely nailed together for ends, and for sides straw rudely tied on. They had no windows, and smoke came out of every crack. They were as unlike the houses which travellers see in southern Japan as a "black hut" in Uist is like a cottage in a trim village in Kent. These peasant proprietors have much to learn of the art of living. At Tsuguriko, the next stage, where the transport office was so dirty that I was obliged to sit in the street in the

---

1 On May 14, 1878, Home Minister Ōkubo Toshimichi was assassinated by Shimada Ichirō and six Kanazawa Domain samurai while on his way to the imperial palace.

rain, they told us that we could only get on a *ri* farther, because the bridges were all carried away and the fords were impassable. But I engaged horses, and, by dint of British doggedness and the willingness of the *mago*, I got the horses singly and without their loads in small punts across the swollen waters of the Hayakuchi, the Yuwase, and the Mochida, and finally forded three branches of my old friend the Yonetsuru-*gawa*, with the foam of its hurrying waters whitening the men's shoulders and the horses' packs, and with a hundred Japanese looking on at the "folly" of the foreigner.

I found kind people everywhere, and the two *mago* were especially so, for, when they found that I was pushing on to Ezo for fear of being laid up in the interior wilds, they did all they could to help me. They lifted me gently from the horse, made steps of their backs for me to mount, and gathered for me handfuls of red berries, which I ate out of politeness, though they tasted of some nauseous drug. They suggested that I should stay at the picturesquely-situated old village of Kawaguchi, but everything about it was mildewed and green with damp. The stench from the green and black ditches with which it abounded was so overpowering, even in passing through, that I was obliged to ride on to Odate, a crowded, forlorn, half-tumbling-to-pieces town of eight thousand people, with bark roofs held down by stones.

The *yadoya* are crowded with storm-staid travellers, and I had a weary tramp from one to another, almost sinking from pain, pressed upon by an immense crowd, and frequently bothered by a policeman, who followed me from one place to the other, making wholly unrighteous demands for my passport at that most inopportune time. After a long search I could get nothing better than this room, with *fusuma* of tissue paper, in the centre of the din of the house, close to the *doma* and *daidokoro*. Fifty travellers, nearly all men, are here, mostly speaking at the top of their voices, and in a provincial jargon which exasperates Itō. Cooking, bathing, eating, and, worst of all, perpetual drawing water from a well with a creaking hoisting apparatus, are going on from half past four in the morning till half past eleven at night, and on both evenings noisy mirth, of alcoholic inspiration, and dissonant performances by *geisha* have added to the dim

In all places lately *hai*, "yes," has been pronounced *he, chi, na, ne*, to Itō's great contempt. It sounds like an expletive or interjection rather than a response, and seems used often as a sign of respect or attention only. Often it is loud and shrill, then guttural, at times little more than a sigh. In these *yadoya* every sound is audible, and I hear low rumbling of mingled voices, and above all the sharp "*hai, hai*" of the teahouse girls in full chorus from every quarter of the house. The habit of saying it is so strong that a man roused out of sleep jumps up with "*hai, hai*", and often, when I speak to Itō in English, someone sitting by answers "*hai.*"

I don't want to convey a false impression of the noise here. It would be at least three times as great were I in equally close proximity to a large hotel kitchen in England, with fifty Britons only separated from me by paper partitions. I had not been long in bed on Saturday night when I was woken by Itō bringing in an old hen which he said he could stew till it was tender. I fell asleep again with its dying squeak in my ears, to be woken a second time by two policemen wanting for some occult reason to see my passport. And a third time by two men with lanterns scrambling and fumbling about the room for the strings of a mosquito net, which they wanted for another traveller. These are among the ludicrous incidents of Japanese travelling. About five Itō woke me by saying he was quite sure that the moxa would be the thing to cure my spine, and, as we were going to stay all day, he would go and fetch an operator. I rejected this as emphatically as the services of the blind man! Yesterday a man came and pasted slips of paper over all the "peep holes" in the *shōji*, and I have been very little annoyed, even though the *yadoya* is so crowded.

The rain continues to come down in torrents, and rumors are hourly arriving of disasters to roads and bridges on the northern route.

Noisy Talk

Early this morning the rain-clouds rolled themselves up and disappeared, and the bright blue sky looked as if it had been well washed. I had to wait till noon before the rivers became fordable, and my day's journey is only seven miles, as it is not possible to go farther till more of the water runs off. We had very limp, melancholy horses, and my *mago* was half tipsy, and sang, talked, and jumped the whole way. *Sake* is frequently taken warm, and in that state produces a very noisy but good-tempered intoxication. I have seen a good many intoxicated persons, but never one in the least degree quarrelsome. The effect very soon passes off, leaving an unpleasant nausea for two or three days as a warning against excess. The abominable concoctions known under the names of beer, wine, and brandy, produce a bad-tempered and prolonged intoxication, and delirium tremens, rarely known as a result of *sake* drinking, is being introduced under their baleful influence.

The sun shone gloriously and brightened the hill-girdled valley in which Odate stands into positive beauty, with the narrow river flinging its bright waters over green and red shingle, lighting it up in glints among the conical hills, some richly wooded with coniferae, and others merely covered with scrub, which were tumbled about in picturesque confusion. When Japan gets the sunshine, its forest-covered hills and garden-like valleys are turned into paradise. In a journey of six hundred miles there has hardly been a patch of country which would not have been beautiful in sunlight.

We crossed five severe fords with the water half-way up the horses' bodies, in one of which the strong current carried my *mago* off his feet. The horse towed him ashore, singing and capering, his drunken glee nothing abated by his cold bath. Everything is in a state of wreck. Several river channels have been formed in places where there was only one. There is not a trace of the road for a considerable distance, not a bridge exists for ten miles, and a great tract of country is covered with boulders, uprooted trees, and logs floated from the mountain sides. Already, however, these industrious peasants are driving piles, carrying soil for embankments in creels on horses' backs, and making ropes of stones to prevent a recurrence of the calamity. About here the female peasants wear for field-work a dress which pleases me much by its suitability—light blue trousers, with a loose sack over them, confined at the waist by a girdle.

On arriving here in much pain, and knowing that the road was not open any farther, I was annoyed by a long and angry conversation between the house master and Itō, during which the horses were not unloaded. The upshot of it was that the man declined to give me shelter, saying that the police had been round the week before giving notice that no foreigner was to be received without first communicating with the nearest police station, which, in this instance, is three hours off. I said that the authorities of Akita prefecture could not by any local regulations override the imperial edict under which passports are issued. But he said he should be liable to a fine and the withdrawal of his license if he violated the rule. No foreigner, he said, had ever lodged in Shirasawa, and I have no doubt that he added that he hoped no foreigner would ever seek lodgings again. My passport was copied and sent off by special runner, as I should have deeply regretted bringing trouble on the poor man by insisting on my rights. In much trepidation he gave me a room open on one side to the village, and on another to a pond, over which, as if to court mosquitoes, it is partially built. I cannot think how the Japanese can regard a hole full of dirty water as an ornamental appendage to a house.

My hotel expenses (including Itō's) are less than three shillings a day, and in nearly every place there has been a cordial desire that I should be comfortable. Considering that I have often put up in small, rough hamlets off the great routes even of Japanese travel, the accommodation, minus the fleas and the odors, has been surprisingly excellent, not to be equalled, I should think, in equally remote regions in any country in the world.

This evening, here, as in thousands of other villages, the men came home from their work, ate their food, had their smoke, enjoyed their children, carried them about, watched their games, twisted straw ropes, made straw sandals, split bamboo, wove straw rain coats, and spent the time universally in those little economical ingenuities and skilful adaptations which our people (the worse for them) practise perhaps less than any other. There was no assembling at the *sake* shop. Poor though the homes are, the men enjoy them. The children are an attraction at any rate, and the brawling and disobedience which often turn our working-class homes into bear gardens are unknown here, where docility and obedience are inculcated from the cradle as a matter of course. The signs of religion become fewer as I travel north, and it appears that the little faith that exists consists mainly in a belief in certain charms and superstitions, which the priests industriously foster.

A low voice is not regarded as a most excellent thing, in man at least, among the lower classes in Japan. The people speak at the top of their voices, and, though most words and syllables end in vowels, the general effect of a conversation is like the discordant gabble of a farmyard. The next room to mine is full of stormbound travellers, and they and the house master kept up what I thought was a most important argument for four hours at the top of their voices. I supposed it must be on the new and important ordinance granting local elective assemblies, of which I heard at Odate. On inquiry I found that it was possible to spend four mortal hours in discussing whether the day's journey from Odate to Noshiro could be made best by road or river.

Japanese women have their own gatherings, where gossip and chit-chat, marked by a truly Oriental indecorum of speech, are the staple of talk. I think that in many things, especially in some which lie on the surface, the Japanese are greatly our superiors, but that in many others they are immeasurably behind us. In living altogether among this courteous, industrious, and civilized people, one comes to forget that one is doing them a gross injustice in comparing their manners and ways with those of a people molded by many centuries of Christianity. Would to God that we were so Christianized that the comparison might always be favorable to us, which it is not!

July 30

In the room on the other side of mine were two men with severe eye-disease, with shaven heads and long and curious rosaries, who beat small drums as they walked. They were on pilgrimage to the shrine of Fudō at Meguro, near Tokyo, a seated, flame-surrounded idol, with a naked sword in one hand and a coil of rope in the other, who has the reputation of giving sight to the blind. At five this morning they began their devotions, which consisted in repeating with great rapidity, and in a high monotonous key for two hours, the invocation of the Nichiren sect of Buddhists, *Namu myōhō rengekyō*, which certainly no Japanese understands, and on the meaning of which even the best scholars are divided. One gave me, "Glory to the salvation-bringing Scriptures;" another, "Hail, precious law and gospel of the lotus flower;" and a third, "Heaven and earth! The teachings of the wonderful lotus flower sect." The invocation of "*Namu Amida Butsu*" was heard at intervals, and two drums were beaten the whole time!

The rain, which began again at eleven last night, fell from five till eight this morning, not in drops, but in streams, and in the middle of it a heavy pall of blackness (said to be a total eclipse) enfolded all things in a lurid gloom. Any detention is exasperating within one day of my journey's end, and I hear without equanimity that there are great difficulties ahead, and that our getting through in three or even four days is doubtful.

Floods

The prophecies concerning difficulties are fulfilled. For six days and five nights the rain has never ceased, except for a few hours at a time, and for the last thirteen hours, as during the eclipse at Shirasawa, it has been falling in such sheets as I have only seen for a few minutes at a time on the equator. I have been here storm-staid for two days, with damp bed, damp clothes, damp everything—boots, bag, books, are all green with mildew. And still the rain falls, and roads, bridges, rice fields, trees, and hillsides are being swept in a common ruin towards the Tsugaru Strait, so tantalizingly near. The simple people are calling on the forgotten gods of the rivers and the hills, on the sun and moon, and all the host of heaven, to save them from this plague of immoderate rain and waters. For myself, to be able to lie down all day is something, and as I cannot get on, I have ceased to chafe, and am rather inclined to magnify the advantages of the detention, a necessary process, as one would think if one saw my surroundings!

The day before yesterday, in spite of severe pain, was one of the most interesting of my journey. As I learned something of the force of fire in Hawaii, I am learning not a little of the force of water in Japan. We left Shirasawa at noon, as it looked likely to clear, taking two horses and three men. It is beautiful scenery—a wild valley, upon which a number of lateral ridges descend, rendered strikingly picturesque by the dark pyramidal cryptomeria, which are truly the glory of Japan. Five of the fords were deep and rapid, and the entrance on them difficult, as the sloping descents were all carried away, leaving steep banks, which had to be levelled by the mattocks of the *mago*. Then the fords themselves were gone. There were shallows where there had been depths, and depths where there had been shallows; new channels were carved, and great beds of shingle had been thrown up. Much wreckage lay about. The road and its small bridges were all gone, trees torn up by the roots or snapped short off by being struck by heavy logs were heaped together like barricades, leaves and even bark being in many cases stripped completely off. Great logs floated down the river in such numbers and with such force that we had to wait half an hour in one place to secure a safe crossing. Hollows were filled with liquid mud, boulders of great size were piled into embankments, causing perilous alterations in the course of the river. A fertile valley had been utterly destroyed, and the men said they could hardly find their way.

At the end of five miles it became impassable for horses. With two of the *mago* carrying the baggage, we set off, wading through water and climbing along the side of a hill, up to our knees in soft wet soil. The hillside and the road were both gone, and there were heavy landslides along the whole valley. Happily there was not much of this exhausting work, for, just as higher and darker ranges, densely wooded with cryptomeria, began to close us in, we emerged upon a fine new road. It is broad enough for a carriage, which, after crossing two ravines on fine bridges, plunges into the depths of a magnificent forest. Then, by a long series of fine zigzags of easy gradients, it ascends the pass of Yadate, on the top of which, in a deep sandstone cutting, is a handsome obelisk marking the boundary between Akita and Aomori prefectures. This is a marvellous road for Japan. It is so well graded and built up, and logs for travellers' rests are placed at convenient distances. Some very heavy work in grading and blasting has been done upon it, but there are only four miles of it, with wretched bridle tracks at each end. I left the others behind, and strolled on alone over the top of the pass and down the other side, where the road is blasted out of rock of a vivid pink and green color, looking brilliant under the trickle of water. I admire this pass more than anything I have seen in Japan. I even long to see it again, but under a bright blue sky. It reminds me much of the finest part of the Brunig Pass, and something of some of the passes in the Rocky Mountains, but the trees are far finer than in either. The pass was lonely, stately, dark, solemn. Its huge cryptomeria, straight as masts, sent their tall spires far aloft in search of light. The ferns, which love damp and shady places, were the only undergrowth. The trees flung their balsamy, aromatic scent liberally upon the air. In the unlighted depths of many a ravine and hollow, clear bright torrents leapt and tumbled, drowning with their thundering bass the musical treble of the lighter streams. Not a traveller disturbed the solitude with his sandalled footfall. There was neither the song of bird nor the hum of insect.

In the midst of this sublime scenery, and at the very top of the pass, the rain, which had been light but steady during the whole day, began to come down in streams and then in sheets. I have been so rained upon for weeks that at first I took little notice of it, but very soon changes occurred before my eyes which concentrated my attention. The rush of waters was heard everywhere, trees of great size slid down, breaking others in their fall. Rocks were rent and carried away trees in their descent, and the waters rose before our eyes. With a boom and roar as of an earthquake a hillside burst, and half the hill, with a noble forest of cryptomeria, was projected outwards. The trees, with the land on which they grew, went down heads foremost, diverting a river from its course. Where the forest-covered hillside had been there was now a great scar, out of which a torrent burst at high pressure, which in half an hour carved for itself a deep ravine, and carried into the valley below an avalanche of stones and sand. Another hillside descended less abruptly, and its noble groves found themselves at the bottom in a perpendicular position, and will doubtless survive their transplantation. Before my eyes, this fine new road was torn away by new torrents, or blocked by landslides in several places. A little lower, in one moment, a hundred yards of it disappeared, and with them a fine bridge, which was deposited aslant across the torrent lower down.

On the descent, when things began to look very bad, and the mountainsides had become cascades bringing trees, logs, and rocks down with them, we were fortunate enough to meet with two packhorses whose leaders were ignorant of the impassability of the road to Odate, and they and my laborers exchanged loads. These were strong horses, and the *mago* were skilful and courageous. They said if we hurried we could just get to the hamlet they had left. Even as they spoke the road and the bridge below were carried away. They insisted on lashing me to the pack saddle. The great stream, whose beauty I had formerly admired, was now a thing of dread, and had to be forded four times without fords. It crashed and thundered, drowning the feeble sound of human voices. The torrents from the heavens hissed through the forest, trees and logs came crashing down the hillsides, a thousand cascades added to the din, and in the bewilderment produced by such an unusual concatenation of sights and sounds we stumbled through the river, the men up to their shoulders, the horses up to their backs. Again and again we crossed. The banks being carried away, it was very hard to get either into or out of the water. The horses had to scramble or jump up places as high as their shoulders, all slippery and crumbling, and twice the men cut steps for them with axes. The rush of the torrent at the last crossing taxed the strength of both men and horses, and, as I was helpless from being tied on, I confess that I shut my eyes!

After getting through, we came upon the lands belonging to this village—rice fields with the dykes burst, and all the beautiful ridge and furrow cultivation of the other crops carried away. The waters were rising fast, the men said we must hurry. They unbound me, so that I might ride more comfortably, spoke to the horses, and went on at a run. My horse, which had nearly worn out his shoes in the fords, stumbled at every step, the *mago* gave me a noose of rope to clutch, the rain fell in such torrents that I speculated on the chance of being washed off my saddle, when suddenly I saw a shower of sparks. I felt unutterable things. I was choked, bruised, stifled, and presently found myself being hauled out of a ditch by three men, and realized that the horse had tumbled down in going down a steepish hill, and that I had gone over his head. To climb again on the soaked *futon* was the work of a moment. With men running and horses stumbling and splashing, we crossed the Hira-*kawa* by one fine bridge, and half a mile farther re-crossed it on another, wishing as we did so that all Japanese bridges were as substantial, for they were both a hundred feet long, and had central piers.

We entered Ikarigaseki from the last bridge, a village of eight hundred people, on a narrow ledge between an abrupt hill and the Hira-*kawa*, a most forlorn and tumble-down place, given up to felling timber and making shingles. Timber in all its forms—logs, planks, faggots, and shingles—is heaped and stalked about. It looks more like a lumberer's encampment than a permanent village, but it is beautifully situated, and unlike any of the innumerable villages that I have ever seen.

The street is long and narrow, with streams in stone channels on either side. These had overflowed, and men, women, and children were constructing square dams to keep the water, which had already reached the *doma*, from rising over the *tatami*. Hardly any house has paper windows, and in the few which have, they are so black with smoke as to look worse than none. The roofs are nearly flat, and are covered with shingles held on by laths and weighted with large stones. Nearly all the houses look like temporary sheds, and most are as black inside as a Barra hut. The walls of many are nothing but rough boards tied to the uprights by straw ropes.

In the drowning torrent, sitting in puddles of water, and drenched to the skin hours before, we reached this very primitive *yadoya*, the lower part of which is occupied by the *daidokoro*, a party of storm-bound students, horses, fowls, and dogs. My room is a wretched loft, reached by a ladder, with such a quagmire at its foot that I have to descend into it in Wellington boots. It was dismally grotesque at first. The torrent on the unceiled roof prevented Itō from hearing what I said, the bed was soaked, and the water, having got into my box, had dissolved the remains of the condensed milk, and had reduced clothes, books, and paper into a condition of universal stickiness. My *kimono* was less wet than anything else, and, borrowing a sheet of oiled paper, I lay down in it, till roused up in half an hour by Itō shrieking above the din on the roof that the people thought that the bridge by which we had just entered would give way. Running to the river bank, we joined a large crowd, far too intensely occupied by the coming disaster to take any notice of the first foreign lady they had ever seen.

The Hira-*kawa*, which an hour before was merely a clear, rapid mountain stream, about four feet deep, was then ten feet deep, they said, and tearing along, thick and muddy, and with a fearful roar. Immense logs of hewn timber, trees, roots, branches, and faggots, were coming down in numbers. The abutment on this side was much undermined, but, except that the central pier trembled whenever a log struck it, the bridge itself stood firm— so firm, indeed, that two men, anxious to save some property on the other side, crossed it after I arrived. Then logs of planed timber of large size, and joints, and much wreckage, came down—fully forty fine timbers, thirty feet long, for the fine bridge above had given way. Most of the harvest of logs cut on the Yadate Pass must have been lost, for over three hundred were carried down in the short time in which I watched the river. This is a very heavy loss to this village, which lives by the timber trade. Efforts were made at a bank higher up to catch them as they drifted by, but they only saved about one in twenty. It was most exciting to see the grand way in which these timbers came down. The moment in which they were to strike or not to strike the pier was one of intense suspense. After an hour of this two superb logs, fully thirty feet long, came down close together, and, striking the central pier nearly simultaneously, it shuddered horribly, the great bridge parted in the middle, gave an awful groan like a living thing, plunged into the torrent, and reappeared in the foam below only as disjointed timbers hurrying to the sea. Not a vestige remained. The bridge below was carried away in the morning, so that, till the river becomes fordable, this little place is completely isolated.

On thirty miles of road, out of nineteen bridges only two remain, and the road itself is almost wholly carried away!

Ikarigaseki

I have well-nigh exhausted the resources of this place. They are to go out three times a day to see how much the river has fallen; to talk with the house master and village chief; to watch the children's games and the making of shingles; to buy toys and sweetmeats and give them away; to apply zinc lotion to a number of sore eyes three times daily, under which treatment, during three days, there has been a wonderful amendment; to watch the cooking, spinning, and other domestic processes in the *daidokoro*; to see the horses, which are also actually in it, making meals of green leaves of trees instead of hay; to see the lepers, who are here for some waters which are supposed to arrest, if not to cure, their terrible malady; to lie on my stretcher and sew, and read the papers of the Asiatic Society, and to go over all possible routes to Aomori. The people have become very friendly in consequence of the eye lotion, and bring many diseases for my inspection, most of which would never have arisen had cleanliness of clothing and person been attended to. The absence of soap, the infrequency with which clothing is washed, and the absence of linen next the skin, cause various cutaneous diseases, which are aggravated by the bites and stings of insects. Scald-head affects nearly half the children here.

I am very fond of Japanese children. I have never yet heard a baby cry, and I have never seen a child troublesome or disobedient. Filial piety is the leading virtue in Japan, and unquestioning obedience is the habit of centuries. The arts and threats by which English mothers cajole or frighten children into unwilling obedience appear unknown. I admire the way in which children are taught to be independent in their amusements. Part of the home education is the learning of the rules of the different games, which are absolute, and when there is a doubt, instead of a quarrelsome suspension of the game, the fiat of a senior child decides the matter. They play by themselves, and don't bother adults at every turn. I usually carry sweeties with me, and give them to the children, but not one has ever received them without first obtaining permission from the father or mother. When that is gained they smile and bow profoundly, and hand the sweeties to those present before eating any themselves. They are gentle creatures, but too formal and precocious.

They have no special dress. This is so queer that I cannot repeat it too often. At three they put on the *kimono* and *obi*, which are as inconvenient to them as to their parents, and childish play in this garb is grotesque. I have never seen what we call child's play—that general abandonment to miscellaneous impulses, which consists in struggling, slapping, rolling, jumping, kicking, shouting, laughing, and quarrelling! Two fine boys are very clever in harnessing paper carts to the backs of beetles with gummed traces, so that eight of them draw a load of rice up an inclined plane. One can imagine what the fate of such a load and team would be at home among a number of snatching hands. Here a number of infants watch the performance with motionless interest, and never need the adjuration, "Don't touch." In most of the houses there are bamboo cages for "the shrill-voiced Katydid," and the children amuse themselves with feeding these vociferous grasshoppers. The channels of swift water in the street turn a number of toy water wheels, which set in motion most ingenious mechanical toys, of which a model of the automatic rice-husker is the commonest, and the boys spend much time in devising and watching these, which are really very fascinating. It is the holidays, but "holiday tasks" are given, and in the evenings you hear the hum of lessons all along the street for about an hour. The school examination is at the re-opening of the school after the holidays, instead of at the end of the session—an arrangement which shows an honest desire to discern the permanent gain made by the scholars.

This afternoon has been fine and windy, and the boys have been flying kites, made of tough paper on a bamboo frame, all of a rectangular shape, some of them five feet square, and nearly all decorated with huge faces of historical heroes. Some of them have a humming arrangement made of whale-bone. There was a very interesting contest between two great kites, and it brought out the whole population. The string of each kite, for thirty feet or more below the frame, was covered with pounded glass, made to adhere very closely by means of tenacious glue, and for two hours the kite-fighters tried to get their kites into a proper position for sawing the adversary's string in two. At last one was successful, and the severed kite became his property, upon which victor and vanquished exchanged three low bows. Silently as the people watched and received the destruction of their bridge, so silently they watched this exciting contest. The boys also flew their kites while walking on stilts—a most dexterous performance, in which few were able to take part—and then a larger number gave a stilt race. The most striking out-of-door games are played at fixed seasons of the year, and are not to be seen now.

There are twelve children in this *yadoya*, and after dark they regularly play at a game which Itō says "is played in the winter in every house in Japan." The children sit in a circle, and the adults look on eagerly, child-worship being more common in Japan than in America, and, to my thinking, the Japanese form is the best.

From proverbial philosophy to personal privation is rather a descent, but owing to the many detentions on the journey my small stock of foreign food is exhausted, and I have been living here on rice, cucumbers, and salt salmon—so salt that, after being boiled in two waters, it produces a most distressing thirst. Even this has failed today, as communication with the coast has been stopped for some time, and the village is suffering under the calamity of its stock of salted fish being completely exhausted. I had an omelette one day, but it was much like musty leather. The Italian ambassador said to me in Tokyo, "No question in Japan is so solemn as that of food," and many others echoed what I thought at the time a most unworthy sentiment. I recognized its truth today when I opened my last resort, a box of Brand's meat lozenges, and found them a mass of moldiness. One can only dry clothes here by hanging them in the wood smoke, so I prefer to let them mildew on the walls, and have bought a straw raincoat, which is more reliable than the paper waterproofs. I hear the hum of the children at their lessons for the last time, for the waters are falling fast, and we shall leave in the morning.

The Tunabata Festival

The waters did not fall as was expected, and I had to spend a fourth day at Ikarigaseki. We left early on Saturday, as we had to travel fifteen miles without halting. The sun shone on all the beautiful country, and on all the wreck and devastation, as it often shines on the dimpling ocean the day after a storm. We took four men, crossed two severe fords where bridges had been carried away, and where I and the baggage got very wet. We saw great devastations and much loss of crops and felled timber. We passed under a cliff, which for two hundred feet was composed of fine columnar basalt in six-sided prisms, and quite suddenly emerged on a great plain, on which green billows of rice were rolling sunlit before a fresh north wind. This plain is liberally sprinkled with wooded villages and surrounded by hills. One low range forming a curtain across the base of Iwakisan, a great snow-streaked dome, which rises to the west of the plain to a supposed height of five thousand feet. The water had risen in most of the villages to a height of four feet, and had washed the lower part of the mud walls away. The people were busy drying their *tatami*, *futon*, and clothing, reconstructing their dykes and small bridges, and fishing for the logs which were still coming down in large quantities.

In one town two very shabby policemen rushed upon us, seized the bridle of my horse, and kept me waiting for a long time in the middle of a crowd, while they toilsomely bored through the passport, turning it up and down, and holding it up to the light, as though there were some nefarious mystery about it. My horse stumbled so badly that I was obliged to walk to save myself from another fall. Just as my powers were failing, we met a *kuruma*, which by good management, such as being carried occasionally, brought me into Kuroishi, a neat town of five and a half thousand people, famous for the making of *geta* and combs. I obtained a very neat, airy, upstairs room, with a good view over the surrounding country and of the doings of my neighbors in their back rooms and gardens. Instead of getting on to Aomori I am spending three days and two nights here, and, as the weather has improved and my room is remarkably cheerful, the rest has been very pleasant. As I have said before, it is difficult to get any information about anything even a few miles off, and even at the post office they cannot give any intelligence as to the date of the sailings of the mail steamer between Aomori, twenty miles off, and Hakodate.

The police were not satisfied with seeing my passport, but must also see me, and four of them paid me a polite but domiciliary visit the evening of my arrival. That evening the sound of drumming was ceaseless, and soon after I was in bed Itō announced that there was something really worth seeing, so I went out in my *kimono* and without my hat, and in this disguise altogether escaped recognition as a foreigner. Kuroishi is unlighted, and I was tumbling and stumbling along in overhaste when a strong arm cleared the way, and the house master appeared with a very pretty lantern, hanging close to the ground from a cane held in the hand.

We soon reached a point for seeing the festival procession advance towards us, and it was so beautiful and picturesque that it kept me out for an hour. It passes through all the streets between seven and ten p.m. each night during the first week in August, with a portable shrine (*mikoshi*), containing slips of paper, on which (as I understand) wishes are written, and each morning at seven this is carried to the river and the slips are cast upon the stream. The procession consisted of three monster drums nearly the height of a man's body, covered with horsehide, and strapped to the drummers, end upwards, and thirty small drums, all beaten rub-a-dub-dub without ceasing. Each drum has the swirling *tomoe* crest painted on its ends. Then there were hundreds of paper lanterns carried on long poles of various lengths round a central lantern, twenty feet high, itself an oblong six feet long, with a front and wings, and all kinds of mythical and mystical creatures painted in bright colors upon it—a transparency rather than a lantern, in fact. Surrounding it were hundreds of beautiful lanterns and transparencies of all sorts of fanciful shapes—fans, fishes, birds, kites, drums. The hundreds of people and children who followed all carried circular lanterns, and rows of lanterns with the *tomoe* crest on one side and two Chinese characters on the other hung from the eaves all along the line of the procession. I never saw anything more completely like a fairy scene, the undulating waves of lanterns as they swayed along, the soft lights and soft tints moving aloft in the darkness, the lantern bearers being in deep shadow. This festival is called the *Tanabata* festival, but I am unable to get any information about it. Itō says that he knows what it means, but is unable to explain, and adds the phrase he always uses when in difficulties, "Mr. Satow would be able to tell you all about it."

A Lady's Toilet

This is a pleasant place, and my room has many advantages besides light and cleanliness, as, for instance, that I overlook my neighbors and that I have seen a lady at her toilet preparing for a wedding! A married girl knelt in front of a black lacquer toilet box with a spray of cherry blossoms in gold sprawling over it, and lacquer uprights at the top, which supported a polished metal mirror. Several drawers in the toilet box were open, and toilet requisites in small lacquer boxes were lying on the floor. A female barber stood behind the lady, combing, dividing, and tying her hair, which, like that of all Japanese women, was glossy black, but neither fine nor long. The coiffure is an erection, a complete work of art. Two divisions, three inches apart, were made along the top of the head, and the lock of hair between these was combed, stiffened with a bandoline, raised two inches from the forehead, turned back, tied, and pinned to the back hair. The rest was combed from each side to the back, and then tied loosely with twine made of paper. Several switches of false hair were then taken out of a long lacquer box, and, with the aid of a quantity of bandoline and a solid pad, the ordinary smooth chignon was produced, to which several loops and bows of hair were added, interwoven with a little dark-blue crepe, spangled with gold. A single, thick, square-sided, tortoiseshell pin was stuck through the whole as an ornament.

The fashions of dressing the hair are fixed. They vary with the ages of female children, and there is a slight difference between the coiffure of the married and unmarried. The two partings on the top of the head and the chignon never vary. The amount of stiffening used is necessary, as the head is never covered out of doors. This arrangement will last in good order for a week or more—thanks to the wooden pillow.

The barber's work was only partially done when the hair was dressed, for every vestige of recalcitrant eyebrow was removed, and every downy hair which dared to display itself on the temples and neck was pulled out with tweezers. This removal of all short hair has a tendency to make even the natural hair look like a wig. Then the lady herself took a box of white powder, and laid it on her face, ears, and neck, till her skin looked like a mask. With a camel's-hair brush she then applied some mixture to her eyelids to make the bright eyes look brighter, the teeth were blackened, or rather reblackened, with a feather brush dipped in a solution of gall-nuts and iron-filings—a tiresome and disgusting process, several times repeated, and then a patch of red was placed upon the lower lip. I cannot say that the effect was pleasing, but the girl thought so, for she turned her head so as to see the general effect in the mirror, smiled, and was satisfied. The remainder of her toilet, which altogether took over three hours, was performed in private, and when she reappeared she looked as if a very unmeaning-looking wooden doll had been dressed up with the exquisite good taste, harmony, and quietness which characterize the dress of Japanese women.

A most rigid social etiquette draws an impassable line of demarcation between the costume of the virtuous woman in every rank and that of her frail sister. The humiliating truth that many of our female fashions are originated by those whose position we the most regret, and are then carefully copied by all classes of women in our country, does not obtain credence among Japanese women, to whom even the slightest approximation in the style of hair-dressing, ornament, or fashion of garments would be a shame.

I was surprised to hear that three Christian students from Hirosaki wished to see me—three remarkably intelligent-looking, handsomely-dressed young men, who all spoke a little English. One of them had the brightest and most intellectual face which I have seen in Japan. They are of the samurai class, as I should have known from the superior type of face and manner. They said that they heard that an English lady was in the house, and asked me if I were a Christian, but apparently were not satisfied till, in answer to the question if I had a Bible, I was able to produce one.

Hirosaki is a castle town of some importance, three and a half *ri* from here, and its ex-*daimyō* supports a high-class school or college there, which has had two Americans successively for its headmasters. These gentlemen must have been very consistent in Christian living as well as energetic in Christian teaching, for under their auspices thirty young men have embraced Christianity. As all of these are well educated, and several are nearly ready to pass as teachers into government employment, their acceptance of the "new way" may have an important bearing on the future of this region.

A Public Bath House

Yesterday was beautiful, and, dispensing for the first time with Itō's attendance, I took a *kuruma* for the day, and had a very pleasant excursion into a cul de sac in the mountains. The one drawback was the infamous road, which compelled me either to walk or be mercilessly jolted. The runner was a nice, kind, merry creature, quite delighted, Itō said, to have a chance of carrying so great a sight as a foreigner into a district in which no foreigner has even been seen. In the absolute security of Japanese travelling, which I have fully realized for a long time, I look back upon my fears at Kasukabe with a feeling of self-contempt.

The scenery, which was extremely pretty, gained everything from sunlight and color—wonderful shades of cobalt and indigo, green blues and blue greens, and flashes of white foam in unsuspected rifts. It looked a simple, home-like region, a very pleasant land.

We passed through several villages of farmers who live in very primitive habitations, built of mud, looking as if the mud had been dabbed upon the framework with the hands. The walls sloped slightly inwards, the thatch was rude, the eaves were deep and covered all manner of lumber. There was a smoke hole (*fukinuke*) in a few, but the majority smoked all over like brick-kilns. They had no windows, and the walls and rafters were black and shiny. Fowls and horses live on one side of the dark interior, and the people on the other. The houses were alive with unclothed children, and as I repassed in the evening unclothed men and women, nude to their waists, were sitting outside their dwellings with the small fry, clothed only in

177

amulets. About them, several big yellow dogs formed part of each family group, and the faces of dogs, children, and people were all placidly contented! These farmers owned many good horses, and their crops were splendid. Probably on *matsuri* days all appear in fine clothes taken from ample hoards. They cannot be so poor, as far as the necessaries of life are concerned; they are only very far back. They know nothing better, and are contented. Their houses are as bad as any that I have ever seen, and the simplicity of Eden is combined with an amount of dirt which makes me sceptical as to the performance of even weekly ablutions.

Upper Nakano is very beautiful, and in the autumn, when its myriads of star-leaved maples are scarlet and crimson, against a dark background of cryptomeria, among which a great white waterfall gleams like a snowdrift before it leaps into the black pool below, it must be well worth a long journey. I have not seen anything which has pleased me more. There is a fine flight of moss-grown stone steps down to the water, a pretty bridge, two superb stone *torii*, some handsome stone lanterns. A grand flight of steep stone steps up a hill-side dark with cryptomeria leads to a small Shinto shrine. Not far off there is a sacred tree, with the token of love and revenge upon it. The whole place is entrancing.

Lower Nakano, which I could only reach on foot, is only interesting as possessing some very hot springs, which are valuable in cases of rheumatism and sore eyes. It consists mainly of teahouses and *yadoya*, and seemed rather gay. It is built round the edge of an oblong depression, at the bottom of which the bathhouses stand, of which there are four, only nominally separated, and with but two entrances, which open directly upon the bathers. In the two end houses women and children were bathing in large tanks, and in the centre ones women and men were bathing together, but at opposite sides, with wooden ledges to sit upon all round. I followed the *kurumaya* blindly to the baths, and when once in I had to go out at the other side, being pressed upon by people from behind. The bathers were too polite to take any notice of my most unwilling intrusion, and the *kurumaya* took me in without the slightest sense of impropriety in so doing. I noticed that formal politeness prevailed in the bathhouse as elsewhere, and that dippers and towels were handed from one to another with profound bows. The public bathhouse is said to be the place in which public opinion is formed, as it is with us in clubs and public- houses, and that the presence of women prevents any dangerous or seditious consequences; but the government is doing its best to prevent promiscuous bathing; and, though the reform may travel slowly into these remote regions, it will doubtless arrive sooner or later. The public bathhouse is one of the features of Japan.

A Stormy Voyage

The journey from Kuroishi to Aomori, though only 22.5 miles, was a tremendous one, owing to the state of the roads. More rain had fallen, and the passage of hundreds of packhorses heavily loaded with salted fish had turned the tracks into quagmires. At the end of the first stage the transport office declined to furnish a *kuruma*, owing to the state of the roads. As I was not well enough to ride farther, I bribed two men for a very moderate sum to take me to the coast. By accommodating each other we got on tolerably, though I had to walk up all the hills and down many, to get out at every place where a little bridge had been carried away, so that the *kuruma* might be lifted over the gap. Often I had to walk for two hundred yards at a time, because it sank up to its axles in the quagmire. In spite of all precautions I was upset into a muddy ditch, with the *kuruma* on the top of me. My air-pillow fortunately fell between the wheel and me, and I escaped with nothing worse than having my clothes soaked with water and mud, which, as I had to keep them on all night, might have given me a cold, but did not. We met strings of packhorses the whole way, carrying salted fish, which is taken throughout the interior.

The mountain-ridge, which runs throughout the main island of Honshu, becomes depressed around Nanbu, but rises again into grand, abrupt hills at Aomori Bay. Between Kuroishi and Aomori it is broken up into low ranges, scantily wooded, mainly with pine, scrub oak, and dwarf bamboo. The sesame bamboo, of which the container for incense sticks are made, covers some hills to the exclusion of all else. Rice grows in the valleys, but there is not much cultivation, and the country looks rough, cold, and hyperborean.

The farming hamlets grew worse and worse, with houses made roughly of mud, with holes scratched in the side for light to get in, or for smoke to get out, and the walls of some were only great pieces of bark and bundles of straw tied to the posts with straw ropes. The roofs were untidy, but this was often concealed by the profuse growth of the watermelons which trailed over them. The people were very dirty, but there was no clear poverty, and a good deal of money must be made on the horses and *mago* required for the transit of fish from Ezo, and for rice to it.

At Namioka occurred the last of the very numerous ridges we have crossed since leaving Nikkō at a point called Tsugarusaka. From it we looked over a rugged country upon a dark-grey sea, nearly landlocked by pine-clothed hills, of a rich purple indigo color. The clouds were drifting, the color was intensifying, the air was fresh and cold, the surrounding soil was peaty, the odors of pines were balsamic. It looked, felt, and smelled like home. The grey sea was Aomori Bay, beyond was the Tsugaru Strait—my long land journey was done. A traveller said a steamer was sailing for Ezo at night, so, in a state of joyful excitement, I engaged four men, and by dragging, pushing, and lifting, they got me into Aomori, a town of grey houses, grey roofs, and grey stones on roofs, built on a beach of grey sand, round a grey bay—a miserable-looking place, though the capital of the prefecture.

It has a great export trade in cattle and rice to Ezo, besides being the outlet of an immense annual emigration from northern Japan to the Ezo fishery, and imports from Hakodate large quantities of fish, skins, and foreign merchandise. It has some trade in a pretty but not valuable variegated lacquer, called Aomori lacquer, but not actually made there, its own speciality being a sweetmeat made of beans and sugar. It has a deep and well-protected harbour, but no piers or conveniences for trade. It has barracks and the usual government buildings, but there was no time to learn anything about it— only a short half-hour for getting my ticket at the Mitsubishi office, where they demanded and copied my passport. I snatched a morsel of fish at a restaurant where "foreign food" was represented by a very dirty table-cloth. And I ran down to the grey beach, where I was carried into a large *bezaisen* crowded with Japanese steerage passengers.

The wind was rising, a considerable surf was running, and the spray was flying over the boat. The steamer had her steam up, and was ringing and whistling impatiently. There was a scud of rain, and I was standing trying to keep my paper waterproof from being blown off, when three inopportune policemen jumped into the boat and demanded my passport. For a moment I wished them and the passport under the waves!

The steamer is a little old paddle-boat of about seventy tons, with no accommodation but a single cabin on deck. She was as clean and trim as a yacht, and, like a yacht, totally unfit for bad weather. Her captain, engineers, and crew were all Japanese, and not a word of English was spoken. My clothes were very wet, and the night was colder than the day had been, but the captain kindly covered me up with several blankets on the floor, so I did not suffer.

We sailed early in the evening, with a brisk northerly breeze, which chopped round to the south-east, and by eleven blew a gale. The sea ran high, the steamer labored and shipped several heavy seas, much water entered the cabin. The captain came below every half-hour, tapped the barometer, sipped some tea, offered me a lump of sugar, and made a face and gesture indicative of bad weather. We were buffeted about mercilessly till 4 a.m., when heavy rain came on, and the gale fell temporarily with it. The boat is not fit for a night passage, and always lies in port when bad weather is expected. As this was said to be the severest gale which has swept the Tsugaru Strait since January, the captain was uneasy about her, but showed much calmness.

The gale rose again after sunrise, and when, after doing sixty miles in fourteen hours, we reached the heads of Hakodate harbour, it was blowing and pouring like a bad day in Argyllshire, the spin-drift was driving over the bay, the Ezo mountains loomed darkly and loftily through rain and mist, and wind and thunder, and "noises of the northern sea," gave me a wild welcome to these northern shores. A rocky head like Gibraltar, a cold-blooded-looking grey town, straggling up a steep hillside, a few coniferae, a great many grey *bezaisen*, a few steamers and vessels of foreign rig at anchor, a number of *bezaisen* riding the rough water easily, seen in flashes between gusts of rain and spin-drift, were all I saw. But somehow it all pleased me from its breezy, northern look.

The steamer was not expected in the gale, so no one met me, and I went ashore with fifty Japanese clustered on the top of a decked *bezaisen* in such a storm of wind and rain that it took us one and a half hours to go half a mile. I waited shelterless on the windy beach till the customs' officers were roused from their late slumbers, and then battled with the storm for a mile up a steep hill. I was expected at the hospitable consulate, but did not know it, and came here to the Church Mission House, to which the Denings kindly invited me when I met them in Tokyo. I was unfit to enter a civilized dwelling. My clothes, besides being soaked, were coated and splashed with mud up to the top of my hat. My gloves and boots were finished, and my mud-splashed baggage was soaked with salt water. But I feel a somewhat legitimate triumph at having conquered all obstacles, and having accomplished more than I intended to accomplish when I left Tokyo.

How musical the clamor of the northern ocean is! How inspiring the shrieking and howling of the boisterous wind! Even the fierce pelting of the rain is home-like, and the cold in which one shivers is stimulating! One cannot imagine the delight of being in a room with a door that will lock, to be in a bed instead of on a stretcher, of finding twenty-three letters containing good news, and of being able to read them in warmth and quietness under the roof of an English home!

A Windy Capital

Hakodate, Ezo, August 13, 1878

After a tremendous bluster for two days the weather has become beautifully fine, and I find the climate here more invigorating than that of the main island. It is Japan, but yet there is a difference somehow. When the mists lift they reveal not mountains smothered in greenery, but naked peaks, volcanoes only recently burnt out, with the red ash flaming under the noonday sun, and passing through shades of pink into violet at sundown. Strips of sand border the bay, ranges of hills, with here and there a patch of pine or scrub, fade into the far-off blue, and the great cloud shadows lie upon their scored sides in indigo and purple. Blue as the Adriatic are the waters of the land-locked bay, and the snowy sails of pale *bezaisen* look whiter than snow against its intense azure. The abruptness of the double peaks behind the town is softened by a belt of cryptomeria, the sandy strip which connects the headland with the mainland heightens the general resemblance of the contour of the ground to Gibraltar. But while one dreams of the western world a *kuruma* passes one at a trot, temple drums are beaten in a manner unlike the roll of the British drum, a Buddhist funeral passes down the street, or a man-cart pulled and pushed by four yellow-skinned, little-clothed mannikins, creaks by, with the monotonous grunt of "*Ha huida.*"

A single look at Hakodate itself makes one feel that it is Japan all over. The streets are very wide and clean, but the houses are mean and low. The city looks as if it had just recovered from a conflagration. The houses are nothing but tinder. The grand tile roofs of some other cities are not to be seen. There is not an element of permanence in the wide and windy streets.

It is an increasing and busy place. It lies for two miles along the shore, and has climbed the hill till it can go no higher. But still houses and people look poor. It has a skeleton aspect too, which is partially due to the number of permanent "clothes-horses" on the roofs. Stones are its prominent feature. Looking down upon it from above you see miles of grey boulders, and realize that every roof in the windy capital is held down by a weight of paving stones. Nor is this all. Some of the flatter roofs are pebbled all over like a courtyard. Others, such as the roof of this house, for instance, are covered with sod and crops of grass, the two latter arrangements being precautions against risks from sparks during fires. These paving stones are certainly the cheapest possible mode of keeping the roofs on the houses in such a windy region, but they look odd.

None of the streets, except one high up the hill, with a row of fine temples and temple grounds, call for any notice. Nearly every house is a shop. Most of the shops supply only the ordinary articles consumed by a large and poor population. Either real or imitated foreign goods abound in Main Street, and the only novelties are furs, skins, and horns, which abound in shops devoted to their sale. I covet the great bear furs and the deep cream-colored furs of Ainu dogs, which are cheap as well as handsome. There are many second-hand, or, as they are called, "curio" shops, and the cheap lacquer from Aomori is also tempting to a stranger.

Missionary Manners

I am enjoying Hakodate so much that, though my tour is all planned and my arrangements are made, I linger on from day to day. There has been an unpleasant eclaircissement about Itō. I engaged him without a character, and he told both Lady Parkes and me that after I had done so his former master, Maries, asked him to go back to him, to which he had replied that he had "a contract with a lady." Maries is here, and I now find that he had a contract with Itō, by which Itō bound himself to serve him as long as he required him, for seven dollars a month. But hearing that I offered twelve, he ran away from him and entered my service with a lie! Maries has been put to the greatest inconvenience by his defection, and has been hindered greatly in completing his botanical collection, for Itō is very clever, and he had not only trained him to dry plants successfully, but he could trust him to go away for two or three days and collect seeds. I am very sorry about it. He says that Itō was a bad boy when he came to him, but he thinks that he cured him of some of his faults, and that he has served me faithfully. I have seen Maries at the consul's, and have arranged that, after my Ezo tour is over, Itō shall be returned to his rightful master, who will take him to China and Formosa for a year and a half, and who, I think, will look after his well-being in every way. The Hepburns, who are here, heard a bad account of the boy after I began my travels and were uneasy about me, but, except for this original lie, I have no fault to find with him, and his Shinto creed has not taught him any better. When I paid him his wages this morning he asked me if I had any fault to find, and I told him of my objection to his manners, which he took in very good part and promised to amend them. "But," he added, "mine are just missionary manners!"

Yesterday I dined at the consulate, to meet Count Charles Theodore Gonzalve de Diesbach de Belleroche, of the French legation, Baron Heinrich von Siebold, of the Austrian legation, and Lieutenant Gustav Ritter von Kreitner, of the Austrian army, who start tomorrow on an exploring expedition in the interior, intending to cross the sources of the rivers which fall into the sea on the southern coast and measure the heights of some of the mountains. They are well stocked in food and claret, but take such a number of pack-ponies with them that I predict that they will fail, and that I, who have reduced my luggage to forty-five pounds, will succeed!

I hope to start on my long-projected tour tomorrow. I have planned it for myself with the confidence of an experienced traveller, and look forward to it with great pleasure, as a visit to the aborigines is sure to be full of novel and interesting experiences.

A Front Horse

I am once again in the wilds! I am sitting outside an upper room built out almost over the lonely Lake Onuma, with wooded points purpling and still shadows deepening in the sinking sun. A number of men are dragging down the nearest hillside the carcass of a bear which they have just despatched with spears. There is no village, and the busy clatter of the cicada and the rustle of the forest are the only sounds which float on the still evening air. The sunset colors are pink and green. On the tinted water lie the waxen cups of great water-lilies, and above the wooded heights the pointed, craggy, and altogether naked summit of the volcano of Komogatake flushes red in the sunset. Not the least of the charms of the evening is that I am absolutely alone, having ridden the eighteen miles from Hakodate without Itō or an attendant of any kind. I have unsaddled my own horse, and by means of much politeness and a dexterous use of Japanese substantives have secured a good room and supper of rice, eggs, and black beans for myself and a mash of beans for my horse, which, as it belongs to the Kaitakushi, and has the dignity of iron shoes, is entitled to special consideration!

I am not yet off the beaten track, but my spirits are rising with the fine weather, the drier atmosphere, and the freedom of Ezo. Ezo is to the main island of Japan what Tipperary is to an Englishman, Barra to a Scotchman, "away down in Texas" to a New Yorker. People can locate all sorts of improbable stories here without much fear of being found out, of which the Ainu and the misdeeds of the ponies furnish the staple, and the queer doings of men and dogs, and adventures with bears, wolves, and salmon, the embroidery. Nobody comes here without meeting with something queer, and one or two tumbles either with or from his horse. Very little is known of the interior except that it is covered with forest matted together by lianas, and with an undergrowth of scrub bamboo impenetrable except to the axe, varied by swamps equally impassable, which give rise to hundreds of rivers well stocked with fish. The glare of volcanoes is seen in different parts of the island. The forests are the hunting-grounds of the Ainu, who are complete savages in everything but their disposition, which is said to be so gentle and harmless that I may go among them with perfect safety.

Kindly interest has been excited by the first foray made by a lady into the country of the aborigines. Richard Eusden, the consul, has worked upon the powers that be with such good effect that the governor has granted me a *shōmon*, a sort of official letter or certificate, giving me a right to obtain horses and laborers everywhere at the government rate of six *sen* a *ri*, with a prior claim to accommodation at the houses kept up for officials on their circuits, and to help and assistance from officials generally. The governor has further telegraphed to the other side of Uchiura Bay desiring the authorities to give me the use of the government *kuruma* as long as I need it, and to detain the steamer to suit my convenience! With this document, which enables me to dispense with my passport, I shall find travelling very easy, and I am very grateful to the consul for procuring it for me.

Here, where rice and tea have to be imported, there is a uniform charge at the *yadoya* of thirty *sen* a day, which includes three meals, whether you eat them or not. Horses are abundant, but small, and not up to heavy weights. They are entirely unshod, and, though their hoofs are very shallow and grow into turned-up points and other singular shapes, they go over rough ground with facility at a scrambling run of over four miles an hour following a leader called a "front horse." If you don't get a front horse and try to ride in front, you find that your horse will not stir till he has another before him. Then you are perfectly helpless, as he follows the movements of his leader without any reference to your wishes. There are no *mago*; a man rides the front horse and goes at whatever pace you please, or, if you get a front horse, you may go without anyone. Horses are cheap and abundant. They drive a number of them down from the hills every morning into corrals in the villages, and keep them there till they are wanted. Because they are so cheap they are very badly used. I have not seen one yet without a sore back, produced by the harsh pack saddle rubbing up and down the spine, as the loaded animals are driven at a run. They are mostly very poor-looking.

As there was some difficulty about getting a horse for me the consul sent one of the Kaitakushi saddle-horses, a handsome, lazy animal, which I rarely succeeded in stimulating into a heavy gallop. Leaving Itō to follow with the baggage, I enjoyed my solitary ride and the possibility of choosing my own pace very much, though the choice was only between a slow walk and the lumbering gallop aforesaid.

I met strings of horses loaded with deer hides, and overtook other strings loaded with *sake* and manufactured goods and in each case had a fight with my sociably inclined animal. In two villages I was interested to see that the small shops contained lucifer matches, cotton umbrellas, boots, brushes, clocks, slates, and pencils, engravings in frames, kerosene lamps, and red and green blankets, all but the last, which are unmistakable British "shoddy," being Japanese imitations of foreign manufactured goods, more or less cleverly executed. The road goes uphill for fifteen miles, and, after passing Nanai, a trim Europeanized village in the midst of fine crops, one of the places at which the government is making acclimatization and other agricultural experiments, it fairly enters the mountains. From the top of a steep hill there is a glorious view of Hakodate Head, looking like an island in the deep blue sea, and from the top of a higher hill, looking northward, a magnificent view of the volcano with its bare, pink summit rising above three lovely lakes densely wooded. These are the flushed scaurs and outbreaks of bare rock for which I sighed amidst the smothering greenery of the main island, and the silver gleam of the lakes takes away the blindness from the face of nature. It was delicious to descend to the water's edge in the dewy silence amidst balsamic odors, to find not a clattering grey village with its monotony, but a single, irregularly-built house, with lovely surroundings.

It is a most displeasing road for most of the way; sides with deep corrugations, and in the middle a high causeway of earth, whose height is being added to by hundreds of creels of earth brought on ponies' backs. It is supposed that carriages and waggons will use this causeway, but a shying horse or a bad driver would overturn them. As it is at present the road is only passable for packhorses, owing to the number of broken bridges. I passed strings of horses laden with *sake* going into the interior. The people of Ezo drink freely, and the poor Ainu outrageously. On the road I dismounted to rest myself by walking uphill, and, the saddle being loosely girthed, the gear behind it dragged it round and under the body of the horse, and it was too heavy for me to lift on his back again. When I had led him for some time two Japanese with a string of packhorses loaded with deer-hides met me. They not only put the saddle on again, but held the stirrup while I remounted, and bowed politely when I went away. Who could help liking such a courteous and kindly people?

Mori, Uchiura Bay, Monday

Even Lake Onuma was not Paradise after dark, and I was actually driven to bed early by the number of mosquitoes. Itō is in an excellent humor on this tour. Like me, he likes the freedom of the Hokkaido. He is much more polite and agreeable also, and very proud of the governor's *shōmon*, with which he swaggers into hotels and transport offices. I never get on so well as when he arranges for me. Saturday was grey and lifeless, and the ride of seven miles here along a sandy road through monotonous forest and swamp, with the volcano on one side and low wooded hills on the other, was wearisome and fatiguing. I saw five large snakes all in a heap, and a number more twisting through the grass. There are no villages, but several very poor teahouses, and on the other side of the road long sheds with troughs hollowed like canoes out of the trunks of trees, containing horse food. Here nobody walks, and the men ride at a quick run, sitting on the tops of their pack saddles with their legs crossed above their horses' necks, and wearing large hats like coal-scuttle bonnets. The horses are infested with ticks, hundreds upon one animal sometimes, and occasionally they become so mad from the irritation that they throw themselves suddenly on the ground, and roll over load and rider. I saw this done twice. The ticks often transfer themselves to the riders.

Mori is a large, ramshackle village, near the southern point of Uchiura Bay—a wild, dreary-looking place on a sandy shore, with a number of *jorōya* (brothels) disreputable characters. Several of the *yadoya* are not respectable, but I rather like this one, and it has a very fine view of the volcano, which forms one point of the bay. Mori has no anchorage, though it has an unfinished pier three hundred and forty-five feet long. The steam ferry across the mouth of the bay is here, and there is a very difficult bridle-track running for nearly a hundred miles round the bay besides, and a road into the interior. But it is a forlorn, decayed place. Last night the inn was very noisy, as some travellers in the next room to mine hired *geisha*, who played, sang, and danced till two in the morning, and the whole party imbibed *sake* freely. In this comparatively northern latitude the summer is already waning. The seeds of the blossoms which were in their glory when I arrived are ripe, and here and there a tinge of yellow on a hillside, or a scarlet spray of maple, heralds the glories and the coolness of autumn.

Yufutsu, Ezo

A loud yell of "steamer," coupled with the information that she could not wait one minute, broke in upon go and everything else, and in a broiling sun we hurried down to the pier. With a heap of Japanese, who filled two scows, we were put on board a steamer not bigger than a large decked steam launch, where the natives were all packed into a covered hole. I was conducted with much ceremony to the forecastle, a place at the bow five feet square, full of coils of rope, shut in, and left to solitude and dignity, and the stare of eight eyes, which perseveringly glowered through the windows. The steamer had been kept waiting for me on the other side for two days, to the infinite disgust of two foreigners, who wished to return to Hakodate, and to mine.

It was a splendid day, with foam crests on the wonderfully blue water, and the red ashes of the volcano, which forms the south point of the bay, glowed in the sunlight. This wretched steamer, whose boilers are so often "sick" that she can never be relied upon, is the only means of reaching the new capital without taking a most difficult and circuitous route. To continue the pier and put a capable good steamer on the ferry would be a useful expenditure of money. The breeze was strong and in our favor, but even with this it took us six weary hours to steam twenty-five miles. It was eight at night before we reached the beautiful and almost land-locked bay of Muroran, with steep, wooded sides, and deep water close to the shore, deep enough for the foreign ships of war which occasionally anchor there, much to the detriment of the town.

We got off in overcrowded *bezaisen*, and several people fell into the water, much to their own amusement. The servants from the different *yadoya* go down to the jetty to tout for guests with large paper lanterns, and the effect of these, one above another, waving and undulating, with their soft colored light, was as bewitching as the reflection of the stars in the motionless water. Muroran is a small town very picturesquely situated on the steep shore of a most lovely bay, with another height, richly wooded, above it, with shrines approached by flights of stone stairs, and behind this hill there is the first Ainu village along this coast.

The long, irregular street is slightly picturesque, but I was impressed both with the unusual sight of loafers and with the dissolute look of the place, arising from the number of *joroya* and *yadoya* that are also haunts of the vicious. I could only get a very small room in a very poor and dirty inn, but there were no mosquitoes, and I got a good meal of fish. On sending to order horses I found that everything was arranged for my journey. The governor sent his card early, to know if there were anything I should like to see or do, but, as the morning was grey and threatening, I wished to push on, and at 9.30 I was in the *kuruma* at the inn door. I call it the *kuruma* because it is the only one, and is kept by the government for the conveyance of hospital patients. I sat there uncomfortably and patiently for half an hour, my only amusement being the flirtations of Itō with a very pretty girl. Loiterers assembled, but no one came to draw the vehicle, and by degrees the dismal truth leaked out that the three laborers who had been impressed for the occasion had all absconded, and that four policemen were in search of them. I walked on in a dawdling way up the steep hill which leads from the town, met Mr. Akboshi, a pleasant young Japanese surveyor, who spoke English and stigmatized Muroran as "the worst place in Ezo." After fuming for two hours at the waste of time, I was overtaken by Itō with the horses, in a boiling rage. "They're the worst and wickedest laborers in all Japan," he stammered. "Two more ran away, and now three are coming, and have got paid for four. The first three who ran away got paid, and the express man's so ashamed for a foreigner, and the governor's in a furious rage."

Except for the loss of time it made no difference to me, but when the *kuruma* did come up the runners were three such ruffianly-looking men, and were dressed so wildly in bark cloth, that, in sending Itō on twelve miles to secure relays, I sent my money along with him. These men, though there were three instead of two, never went out of a walk. As if on purpose, they took the vehicle over every stone and into every rut, and kept up a savage chorus of "*haesha, haeshora*" the whole time, as if they were pulling stone-carts. There are really no runners out of Hakodate, and the men don't know how to pull, and hate doing it.

Muroran Bay is truly beautiful from the top of the ascent. The coast scenery of Japan generally is the loveliest I have ever seen, except that of a portion of windward Hawaii, and this yields in beauty to none. The irregular grey town, with a grey temple on the height above, straggles round the little bay on a steep, wooded terrace. Hills, densely wooded, and with a perfect entanglement of large-leaved trailers, descend abruptly to the water's edge. The festoons of the vines are mirrored in the still waters. Above the dark forest, and beyond the gleaming sea, rises the red, peaked top of the volcano. Then the road dips abruptly to sandy swellings, rising into bold headlands here and there. For the first time I saw the surge of five thousand miles of unbroken ocean break upon the shore. Glimpses of the Pacific, an uncultivated, swampy level quite uninhabited, and distant hills mainly covered with forest, made up the landscape till I reached Horobetsu, a mixed Japanese and Ainu village built upon the sand near the sea.

In these mixed villages the Ainu are compelled to live at a respectful distance from the Japanese, and frequently out-number them, as at Horobetsu, where there are forty-seven Ainu and only eighteen Japanese houses. The Ainu village looks larger than it really is, because nearly every house has a *kura*, raised six feet from the ground by wooden stilts. When I am better acquainted with the houses I shall describe them. At present I will only say that they do not resemble the Japanese houses so much as the Polynesian, as they are made of reeds very neatly tied upon a wooden frame-work. They have small windows, and roofs of a very great height, and steep pitch, with the thatch in a series of very neat frills, and the ridge poles covered with reeds, and ornamented. The coast Ainu are nearly all engaged in fishing, but at this season the men hunt deer in the forests. On this coast there are several names compounded with *betsu*, the Ainu word for river.

I found that Itō had been engaged for a whole hour in a violent altercation, which was caused by the transport agent refusing to supply runners for the *kuruma*, saying that no one in Horobetsu would draw one. But on my producing the *shōmon* I was at once started on my journey of sixteen miles with three Japanese lads, Itō riding on to Shiraoi to get my room ready. I think that the transport offices in Ezo are in government hands. In a few minutes three Ainu ran out of a house, took the *kuruma*, and went the whole stage without stopping. They took a boy and three saddled horses along with them to bring them back, and rode and hauled alternately, two youths always attached to the shafts, and a man pushing behind. They were very kind, and so courteous, after a new fashion, that I quite forgot that I was alone among savages. The lads were young and beardless, their lips were thick, and their mouths very wide, and I thought that they approached more nearly the Eskimo type than to any other. They had masses of soft black hair falling on each side of their faces. The adult man was not a pure Ainu. His dark hair was not very thick, and both it and his beard had an occasional auburn gleam. I think I never saw a face more completely beautiful in features and expression, with a lofty, sad, far-off, gentle, intellectual look. His manner was most graceful, and he spoke both Ainu and Japanese in the low musical tone which I find is a characteristic of Ainu speech. These Ainu never took off their clothes, but merely let them fall from one or both shoulders when it was very warm.

The road from Horobetsu to Shiraoi is very solitary, with not more than four or five houses the whole way. It is broad and straight, except when it ascends hills or turns inland to cross rivers, and is carried across a broad swampy level, covered with tall wild flowers, which extends from the high beach thrown up by the sea for two miles inland, where there is a lofty wall of wooded rock. Beyond are the forest-covered mountains of the interior. At the top of the raised beach there were Ainu hamlets, and occasionally a nearly overpowering stench came across the level from the sheds and apparatus used for extracting fish oil.

I enjoyed the afternoon thoroughly. It is so good to have got beyond the confines of stereotyped civilisation and the trammels of Japanese travelling to the solitude of nature and an atmosphere of freedom. It was grey, with a hard, dark line of ocean horizon, and over the weedy level the grey road, with grey telegraph-poles along it, stretched wearisomely like a grey thread. The breeze came up from the sea, rustled the reeds, and waved the tall plumes of tall grass, and the thunder of the Pacific surges boomed through the air with its grand, deep bass. Poetry and music pervaded the solitude, and my spirit was rested.

Going up and then down a steep, wooded hill, the road appeared to return to its original state of brushwood. The men stopped at the broken edge of a declivity which led down to a shingle bank and a foam-crested river of clear, blue-green water, strongly impregnated with sulphur from some medicinal springs above, with a steep bank of tangle on the opposite side. This beautiful stream was crossed by two round poles, a foot apart, on which I attempted to walk with the help of an Ainu hand. The poles were very unsteady, and I doubt whether anyone, even with a strong head, could walk on them in boots. Then the beautiful Ainu signed to me to come back and mount on his shoulders. But when he had got a few feet out the poles swayed and trembled so much that he was obliged to retrace his way cautiously, during which process I endured miseries from dizziness and fear. Then he carried me through the rushing water, which was up to his shoulders, and through a bit of swampy jungle, and up a steep bank, to the great fatigue both of body and mind, hardly mitigated by the enjoyment of the ludicrous in riding a savage through these Ezo waters. They dexterously carried the *kuruma* through, on the shoulders of four, and showed extreme anxiety that neither it nor I should get wet. After this we crossed two deep, still rivers in scows, and far above the grey level and the grey sea the sun was setting in gold and vermilion-streaked green behind a glorified mountain of great height, at whose feet the forest-covered hills lay in purple gloom. At dark we reached Shiraoi, a village of eleven Japanese houses, with a village of fifty-one Ainu houses, near the sea. There is a large *yadoya* of the old style there. But I found that Itō had chosen a very pretty new one, with four stalls open to the road, in the centre one of which I found him, with the welcome news that a steak of fresh salmon was broiling on the coals. The room was clean and sweet and I was very hungry, and I enjoyed my meal by the light of a rush in a saucer of fish oil as much as any part of the day.

Sarufuto

The night was too cold for sleep, and at daybreak, hearing a great din, I looked out, and saw a drove of fully a hundred horses all galloping down the road, with two Ainu on horseback, and a number of big dogs after them. Hundreds of horses run nearly wild on the hills, and the Ainu, getting a large drove together, skilfully head them for the entrance into the corral, in which a selection of them is made for the day's needs. The remainder—that is, those with the deepest sores on their backs—are turned loose. This dull rattle of shoeless feet is the first sound in the morning in these Ezo villages. I sent Itō on early, and followed at nine with three Ainu. The road is perfectly level for thirteen miles, through gravel flats and swamps, very monotonous, but with a wild charm of its own. There were swampy lakes, with wild ducks and small white water-lilies, and the surrounding levels were covered with reedy grass, flowers, and weeds. The early autumn has withered a great many of the flowers. But enough remains to show how beautiful the now russet plains must have been in the early summer. A dwarf rose, of a deep crimson color, with orange, medlar-shaped hips, as large as crabs, and corollas three inches across, is one of the features of Ezo. Besides, there is a large rose-red convolvulus, a blue campanula, with tiers of bells, a blue monkshood, the flaunting bindweed, purple asters, grass of Parnassus, yellow lilies, and a remarkable trailer. Its delicate leafage looked quite out of place among its coarse surroundings, with a purplish-brown campanulate blossom, only remarkable for a peculiar arrangement of the pistil, green stamens, and a most offensive carrion-like odor, which is probably to attract to it a very objectionable-looking fly, for purposes of fertilisation.

We overtook four Ainu women, young and comely, with bare feet, striding firmly along. After a good deal of laughing with the men, they took hold of the *kuruma*, and the whole seven raced with it at full speed for half a mile, shrieking with laughter. Soon after we came upon a little teahouse, and the Ainu showed me a straw package, and pointed to their open mouths, by which I understood that they wished to stop and eat. Later we overtook four Japanese on horseback, and the Ainu raced with them for a considerable distance. The result of these spurts was that I reached Tomakomai at noon— a wide, dreary place, with houses roofed with sod, bearing luxuriant crops of weeds. Near this place is the volcano of Tarumae, a calm-looking, grey cone, whose skirts are draped by tens of thousands of dead trees. So calm and grey had it looked for many a year that people supposed it had passed into endless rest, when quite lately, on a sultry day, it blew off its cap and covered the whole country for many a mile with cinders and ashes, burning up the forest on its sides, adding a new covering to the Tomakomai roofs, and depositing fine ash as far as Cape Erimo, fifty miles off.

At this place the road and telegraph wires turn inland to Sapporo. A track for horses only turns to the north-east, and straggles round the island for about seven hundred miles. From Muroran to Sarufuto there are everywhere traces of new and old volcanic action—pumice, tufas, conglomerates, and occasional beds of hard basalt, all covered with recent pumice, which, from Shiraoi eastwards, conceals everything. At Tomakomai we took horses, and, as I brought my own saddle, I have had the nearest approach to real riding that I have enjoyed in Japan. The wife of a Sapporo doctor was there, who was travelling for two hundred miles astride on a pack saddle, with rope-loops for stirrups. She rode well, and vaulted into my saddle with circus-like dexterity, and performed many equestrian feats upon it, telling me that she should be quite happy if she owned it.

I was happy when I left the beaten track to Sapporo, and saw before me, stretching for I know not how far, rolling, sandy plains like those of the Outer Hebrides, desert-like and lonely, covered almost altogether with dwarf roses and campanulas, a prairie land on which you can make any tracks you please. Sending the others on, I followed them at the Ezo scramble, and soon ventured on a long gallop, and revelled in the music of the thud of shoeless feet over the elastic soil. But I had not realized the peculiarities of Ezo steeds, and had forgotten to ask whether mine was a front horse. Just as we were going at full speed we came nearly up with the others, and my horse coming abruptly to a full stop, I went six feet over his head among the rose bushes. Itō looking back saw me tightening the saddle-girths, and I never divulged this escapade.

After riding eight miles along this breezy belt, with the sea on one side and forests on the other, we came upon Yufutsu, a place which has fascinated me so much that I intend to return to it. But I must confess that its fascinations depend rather upon what it has not than upon what it has, and Itō says that it would kill him to spend even two days there. It looks like the end of all things, as if loneliness and desolation could go no farther. A sandy stretch on three sides, a river arrested in its progress to the sea, and compelled to wander tediously in search of an outlet by the height and mass of the beach thrown up by the Pacific, a distant forest belt rising into featureless, wooded ranges in shades of indigo and grey, and a never-absent consciousness of a vast ocean just out of sight, are the environments of two high look-outs. There are some sheds for fish oil purposes, four or five Japanese houses, four Ainu huts on the top of the beach across the river, and a grey barrack, consisting of a polished passage eighty feet long, with small rooms on either side, at one end a gravelled yard, with two quiet rooms opening upon it, and at the other an immense *daidokoro*, with dark recesses and blackened rafters—a haunted-looking abode. One would suppose that there had been a special object in setting the houses down at weary distances from each other. Few as they are, they are not all inhabited at this season, and all that can be seen is grey sand, sparse grass, and a few savages creeping about.

Nothing that I have seen has made such an impression upon me as that ghostly, ghastly fishing station. In the long grey wall of the long grey barrack there were many dismal windows. When we hooted for admission a stupid face appeared at one of them and disappeared. Then a grey gateway opened, and we rode into a yard of grey gravel, with some silent rooms opening upon it. The solitude of the thirty or forty rooms which lie between it and the kitchen, and which are now filled with nets and fishing tackle, was something awful. The wind swept along the polished passage, rattling the *fusuma* and lifting the shingles on the roof, and the rats careered from end to end. I went to the great black *daidokoro* in search of social life, and found a few embers and an *andon*, and nothing else but the stupid-faced man deploring his fate, and two orphan boys whose lot he makes more wretched than his own. In the fishing season this barrack accommodates from two to three hundred men.

I started to the seashore, crossing the dreary river, and found open sheds much blackened, deserted huts of reeds, long sheds with a nearly insufferable odor from caldrons in which oil had been extracted from last year's fish. There were two or three Ainu huts, and two or three grand-looking Ainu, clothed in skins, striding like ghosts over the sandbanks, a number of wolfish dogs, some log canoes or "dug-outs," the bones of a wrecked *bezaisen*, and a quantity of bleached drift-wood. A beach of dark-grey sand ran along a tossing expanse of dark-grey ocean under a dull and windy sky.

On this part of the coast the Pacific spends its fury, and has raised up at a short distance above high-water mark a sandy sweep of such a height that when you descend its seaward slope you see nothing but the sea and the sky. A grey, curving shore, is covered thick for many a lonely mile with fantastic forms of whitened drift-wood, the shattered wrecks of forest-trees, which are carried down by the innumerable rivers:

> And from wrecks of ships, and drifting
> Spars, uplifting
> On the desolate, rainy seas; —
>
> Ever drifting, drifting, drifting
> On the shifting
> Currents of the restless main;
> Till in sheltered coves, and reaches
> Of sandy beaches,
> All have found repose again

The deep boom of the surf was music, and the strange cries of sea birds, and the hoarse notes of the audacious black crows, were all harmonious, for nature, when left to herself, never produces discords either in sound or color.

Sarufuto

No! Nature has no discords. This morning, to the far horizon, diamond-flashing blue water shimmered in perfect peace, outlined by a line of surf which broke lazily on a beach scarcely less snowy than itself. The deep, perfect blue of the sky was only broken by a few radiant white clouds, whose shadows trailed slowly over the plain on whose broad bosom a thousand corollas, in the glory of their brief but passionate life, were drinking in the sunshine. Wavy ranges slept in depths of indigo, and higher hills beyond were painted in faint blue on the dreamy sky. Even the few grey houses of Yufutsu were spiritualized into harmony by a faint blue veil that was not a mist, and the loud croak of the loquacious and impertinent crows had a cheeriness about it, a hearty mockery, which I liked.

Above all, I had a horse so good that he was always trying to run away, and galloped so lightly over the flowery grass that I rode the seventeen miles here with great enjoyment. Truly a good horse, good ground to gallop on, and sunshine, make up the sum of enjoyable travelling. The discord in the general harmony was produced by the sight of the Ainu, a harmless people without the instinct of progress, descending to that vast tomb of conquered and unknown races which has opened to receive so many before them.

A mounted policeman started with us from Yufutsu, and rode the whole way here, keeping exactly to my pace, but never speaking a word. We forded one broad, deep river, and crossed another, partly by fording and partly in a scow, after which the track left the level. After passing through reedy grass as high as the horse's ears, went for some miles up and downhill, through woods composed entirely of trees of heaven, with leaves much riddled by the mountain silkworm, and a ferny undergrowth.

The deep shade and glancing lights of this open copsewood were very pleasant. The horse tripped gaily up and down the little hills, and the sea murmur mingled with the rustle of the breeze. A glint of white surf sometimes flashed through the greenery, and dragonflies and butterflies in suits of crimson and black velvet crossed the path continually like living flashes of light. I was reminded, though faintly, of windward Hawaii.

We emerged upon an Ainu hut and a beautiful placid river, and two Ainu ferried the four people and horses across in a scow, the third wading to guide the boat. They wore no clothing, but only one was hairy. They were superb-looking men, gentle, and extremely courteous, handing me in and out of the boat, and holding the stirrup while I mounted, with much natural grace. On leaving they extended their arms and waved their hands inwards twice, stroking their grand beards afterwards, which is their usual salutation.

A short distance over shingle brought us to this Japanese village of sixty-three houses, a colonization settlement, mainly of samurai from Sendai, who are raising very fine crops on the sandy soil. The mountains, twelve miles in the interior, have a large Ainu population. Only a few Ainu live near this village and are held in great contempt by its inhabitants. My room is on the village street, and, as it is too warm to close the *shōji*, the aborigines stand looking in at the lattice hour after hour.

A short time ago Von Siebold and Diesbach galloped up on their return from Biratori, the Ainu village to which I am going. Diesbach, throwing himself from his horse, rushed up to me with the exclamation, *Les puces! les puces!* (The flees! The flees!). They have brought down with them the chief, Benri, a superb but dissipated-looking savage. Von Siebold called on me this evening, and I envied him his fresh, clean clothing as much as he envied me my stretcher and mosquito net. They have suffered terribly from fleas, mosquitoes, and general discomfort, and are much exhausted. Von Siebold thinks that, in spite of all, a visit to the mountain Ainu is worth a long journey. As I expected, they have completely failed in their explorations, and have been deserted by Lieutenant Kreitner. I asked Von Siebold to speak to Itō in Japanese about the importance of being kind and courteous to the Ainu whose hospitality I shall receive. Itō is very indignant at this. "Treat Ainu politely?! They're just dogs, not men!" Ever since, he has regaled me with all the scandal concerning them which he has been able to rake together in the village.

We have to take not only food for both Itō and myself, but cooking utensils. I have been introduced to Benri, the chief. And, though he does not return for a day or two, he will send a message along with us which will ensure me hospitality.

Ainu Courtesy

I am in the lonely Ainu land, and I think that the most interesting of my travelling experiences has been the living for three days and two nights in an Ainu hut, and seeing and sharing the daily life of complete savages, who go on with their ordinary occupations just as if I were not among them. I found yesterday a most fatiguing and over-exciting day. Everything was new and interesting, even the extracting from men who have few if any ideas in common with me all I could concerning their religion and customs, and that through an interpreter.

I got up at six this morning to write out my notes, and have been writing for five hours, and there is shortly the prospect of another savage seance. The distractions are many. At this moment a savage is taking a cup of *sake* by the fire in the centre of the floor. He salutes me by extending his hands and waving them towards his face, and then dips a rod in the *sake*, and makes six libations to the god—an upright piece of wood with a fringe of shavings planted in the floor of the room. Then he waves the cup several times towards himself, makes other libations to the fire, and drinks. Ten other men and women are sitting along each side of the fire hole. The chief's wife is cooking, and the men are apathetically contemplating the preparation of their food. The other women, who are never idle, are splitting the bark of which they make their clothes. I occupy the guest seat—a raised platform at one end of the fire, with the skin of a black bear thrown over it.

Itō is very greedy and self-indulgent, and whimpered very much about coming to Biratori at all—one would have thought he was going to the stake. He actually borrowed for himself a sleeping mat and *futon*, and has brought a chicken, onions, potatoes, French beans, soy sauce, tea, rice, a kettle, a stew pan, and a rice pan. I contented myself with a cold fowl and potatoes.

We took three horses and a mounted Ainu guide, and found a beaten track the whole way. It turns into the forest at once on leaving Sarufuto, and goes through forest the entire distance, with an abundance of reedy grass higher than my hat on horseback along it. As it is only twelve inches broad and much overgrown and the horses were constantly pushing through leafage soaking from a night's rain, I was soon wet up to my shoulders. The forest trees are almost solely trees of heaven and the keaki, often matted together with a white-flowered trailer of the hydrangea genus. The undergrowth is simply hideous, consisting mainly of coarse reedy grass, monstrous docks, the large-leaved knotweed, several umbelliferous plants, and a ragweed that, like most of its gawky fellows, grows from five to six feet high. The forest is dark and very silent, threaded by this narrow path, and by others as narrow, made by the hunters in search of game. The main road sometimes plunges into deep bogs. At others it is roughly corduroyed by the roots of trees, and frequently hangs over the edge of abrupt and much-worn declivities. Going up one the baggage horse rolled down a bank fully thirty feet high, and nearly all the tea was lost. At another the guide's pack saddle lost its balance, and man, horse, and saddle went over the slope, pots, pans, and packages flying after them. At one stage my horse sank up to his chest in a very bad bog. He was totally unable to extricate himself, and I was obliged to scramble upon his neck and jump to the ground over his ears.

There is something very gloomy in the solitude of this silent land, with its beast-haunted forests, its great patches of pasture, the resort of wild animals that haunt the lower regions in search of food when the snow drives them down from the mountains, and its narrow track, indicating the single file in which the savages of the interior walk with their bare, noiseless feet. Reaching the Sarufuto-*gawa*, a river with a treacherous bottom, in which Von Siebold and his horse came to grief, I hailed an Ainu boy, who took me up the stream in a dug-out. After that we passed through Biroka, Saruba, and Mina, all purely Ainu villages, situated among small patches of millet, tobacco, and pumpkins, so choked with weeds that it was doubtful whether they were crops. I was much surprised with the extreme neatness and cleanliness outside the houses. Model villages they are in these respects, with no litter lying in sight anywhere, nothing indeed but dog troughs, hollowed out of logs, like dug-outs, for the numerous yellow dogs, which are a feature of Ainu life. There are neither puddles nor heaps, but the houses, all trim and in good repair, rise clean out of the sandy soil.

Biratori, the largest of the Ainu settlements in this region, is very prettily situated among forests and mountains, on rising ground, with a very sinuous river winding at its feet and a wooded height above. A lonelier place could scarcely be found. As we passed among the houses the yellow dogs barked, the women looked shy and smiled, and the men made their graceful salutation. We stopped at the chief's house, where, of course, we were unexpected guests. Shinondi, his nephew, and two other men came out, saluted us, and with most hospitable intent helped Itō to unload the horses. Indeed their eager hospitality created quite a commotion, one running hither and the other thither in their anxiety to welcome a stranger. It is a large house, the room being thirty-five by twenty-five, and the roof twenty feet high. You enter by an ante-chamber, in which are kept the millet-mill and other articles. There is a doorway in this, but the inside is pretty dark, and Shinondi, taking my hand, raised the reed curtain bound with hide, which concealed the entrance into the actual house. Leading me into it, he retired a footstep, extended his arms, waved his arms inwards three times, and then stroked his beard several times, after which he indicated by a sweep of his hand and a beautiful smile that the house and all it contained were mine. An aged woman, the chief's mother, who was splitting bark by the fire, waved her hands also. She is the queen-regnant of the house.

Again taking my hand, Shinondi led me to the place of honor at the head of the fire—a crude, movable platform six feet long by four broad, and a foot high, on which he laid an ornamental mat, apologizing for not having at that moment a bearskin to cover it. The baggage was speedily brought in by several willing pairs of hands. Some reed mats fifteen feet long were laid down upon the very coarse ones which covered the whole floor. When they saw Itō putting up my stretcher they hung a fine mat along the rough wall to conceal it, and suspended another on the beams of the roof for a canopy.

The alacrity and instinctive hospitality with which these men rushed about to make things comfortable were fascinating, though comfort is a word misapplied in an Ainu hut. The women only did what the men told them.

They offered food at once, but I told them that I had brought my own, and would only ask leave to cook it on their fire. I need not have brought any cups, for they have many lacquer bowls. Shinondi brought me on a lacquer tray a bowl full of water from one of their four wells. They said that Benri, the chief, would wish me to make his house my own for as long as I cared to stay, and I must excuse them in all things in which their ways were different from my own.

Shinondi and four others in the village speak tolerable Japanese, and this of course is the medium of communication. Itō has exerted himself nobly as an interpreter, and has entered into my wishes with a cordiality and intelligence which have been invaluable. Though he did growl at Von Siebold's injunctions regarding politeness, he has carried them out to my satisfaction, and even admits that the mountain Ainu are better than he expected. "But," he added "they have learned their politeness from the Japanese!"

They have never seen a foreign woman, and only three foreign men, but there is neither crowding nor staring as among the Japanese, possibly in part from apathy and want of intelligence. For three days they have kept up their graceful and kindly hospitality, going on with their ordinary life and occupations. Though I have lived among them in this room by day and night, there has been nothing which in any way could offend the most fastidious sense of delicacy.

They said they would leave me to eat and rest, and all retired but the chief's mother, a weird, witch-like woman of eighty, with shocks of yellow-white hair, and a stern suspiciousness in her wrinkled face. I have come to feel as if she had the evil eye, as she sits there watching, watching always, and forever knotting the bark thread like one of the Fates, keeping a jealous watch on her son's two wives, and on other young women who come in to weave—neither the dulness nor the repose of old age about her. Her eyes gleam with a greedy light when she sees *sake*, of which she drains a bowl without taking breath. She alone is suspicious of strangers, and she thinks that my visit bodes no good to her tribe. I see her eyes fixed upon me now, and they make me shudder.

I had a good meal seated in my chair on the top of the guest-seat to avoid the fleas, which are truly legion. At dusk Shinondi returned, and soon people began to drop in, till eighteen were assembled, including the sub-chief and several very grand-looking old men, with full, grey, wavy beards. Age is held in much reverence, and it is etiquette for these old men to do honor to a guest in the chief's absence. As each entered he saluted me several times, and after sitting down turned towards me and saluted again, going through the same ceremony with every other person. They said they had come "to bid me welcome." They took their places in rigid order at each side of the fireplace, which is six feet long, Benri's mother in the place of honor at the right, then Shinondi, then the sub-chief, and on the other side the old men. Besides these, seven women sat in a row in the background splitting bark. A large iron pan hung over the fire from a blackened arrangement above, and Benri's principal wife cut wild roots, green beans, and seaweed. She shred dried fish and venison among them, adding millet, water, and some strong-smelling fish oil, and set the whole on to simmer for three hours, stirring the stew now and then with a wooden spoon.

Several of the older people smoked, and I handed round some mild tobacco, which they received with waving hands. I told them that I came from a land in the sea, very far away, where they saw the sun go down— so very far away that a horse would have to gallop day and night for five weeks to reach it—. I said that I had come a long journey to see them, and that I wanted to ask them many questions, so that when I went home I might tell my own people something about them. Shinondi and another man, who understood Japanese, bowed, and (as on every occasion) translated what I said into Ainu for the venerable group opposite. Shinondi then said "that he and Shinrichi, the other Japanese speaker, would tell me all they knew, but they were but young men, and only knew what was told to them. They would speak what they believed to be true, but the chief knew more than they, and when he came back he might tell me differently, and then I should think that they had spoken lies." I said that no one who looked into their faces could think that they ever told lies. They were very much pleased, and waved their hands and stroked their beards repeatedly. Before they told me anything they begged and prayed that I would not inform the Japanese government that they had told me of their customs, or harm might come to them!

For the next two hours, and for two more after supper, I asked them questions concerning their religion and customs, and again yesterday for a considerable time. This morning, after Benri's return, I went over the same subjects with him, and have also employed a considerable time in getting about three hundred words from them, which I have spelt phonetically of course, and intend to go over again when I visit the coast Ainu. I went over them with the Ainu of a remote village on Uchiura Bay, and found the differences in pronunciation very slight, except that the definiteness of the sound which I have represented by "tshi" was more strongly marked. I afterwards went over them with Walter Dening, and with Von Siebold at Tokyo, who have made a larger collection of words than I have, and it is satisfactory to find that we have represented the words in the main by the same letters, with the single exception that usually the sound represented by them by the letters :ch" I have given as "tch", and I venture to think that is the most correct rendering.

The process was slow, as both question and answer had to pass through three languages. There was a very manifest desire to tell the truth, and I think that their statements concerning their few and simple customs may be relied upon. I shall give what they told me separately when I have time to write out my notes in an orderly manner. I can only say that I have seldom spent a more interesting evening.

About nine the stew was ready, and the women ladled it into lacquer bowls with wooden spoons. The men were served first, but all ate together. Afterwards *sake*, their curse, was poured into lacquer bowls, and across each bowl a finely-carved "*sake*-stick" was laid. These sticks are very highly prized. The bowls were waved several times with an inward motion, then each man took his stick and, dipping it into the *sake*, made six libations to the fire and several to the "god"—a wooden post, with a quantity of spiral white shavings falling from near the top The Ainu are not affected by *sake* nearly so easily as the Japanese. They took it cold, it is true, but each drank about three times as much as would have made a Japanese foolish, and it had no effect upon them.

After two hours more talk one after another got up and went out, making profuse salutations to me and to the others. My candles had been forgotten, and our seance was held by the fitful light of the big logs on the fire, aided by a succession of chips of birch bark, with which a woman replenished a cleft stick that was stuck into the fire hole. I never saw such a strangely picturesque sight as that group of magnificent savages with the fitful firelight on their faces, and for adjuncts the flare of the torch, the strong lights, the blackness of the recesses of the room and of the roof, at one end of which the stars looked in, and the row of savage women in the background—eastern savagery and western civilisation met in this hut, savagery giving and civilisation receiving, the yellow-skinned Itō the connecting-link between the two, and the representative of a civilisation to which our own is but an infant of days.

I found it very exciting, and when all had left crept out into the starlight. The lodges were all dark and silent, and the dogs, mild like their masters, took no notice of me. The only sound was the rustle of a light breeze through the surrounding forest.

I crept back again and into my mosquito net, and suffered not from fleas or mosquitoes, but from severe cold. Shinondi conversed with Itō for some time in a low musical voice, having previously asked if it would keep me from sleeping. No Japanese ever intermitted his ceaseless chatter at any hour of the night for a similar reason. Later, the chief's principal wife, Noma, stuck a triply-cleft stick in the fire hole, put a potsherd with a wick and some fish oil upon it, and by the dim light of this rude lamp sewed until midnight at a garment of bark cloth which she was ornamenting for her lord with strips of blue cloth, and when I opened my eyes the next morning she was at the window sewing by the earliest daylight. She is the most intelligent-looking of all the women, but looks sad and almost stern, and speaks seldom. Although she is the principal wife of the chief she is not happy, for she is childless, and I thought that her sad look darkened into something evil as the other wife caressed a fine baby boy. Benri seems to me something of a brute, and the mother-in-law obviously holds the reins of government pretty tight. After sewing till midnight she swept the mats with a bunch of twigs, and then crept into her bed behind a hanging mat. For a moment in the stillness I felt a feeling of panic, as if I were incurring a risk by being alone among savages, but I conquered it, and, after watching the fire till it went out, fell asleep till I was woken by the severe cold of the next day's dawn.

When I crept from under my net much benumbed with cold, there were about eleven people in the room, who all made their graceful salutation. It did not seem as if they had ever heard of washing, for, when water was asked for, Shinondi brought a little in a lacquer bowl, and held it while I bathed my face and hands, supposing the performance to be an act of worship. I was about to throw some cold tea out of the window by my bed when he arrested me with an anxious face, and I saw, what I had not observed before, that there was a god at that window—a stick with festoons of shavings hanging from it, and beside it a dead bird.

The Ainu have two meals a day, and their breakfast was a repetition of the previous night's supper. We all ate together, and I gave the children the remains of my rice, and it was most amusing to see little creatures of three, four, and five years old, with no other clothing than a piece of pewter hanging round their necks, first formally asking leave of the parents before taking the rice, and then waving their hands. The obedience of the children is instantaneous. Their parents are more demonstrative in their affection than the Japanese are, caressing them a good deal, and two of the men are devoted to children who are not their own. These little ones are as grave and dignified as Japanese children, and are very gentle.

I went out soon after five, when the dew was glittering in the sunshine, and the mountain hollow in which Biratori stands was looking its very best. The silence of the place, even though the people were all astir, was as impressive as that of the night before. What a strange life! knowing nothing, hoping nothing, fearing a little, the need for clothes and food the one motive principle, *sake* in abundance the one good. How very few points of contact it is possible to have! I was just thinking so when Shinondi met me, and took me to his house to see if I could do anything for a child sorely afflicted with skin disease, and his extreme tenderness for the child made me feel that human affections were the same among them as with us. He had carried it on his back from a village, five miles distant, that morning, in the hope that it might be cured. As soon as I entered he laid a fine mat on the floor, and covered the guest-seat with a bearskin. After breakfast he took me to the lodge of the sub-chief, the largest in the village, forty-five feet square, and into about twenty others all constructed in the same way, but some of them were not more than twenty feet square. In all I was received with the same courtesy, but a few of the people asked Shinondi not to take me into their houses, as they did not want me to see how poor they are. In every house there was the low shelf with more or fewer curios upon it. Besides these, none but the barest necessaries of life, though the skins which they sell or barter every year would enable them to surround themselves with comforts, were it not that their gains represent to them *sake*, and nothing else. They are not nomads. On the contrary, they cling tenaciously to the sites on which their fathers have lived and died. But anything more deplorable than the attempts at cultivation which surround their lodges could not be seen. The soil is little better than white sand, on which without manure they attempt to grow millet, which is to them in the place of rice, pumpkins, onions, and tobacco. The look of their plots is as if they had been cultivated ten years ago, and some chance-sown grain and vegetables had come up among the weeds. When nothing more will grow, they partially clear another bit of forest, and exhaust that in its turn.

In every house the same honor was paid to a guest. This seems a savage virtue which is not strong enough to survive much contact with civilisation. Before I entered one lodge the woman brought several of the finer mats, and arranged them as a pathway for me to walk to the fire. They will not accept anything for lodging, or for anything that they give, so I was anxious to help them by buying some of their handiwork, but found even this a difficult matter. They were very anxious to give, but when I desired to buy they said they did not wish to part with their things. I wanted what they had in actual use, such as a tobacco-box and pipe-sheath, and knives with carved handles and scabbards, and for three of these I offered two and a half dollars. They said they did not care to sell them, but in the evening they came saying they were not worth more than one dollar ten cents, and they would sell them for that. I could not get them to take more. They said it was "not their custom."

I bought a bow and three poisoned arrows, two reed-mats, with a diamond pattern on them in reeds stained red, some knives with sheaths, and a bark cloth dress. I tried to buy the *sake*-sticks with which they make libations to their gods, but they said it was "not their custom" to part with the *sake*-stick of any living man. However, this morning Shinondi has brought me, as a very valuable present, the stick of a dead man! This morning the man who sold the arrows brought two new ones, to replace two which were imperfect. I found them, as Von Siebold had done, punctiliously honest in all their transactions. They wear very large earrings with hoops an inch and a half in diameter, a pair constituting the dowry of an Ainu bride, but they would not part with these.

A house was burned down two nights ago, and custom in such a case requires that all the men should work at rebuilding it, so in their absence I got two boys to take me in a dug-out as far as we could go up the Sarufuto-gawa—a lovely river, which winds tortuously through the forests and mountains in unspeakable loveliness. I had much of the feeling of the ancient mariner: "We were the first Who ever burst Into that silent sea." For certainly no European had ever previously floated on the dark and forest-shrouded waters. I enjoyed those hours thoroughly, for the silence was profound, and the faint blue of the autumn sky, and the soft blue veil which spiritualized the distances, were so exquisitely like the Indian summer.

The evening was spent like the previous one, but the hearts of the savages were sad, for there was no more *sake* in Biratori, so they could not drink to their god, and the fire and the post with the shavings had to go without libations. There was no more oil, so after the strangers retired the hut was in complete darkness.

Yesterday morning we all breakfasted soon after daylight, and the able-bodied men went away to hunt. Hunting and fishing are their occupations, and for indoor recreation they carve tobacco-boxes, knife-sheaths, *sake*-sticks, and shuttles. It is quite unnecessary for them to do anything. They are quite contented to sit by the fire, and smoke occasionally, and eat and sleep, this apathy being varied by spasms of activity when there is no more dried flesh in the *kura*, and when skins must be taken to Sarufuto to pay for *sake*.

The women seem never to have an idle moment. They rise early to sew, weave, and split bark, for they not only clothe themselves and their husbands in this nearly indestructible cloth, but weave it for barter, and the lower class of Japanese are often seen wearing the product of Ainu industry. They do all the hard work, such as drawing water, chopping wood, grinding millet, and cultivating the soil, after their fashion. To do the men justice, I often see them trudging along carrying one and even two children. The women take the exclusive charge of the *kura*, which are never entered by men.

I was left for some hours alone with the women, of whom there were seven in the hut, with a few children. On the one side of the fire the chief's mother sat like a Fate, for ever splitting and knotting bark, and petrifying me by her cold, fateful eyes. Her thick, grey hair hangs in shocks, the tattooing round her mouth has nearly faded, and no longer disguises her really handsome features. She is dressed in a much ornamented bark cloth dress, and wears two silver beads tied round her neck by a piece of blue cotton, in addition to very large earrings. She has much sway in the house, sitting on the men's side of the fire, drinking plenty of *sake*, and occasionally chiding her grandson Shinondi for telling me too much, saying that it will bring harm to her people. Though her expression is so severe and forbidding, she is certainly very handsome, and it is a European, not an Asiatic, beauty.

The younger women were all at work; two were seated on the floor weaving without a loom, and the others were making and mending the bark coats which are worn by both sexes. Noma, the chief's principal wife, sat apart, seldom speaking. Two of the youngest women are very pretty—as fair as ourselves, and their comeliness is of the rosy, peasant kind. It turns out that two of them, though they would not divulge it before men, speak Japanese, and they prattled to Itō with great vivacity and merriment, the ancient Fate scowling at them the while from under her shaggy eyebrows. I got a number of words from them, and they laughed heartily at my erroneous pronunciation. They even asked me a number of questions regarding their own sex among ourselves, but few of these would bear repetition, and they answered a number of mine. As the merriment increased the old woman looked increasingly angry and restless, and at last rated them sharply, as I have heard since, telling them that if they spoke another word she should tell their husbands that they had been talking to strangers. After this not another word was spoken, and Noma, who is an industrious housewife, boiled some millet into a mash for a mid-day lunch.

During the afternoon a very handsome young Ainu, with a washed, richly-colored skin and fine clear eyes, came up from the coast, where he had been working at the fishing. He saluted the old woman and Benri's wife on entering, and presented the former with a gourd of *sake*, bringing a greedy light into her eyes as she took a long draught. Saluting me, he threw himself down in the place of honor by the fire, with the easy grace of a staghound, a savage all over. His name is Pipichari, and he is the chief's adopted son. He had cut his foot badly with a root, and asked me to cure it, and I stipulated that it should be bathed for some time in warm water before anything more was done, after which I bandaged it with lint. He said "he did not like me to touch his foot, it was not clean enough, my hands were too white." But when I had dressed it, and the pain was much relieved, he bowed very low and then kissed my hand! He was the only one among them all who showed the slightest curiosity regarding my things. He looked at my scissors, touched my boots, and watched me, as I wrote, with the simple curiosity of a child. He could speak a little Japanese, but he said he was "too young to tell me anything; the older men would know." He is a total abstainer from *sake*, and he says that there are four such besides himself among the large number of Ainu who are just now at the fishing at Hidaka Monbetsu, and that the others keep separate from them, because they think that the gods will be angry with them for not drinking.

Several patients, mostly children, were brought in during the afternoon. Itō was much disgusted by my interest in these people, who, he repeated, "are just dogs," referring to their legendary origin, of which they are not ashamed. His assertion that they have learned politeness from the Japanese is simply baseless. Their politeness, though of quite another and more manly stamp, is savage, not civilized. The men came back at dark, the meal was prepared, and we sat round the fire as before. There was no *sake*, except in the possession of the old woman. And again the hearts of the savages were sad. I could multiply instances of their politeness. As we were talking, Pipichari, who is a very untutored savage, dropped his coat from one shoulder, and at once Shinondi signed to him to put it on again. Again, a woman was sent to a distant village for some oil as soon as they heard that I usually burned a light all night. Little acts of courtesy were constantly being performed. But I really appreciated nothing more than the quiet way in which they went on with the routine of their ordinary lives.

During the evening a man came to ask if I would go and see a woman who could hardly breathe. I found her very ill of bronchitis, accompanied with much fever. She was lying in a coat of skins, tossing on the hard boards of her bed, with a matting-covered roll under her head, and her husband was trying to make her swallow some salted fish. I took her dry, hot hand—

such a small hand, tattooed all over the back—and it gave me a strange thrill. The room was full of people, and they all seemed very sorry. A medical missionary would be of little use here. But a medically-trained nurse, who would give medicines and proper food, with proper nursing, would save many lives and much suffering. It is of no use to tell these people to do anything which requires to be done more than once: they are just like children. I gave her some chlorodyne, which she swallowed with difficulty, and left another dose ready mixed, to give her in a few hours. About midnight they came to tell me that she was worse. On going I found her very cold and weak, and breathing very hard, moving her head wearily from side to side. I thought she could not live for many hours, and was much afraid that they would think that I had killed her. I told them that I thought she would die, but they urged me to do something more for her. As a last hope I gave her some brandy, with twenty-five drops of chlorodyne, and a few spoonfuls of very strong beef tea. She was unable, or more probably unwilling, to make the effort to swallow it, and I poured it down her throat by the wild glare of strips of birch bark. An hour later they came back to tell me that she felt as if she were very drunk. Going back to her house, I found that she was sleeping quietly, and breathing more easily. Creeping back just at dawn, I found her still sleeping, and with her pulse stronger and calmer. She is now decidedly better and quite sensible, and her husband, the sub-chief, is much delighted. It seems so sad that they have nothing fit for a sick person's food. Though I have made a bowl of beef-tea with the remains of my stock, it can only last one day.

I was so tired with these nocturnal expeditions and anxieties that on lying down I fell asleep, and on waking found more than the usual assemblage in the room, and the men were obviously agog about something. They have a singular, and I hope an unreasonable, fear of the Japanese government. Von Siebold thinks that the officials threaten and knock them about. This is possible, but I really think that the Hokkaido Colonization Bureau means well by them Removing the oppressive restrictions by which, as a conquered race, they were fettered, it treats them far more humanely and equitably than the U.S. government, for instance, treats the North American indians. However, they are ignorant; one of the men, who had been most grateful because I said I would get Dr. Hepburn to send some medicine for his child, came this morning and begged me not to do so, as, he said, "the Japanese government would be angry." After this they again prayed me not to tell the Japanese government that they had told me their customs and then they began to talk earnestly together.

The sub-chief then spoke, and said that I had been kind to their sick people, and they would like to show me their temple, which had never been seen by any foreigner. They were very much afraid of doing so, and they asked me many times "not to tell the Japanese government that they showed it to me, lest some great harm should happen to them." The sub-chief put on a sleeveless Japanese war-cloak to go up, and he, Shinondi, Pipichari, and two others accompanied me. It was a beautiful but very steep walk, or rather climb, to the top of an abrupt acclivity beyond the village, on which the temple or shrine stands. It would be impossible to get up were it not for the remains of a wooden staircase, not of Ainu construction. Forest and mountain surround Biratori, and the only breaks in the dense greenery are glints of the shining waters of the Sarufuto-*gawa*, and the tawny roofs of the Ainu lodges. It is a lonely and a silent land, fitter for the *hiding* place than the *dwelling* place of men.

When the splendid young savage, Pipichari, saw that I found it difficult to get up, he took my hand and helped me up, as gently as an English gentleman would have done. When he saw that I had greater difficulty in getting down, he all but insisted on my riding down on his back, and certainly would have carried me had not Benri, the chief, who arrived while we were at the shrine, made an end of it by taking my hand and helping me down himself. Their instinct of helpfulness to a foreign woman strikes me as so odd, because they never show any courtesy to their own women, whom they treat (though to a less extent than is usual among savages) as inferior beings.

On the very edge of the cliff, at the top of the zigzag, stands a wooden temple or shrine, such as one sees in any grove, or on any high place on the main island, obviously of Japanese construction, but concerning which Ainu tradition is silent. No European had ever stood where I stood, and there was a solemnity in the knowledge. The sub-chief drew back the sliding doors, and all bowed with much reverence, It was a simple shrine of unlacquered wood, with a broad shelf at the back, on which there was a small shrine containing a figure of the historical hero Yoshitsune, in a suit of inlaid brass armour, some metal *gohei* (sacred wand), a pair of tarnished brass candle-sticks, and a colored picture representing a *bezaisen*. Here, then, I was introduced to the great god of the mountain Ainu. There is something very pathetic in these people keeping alive the memory of Yoshitsune, not on account of his martial exploits, but simply because their tradition tells them that he was kind to them. They pulled the bell three times to attract his attention, bowed three times, and made six libations of *sake*, without which he cannot be approached. They asked me to worship their god, but when I declined on the ground that I could only worship my own God, of the dead and of the living, they were too courteous to press their request. As to Itō, it did not signify to him whether or not he added another god to his already crowded pantheon, and he worshipped, i.e. bowed down, most willingly before the great hero of his own, the conquering race.

While we were crowded there on the narrow ledge of the cliff, Benri, the chief, arrived—a square-built, broad-shouldered, elderly man, strong as an ox, and very handsome, but his expression is not pleasing, and his eyes are bloodshot with drinking. The others saluted him very respectfully, but I noticed then and since that his manner is very arbitrary, and that a blow not infrequently follows a word. He had sent a message to his people by Itō that they were not to answer any questions till he returned, but Itō very tactfully neither gave it nor told me of it, and he was displeased with the young men for having talked to me so much. His mother had evidently peached. I like him less than any of his tribe. He has some fine qualities, truthfulness among others, but he has been contaminated by the four or five foreigners that he has seen, and is a brute and a sot. The hearts of his people are no longer sad, for there is *sake* in every house tonight.

Female Comeliness

Biratori, Ezo, August 24
I expected to have written out my notes on the Ainu in the comparative quiet and comfort of Sarufuto, but the delay in Benri's return, and the non-arrival of the horses, have compelled me to accept Ainu hospitality for another night. This involves living on tea and potatoes, for my stock of food is exhausted. In some respects I am glad to remain longer, as it enables me to go over my stock of words and notes with the chief, who is intelligent, and it is a pleasure to find that his statements confirm those which have been made by the young men. The glamour which at first disguises the inherent barrenness of savage life has had time to pass away, and I see it in all its nakedness as a life not much raised above the necessities of animal existence: timid, monotonous, barren of good, dark, dull. Yet at its lowest and worst it is still considerably higher and better than that of many other aboriginal races, and— must I say it?—considerably higher and better than that of thousands of the lapsed masses of our own great cities. The Ainu are truthful and, on the whole, chaste, hospitable, honest, reverent, and kind to the aged. Drinking, their great vice, is not, as among us, in antagonism to their religion, but is actually a part of it, and as such would be exceptionally difficult to eradicate.

The early darkness has once again come on, and once again the elders have assembled round the fire in two long lines, with the younger men at the ends. Pipichari, who yesterday sat in the place of honor and was helped to food first as the newest arrival, took his place as the youngest at the end of the right-hand row. The birch-bark chips beam with fitful glare, the evening *sake* bowls are filled, and the fire-god and the garlanded god receive their libations. The ancient woman, still sitting like a Fate, splits bark, and the younger women knot it. And the log-fire lights up as magnificent a set of venerable heads as painter or sculptor would desire to see, their heads, full of—what? They have no history, their traditions are scarcely worthy the name, they claim descent from a dog, their houses and persons swarm with vermin, they are sunk in the grossest ignorance, they have no letters or any numbers above a thousand, they are clothed in the bark of trees and the untanned skins of beasts, they worship the bear, the sun, moon, fire, water, and I know not what, they are uncivilizable and altogether irreclaimable savages. Yet they are attractive, and in some ways fascinating, and I hope I shall never forget the music of their low, sweet voices, the soft light of their mild, brown eyes, and the wonderful sweetness of their smile.

After the yellow skins, the stiff horse hair, the feeble eyelids, the elongated eyes, the sloping eyebrows, the flat noses, the sunken chests, the Mongolian features, the puny physique, the shaky walk of the men, the restricted totter of the women, and the general impression of degeneracy conveyed by the appearance of the Japanese, the Ainu make a very singular impression. All but two or three that I have seen are the most ferocious-looking of savages, with a physique vigorous enough for carrying out the most ferocious intentions. But as soon as they speak the countenance brightens into a smile as gentle as that of a woman, something which can never be forgotten.

The men are about middle height, broad-chested, broad-shouldered, thick set, very strongly built, the arms and legs short, thick, and muscular, the hands and feet large. The bodies, and especially the limbs, of many are covered with short bristly hair. I have seen two boys whose backs are covered with fur as fine and soft as that of a cat. The heads and faces are very striking. The foreheads are very high, broad, and prominent, and at first sight give one the impression of an unusual capacity for intellectual development. The ears are small and set low; the noses are straight but short, and broad at the nostrils; the mouths are wide but well formed; and the lips rarely show a tendency to fulness. The neck is short, the cranium rounded, the cheek-bones low, and the lower part of the face is small as compared with the upper, the peculiarity called a "jowl" being unknown. The eyebrows are full, and form a straight line nearly across the face. The eyes are large, tolerably deeply set, and very beautiful, the color a rich liquid brown, the expression singularly soft, and the eyelashes long, silky, and abundant. The skin has the Italian olive tint, but in most cases is thin, and light enough to show the changes of color in the cheek. The features, expression, and aspect, are European rather than Asiatic.

The "ferocious savagery" of the appearance of the men is produced by a profusion of thick, soft, black hair, divided in the middle, and falling in heavy masses nearly to the shoulders. Out of doors it is kept from falling over the face by a fillet round the brow. The beards are equally profuse, quite magnificent, and generally wavy, and in the case of the old men they give a truly patriarchal and venerable aspect, in spite of the yellow tinge produced by smoke and want of cleanliness. The savage look produced by the masses of hair and beard, and the thick eyebrows, is mitigated by the softness in the dreamy brown eyes, and is altogether obliterated by the exceeding sweetness of the smile, which belongs in greater or lesser degree to all the rougher sex.

Passing travellers who have seen a few of the Ainu women on the road to Sapporo speak of them as very ugly, but as making amends for their ugliness by their industry and conjugal fidelity. Of the latter there is no doubt, but I am not disposed to admit the former. The ugliness is certainly due to art and dirt. The Ainu women seldom exceed five feet in height, but they are beautifully formed, straight, lithe, and well-developed, with small feet and hands, well-arched insteps, rounded limbs, well-developed busts, and a firm, elastic gait. Their heads and faces are small; but the hair, which falls in masses on each side of the face like that of the men, is equally redundant. They have superb teeth, and display them liberally in smiling. Their mouths are somewhat wide, but well formed, and they have a ruddy comeliness about them which is pleasing, in spite of the disfigurement of the band which is tattooed both above and below the mouth, and which, by being united at the corners, enlarges its apparent size and width. A girl at Shiraoi, who, for some reason, has not been subjected to this process, is the most beautiful creature in features, coloring, and natural grace of form, that I have seen for a long time. Their complexions are lighter than those of the men. There are not many here even as dark as our European brunettes. A few unite the eyebrows by a streak of tattooing, so as to produce a straight line. Like the men, they cut their hair short for two or three inches above the nape of the neck, but instead of using a fillet they take two locks from the front and tie them at the back.

They are universally tattooed, not only with the broad band above and below the mouth, but with a band across the knuckles, succeeded by an elaborate pattern on the back of the hand, and a series of bracelets extending to the elbow. The process of disfigurement begins at the age of five, when some of the sufferers are yet unweaned. I saw the operation performed on a dear little bright girl this morning. A woman took a large knife with a sharp edge, and rapidly cut several horizontal lines on the upper lip, following closely the curve of the very pretty mouth, and before the slight bleeding had ceased carefully rubbed in some of the shiny soot which collects on the mat above the fire. In two or three days the scarred lip will be washed with the decoction of the bark of a tree to fix the pattern, and give it that blue look which makes many people mistake it for a daub of paint. A child who had this second process performed yesterday has her lip fearfully swollen and inflamed. The latest victim held her hands clasped tightly together while the cuts were inflicted, but never cried. The pattern on the lips is deepened and widened every year up to the time of marriage, and the circles on the arm are extended in a similar way. The men cannot give any reason for the universality of this custom. It is an old custom, they say, and part of their religion, and no woman could marry without it. Benri fancies that the Japanese custom of blackening the teeth is equivalent to it. But he is mistaken, as that ceremony usually succeeds marriage. They begin to tattoo the arms when a girl is five or six, and work from the elbow downwards. They expressed themselves as very much grieved and tormented by the recent prohibition of tattooing. They say the gods will be angry, and that the women can't marry unless they are tattooed. They implored both Von Siebold and me to intercede with the Japanese government on their behalf in this respect. They are less apathetic on this than on any subject, and repeat frequently, "It's a part of our religion."

The children are very pretty and attractive, and their faces give promise of an intelligence which is lacking in those of the adults. They are much loved, and are caressing as well as caressed. The infants of the mountain Ainu have seeds of millet put into their mouths as soon as they are born, and those of the coast Ainu a morsel of salted fish. Whatever the hour of birth, custom requires that they shall not be fed until a night has passed. They are not weaned until they are at least three years old. Boys are preferred to girls, but both are highly valued, and a childless wife may be divorced.

Children do not receive names till they are four or five years old, and then the father chooses a name by which his child is afterwards known. Young children when they travel are either carried on their mothers' backs in a net, or in the back of the loose garment. In both cases the weight is mainly supported by a broad band which passes round the woman's forehead. When men carry them they hold them in their arms. The hair of very young children is shaven, and from about five to fifteen the boys wear either a large tonsure or tufts above the ears, while the girls are allowed to grow hair all over their heads.

Implicit and prompt obedience is required from infancy. From a very early age the children are utilised by being made to fetch and carry and go on messages. I have seen children apparently not more than two years old sent for wood. Even at this age they are so thoroughly trained in the observances of etiquette that babies just able to walk never toddle into or out of this house without formal salutations to each person within it, the mother alone excepted. They don't wear any clothing till they are seven or eight years old, and are then dressed like their elders. Their manners to their parents are very affectionate. Even today, in the chief's awe-inspiring presence, one dear little nude creature, who had been sitting quietly for two hours staring into the fire with her big brown eyes, rushed to meet her mother when she entered, and threw her arms round her, to which the woman responded by a look of true maternal tenderness and a kiss. These little creatures, in the absolute unconsciousness of innocence, with their beautiful faces, olive-tinted bodies—all the darker, sad to say, from dirt—their perfect docility, and absence of prying curiosity, are very bewitching. They all wear silver or pewter ornaments tied round their necks by a wisp of blue cotton.

Apparently the ordinary infantile maladies, such as whooping-cough and measles, do not afflict the Ainu fatally. But the children suffer from a cutaneous affection, which wears off as they reach the age of ten or eleven years, as well as from severe toothache with their first teeth.

Ainu clothing, for savages, is exceptionally good. In the winter it consists of one, two, or more coats of skins, with hoods of the same, to which the men add rude moccasins when they go out hunting. In summer they wear loose coats, made of cloth woven from the split bark of a forest tree. This is a durable and beautiful fabric in various shades of natural buff, and somewhat resembles what is known to fancy workers as "Panama canvas." Under this a skin or bark cloth vest may or may not be worn. The men wear these coats reaching a little below the knees, folded over from right to left, and confined at the waist by a narrow girdle of the same cloth, to which is attached a rude, dagger-shaped knife, with a carved and engraved wooden handle and sheath. Smoking is by no means a general practice. Consequently the pipe and tobacco-box are not, as with the Japanese, a part of ordinary male attire. Tightly-fitting leggings, either of bark cloth or skin, are worn by both sexes, but neither shoes nor sandals.

The coat worn by the women reaches half-way between the knees and ankles, and is quite loose and without a girdle. It is fastened the whole way up to the collar-bone. Not only is the Ainu woman completely covered, but she will not change one garment for another except alone or in the dark. Lately a Japanese woman at Sarufuto took an Ainu woman into her house, and insisted on her taking a bath, which she absolutely refused to do till the bathhouse had been made quite private by means of screens. On the Japanese woman going back a little later to see what had become of her, she found her sitting in the water in her clothes. On being remonstrated with, she said that the gods would be angry if they saw her without clothes!

Many of the garments for holiday occasions are exceedingly handsome, being decorated with geometrical patterns, in which the Greek fret takes part, in coarse blue cotton, braided most dexterously with scarlet and white thread. Some of the handsomest take half a year to make. The masculine dress is completed by an apron of oblong shape decorated in the same elaborate manner. These handsome savages, with their powerful physique, look remarkably well in their best clothes. I have not seen a boy or girl above nine who is not thoroughly clothed. The jewelery of the women is large, hoop earrings of silver or pewter, with attachments of a classical pattern, and silver neck ornaments, and a few have brass bracelets soldered upon their arms. The women have a perfect passion for every hue of red, and I have made friends with them by dividing among them a large turkey-red silk handkerchief, strips of which are already being utilised for the ornamenting of coats.

The houses in the five villages up here are very good. So they are at Horobetsu, but at Shiraoi, where the Ainu suffer from the close proximity of several grog shops, they are inferior. They differ in many ways from any that I have seen before, approaching most nearly to the grass houses of the natives of Hawaii. Custom does not appear to permit either of variety or innovations; in all the style is the same, and the difference consists in the size and plenishings. The dwellings seem ill-fitted for a rigorous climate, but the same thing may be said of those of the Japanese. In their houses, as in their faces, the Ainu are more European than their conquerors, as they possess doorways, windows, central fireplaces, like those of the Highlanders of Scotland, and raised sleeping places.

The usual appearance is that of a small house built on at the end of a larger one. The small house is the vestibule or ante-room, and is entered by a low doorway screened by a heavy mat of reeds. It contains the large wooden mortar and pestle with two ends, used for pounding millet, a wooden receptacle for millet, nets or hunting gear, and some bundles of reeds for repairing roof or walls. This room never contains a window. From it the large room is entered by a doorway, over which a heavy reed-mat, bound with hide, invariably hangs. This room in Benri's case is thirty-five feet long by twenty-five feet broad, another is forty-five feet square, the smallest measures twenty by fifteen feet. On entering, one is much impressed by the great height and steepness of the roof, altogether out of proportion to the height of the walls.

The frame of the house is of posts, four feet ten inches high, placed four feet apart, and sloping slightly inwards. The height of the walls is apparently regulated by that of the reeds, of which only one length is used, and which never exceed four feet ten inches. The posts are scooped at the top, and heavy poles, resting on the scoops, are laid along them to form the top of the wall. The posts are again connected twice by slighter poles tied on horizontally. The wall is double; the outer part being formed of reeds tied very neatly to the framework in small, regular bundles, the inner layer or wall being made of reeds attached singly. From the top of the pole, which is secured to the top of the posts, the framework of the roof rises to a height of twenty-two feet, made, like the rest, of poles tied to a heavy and roughly-hewn ridge beam. At one end under the ridge beam there is a large triangular aperture for the exit of smoke. Two very stout, roughly-hewn beams cross the width of the house, resting on the posts of the wall, and on props let into the floor, and a number of poles are laid at the same height, by means of which a secondary roof formed of mats can be at once extemporized, but this is only used for guests. These poles answer the same purpose as shelves. Very great care is bestowed upon the outside of the roof, which is a marvel of neatness and prettiness, and has the appearance of a series of frills being thatched in ridges. The ridge-pole is very thickly covered, and the thatch both there and at the corners is elaborately laced with a pattern in strong peeled twigs. The poles, which for much of the room run from wall to wall, compel one to stoop to avoid fracturing one's skull and bringing down spears, bows and arrows, arrow traps, and other primitive property. The roof and rafters are black and shiny from wood smoke. Immediately under them, at one end and one side, are small, square windows, which are closed at night by wooden shutters, which during the daytime hang by ropes. Nothing is a greater insult to an Ainu than to look in at his window.

On the left of the doorway is invariably a fixed wooden platform, eighteen inches high, and covered with a single mat, which is the sleeping-place. The pillows are small stiff bolsters, covered with ornamental matting. If the family is large there are several of these sleeping platforms. A pole runs horizontally at a fitting distance above the outside edge of each, over which mats are thrown to conceal the sleepers from the rest of the room. The inside half of these mats is plain, but the outside, which is seen from the room, has a diamond pattern woven into it in dull reds and browns. The whole floor is covered with a very coarse reed mat, with interstices half an inch wide. The fireplace, which is six feet long, is oblong. Above it, on a very black and elaborate framework, hangs a very black and shiny mat, whose superfluous soot forms the basis of the stain used in tattooing, and whose apparent purpose is to prevent the smoke ascending, and to diffuse it equally throughout the room. From this framework hangs the great cooking pot, which plays a most important part in Ainu economy.

Household gods form an essential part of the furnishing of every house. In this one, at the left of the entrance, there are ten white wands, with shavings suspended from the upper end, stuck in the wall. Another projects from the window that faces the sunrise. The great god—a white post, two feet high, with spirals of shavings depending from the top—is always planted in the floor, near the wall, on the left side, opposite the fire, between the platform bed of the householder and the low, broad shelf placed invariably on the same side. It is a singular feature of all Ainu houses, coast and mountain, down to the poorest, containing, as it does, Japanese curios, many of them very valuable objects of antique art, though much destroyed by damp and dust. They are true curiosities in the dwellings of these northern aborigines, and look almost solemn ranged against the wall. In this house there are twenty-four lacquered urns, or tea-chests, or seats, each standing two feet high on four small legs, shod with engraved or filigree brass. Behind these are eight lacquered tubs, and a number of bowls and lacquer trays, and above are spears with inlaid handles, and fine Kaga and Awata bowls. The lacquer is good, and several of the urns have *daimyō*'s crests in gold upon them. One urn and a large covered bowl are beautifully inlaid with Venus' ear. The great urns are to be seen in every house, and in addition there are suits of inlaid armour, and swords with inlaid hilts, engraved blades, and repousse scabbards, for which a collector would give almost anything.

No offers, however liberal, can tempt the Ainu to sell any of these antique possessions. "They were presents," they say in their low, musical voices; "they were presents from those who were kind to our fathers; no, we cannot sell them; they were presents." And so gold lacquer, and pearl inlaying, and gold niello-work, and *daimyō*'s crests in gold, continue to gleam in the smoky darkness of their huts. Some of these items were doubtless gifts to their fathers when they went to pay tribute to the representative of the *shōgun* and the Prince of Matsumae, soon after the conquest of Ezo. Others were probably gifts from samurai, who took refuge here during the rebellion, and some must have been obtained by barter. They are the one possession which they will not barter for *sake*, and are only parted with in payment of fines at the command of a chief, or as the dower of a girl.

Except in the poorest houses, where the people can only afford to lay down a mat for a guest, they cover the coarse mat with fine ones on each side of the fire. These mats and the bark cloth are really their only manufactures. They are made of fine reeds, with a pattern in dull reds or browns, and are fourteen feet long by three feet six inches wide. It takes a woman eight days to make one of them. In every house there are one or two movable platforms six feet by four and fourteen inches high, which are placed at the head of the fireplace, and on which guests sit and sleep on a bearskin or a fine mat. In many houses there are broad seats a few inches high, on which the elder men sit cross-legged, as their custom is, not squatting Japanese fashion on the heels. A water tub always rests on a stand by the door, and the dried fish and venison or bear for daily use hang from the rafters, as well as a few skins. Besides these things there are a few absolute necessaries,—lacquer or wooden bowls for food and *sake*, a chopping board and rude chopping knife, a cleft stick for burning strips of birchbark, a triply-cleft stick for supporting the potsherd in which, on rare occasions, they burn a wick with oil. Then there are the component parts of their rude loom, the bark of which they make their clothes, the reeds of which they make their mats,—and the inventory of the essentials of their life is nearly complete. No iron enters into the construction of their houses, its place being taken by a remarkably tenacious fiber.

I have before described the preparation of their food, which usually consists of a stew of abominable things. They eat salt and fresh fish, dried fish, seaweed, slugs, the various vegetables which grow in the wilderness of tall weeds which surrounds their villages, wild roots and berries, fresh and dried venison and bear. Their carnival consists of fresh bear's flesh and *sake*, seaweed, mushrooms, and anything they can get, in fact, which is not poisonous, mixing everything up together. They use a wooden spoon for stirring, and eat with chopsticks. They have only two regular meals a day, but eat very heartily. In addition to the edibles just mentioned they have a thick soup made from a putty-like clay which is found in one or two of the valleys. This is boiled with the bulb of a wild lily, and, after much of the clay has been allowed to settle, the liquid, which is very thick, is poured off. In the north, a valley where this earth is found is called Tsietoinai, literally "Eat-earth-valley."

The men spend the autumn, winter, and spring in hunting deer and bears. Part of their tribute or taxes is paid in skins, and they subsist on the dried meat. Up to about this time the Ainu have obtained these beasts by means of poisoned arrows, arrow traps, and pitfalls, but the Japanese government has prohibited the use of poison and arrow traps, and these men say that hunting is becoming extremely difficult, as the wild animals are driven back farther and farther into the mountains by the sound of the guns. But, they add significantly, "the eyes of the Japanese government are not in every place!"

Their bows are only three feet long, and are made of stout saplings with the bark on, and there is no attempt to render them light or shapely at the ends. The wood is singularly inelastic. The arrows (of which I have obtained a number) are very peculiar, and are made in three pieces, the point consisting of a sharpened piece of bone with an elongated cavity on one side for the reception of the poison. This point or head is very slightly fastened by a lashing of bark to a fusiform piece of bone about four inches long, which is in turn lashed to a shaft about fourteen inches long, the other end of which is sometimes equipped with a triple feather and sometimes is not.

The poison is placed in the elongated cavity in the head in a very soft state, and hardens afterwards. In some of the arrow-heads fully half a teaspoonful of the paste is inserted. From the nature of the very slight lashings which attach the arrow-head to the shaft, it constantly remains fixed in the slight wound that it makes, while the shaft falls off.

Pipichari has given me a small quantity of the poisonous paste, and has also taken me to see the plant from the root of which it is made, a monkshood, whose tall spikes of blue flowers are brightening the brushwood in all directions. The root is pounded into a pulp, mixed with a reddish earth like an iron ore pulverized, and again with animal fat, before being placed in the arrow. It has been said that the poison is prepared for use by being buried in the earth, but Benri says that this is needless. They claim for it that a single wound kills a bear in ten minutes, but that the flesh is not rendered unfit for eating, though they take the precaution of cutting away a considerable quantity of it round the wound.

Dr. Eldridge, formerly of Hakodate, obtained a small quantity of the poison. After trying some experiments with it, came to the conclusion that it is less virulent than other poisons employed for a like purpose, as by the natives of Java, the Bushmen, and certain tribes of the Amazon and Orinoco. The Ainu say that if a man is accidentally wounded by a poisoned arrow the only cure is immediate excision of the part.

I do not wonder that the government has prohibited arrow traps, for they made locomotion unsafe, and it is still unsafe a little farther north, where the hunters are more out of observation than here. The traps consist of a large bow with a poisoned arrow, fixed in such a way that when the bear walks over a cord which is attached to it he is simultaneously transfixed. I have seen as many as fifty in one house. The simple contrivance for inflicting this silent death is most ingenious.

The women are occupied all day, as I have before said. They look cheerful, and even merry when they smile, and are not like the Japanese, prematurely old, partly perhaps because their houses are well ventilated, and the use of charcoal is unknown. I do not think they undergo the unmitigated drudgery which falls to the lot of most savage women, though they work hard. The men do not like them to speak to strangers and say that their place is to work and rear children. They eat of the same food, and at the same time as the men, laugh and talk before them, and receive equal support and respect in old age. They sell mats and bark cloth in the piece, and made up, when they can, and their husbands do not take their earnings from them. All Ainu women understand the making of bark cloth. The men bring in the bark in strips, five feet long, having removed the outer coating. This inner bark is easily separated into several thin layers, which are split into very narrow strips by the older women, very neatly knotted, and wound into balls weighing about a pound each. No preparation of either the bark or the thread is required to fit it for weaving, but I observe that some of the women steep it in a decoction of a bark which produces a brown dye to deepen the buff tint.

The loom is so simple that I almost fear to represent it as complicated by description. It consists of a stout hook fixed in the floor, to which the threads of the far end of the web are secured. A cord fastens the near end to the waist of the worker, who supplies, by dexterous rigidity, the necessary tension. In addition there are a frame like a comb resting on the ankles, through which the threads pass; a hollow roll for keeping the upper and under threads separate; a spatula-shaped shuttle of engraved wood; and a roller on which the cloth is rolled as it is made. The length of the web is fifteen feet, and the width of the cloth fifteen inches. It is woven with great regularity, and the knots in the thread are carefully kept on the under side.

The weaving is a very slow and fatiguing process, and a woman cannot do much more than a foot a day. The weaver sits on the floor with the whole arrangement attached to her waist, and the loom, if such it may be called, on her ankles. It takes long practice before she can supply the necessary tension by spinal rigidity. As the work proceeds she drags herself almost imperceptibly nearer the hook. In this house and other large ones two or three women bring in their webs in the morning, fix their hooks, and weave all day, while others, who have not equal advantages, put their hooks in the ground and weave in the sunshine. The web and loom can be bundled up in two minutes, and carried away quite as easily as a knitted soft blanket. It is the simplest and perhaps the most primitive form of hand-loom, and comb, shuttle, and roll, are all easily fashioned with an ordinary knife.

There cannot be anything more vague and destitute of cohesion than Ainu religious notions. With the exception of the hill shrines of Japanese construction dedicated to Yoshitsune, they have no temples, and they have neither priests, sacrifices, nor worship. Apparently through all traditional time their cultus has been the rudest and most primitive form of nature-worship, the attaching of a vague sacredness to trees, rivers, rocks, and mountains, and of vague notions of power for good or evil to the sea, the forest, the fire, and the sun and moon. I cannot make out that they possess a trace of the deification of ancestors, though their rude nature worship may well have been the primitive form of Japanese Shinto.

The solitary exception to their adoration of animate and inanimate nature appears to be the reverence paid to Yoshitsune, to whom they believe they are greatly indebted, and who, it is supposed by some, will yet interfere on their behalf. Yoshitsune is the most popular hero of Japanese history, and the special favorite of boys. He was the brother of Yoritomo, who was appointed by the emperor in 1192 *Sei-i Tai Shōgun* (Barbarian-subjugating General) for his victories, and was the first of that series of great *shōguns* whom our European notions distorted into "Temporal Emperors" of Japan. Yoshitsune, to whom the real honor of these victories belonged, became the object of the jealousy and hatred of his brother, and was hunted from province to province, till, according to popular belief, he committed *harakiri*, after killing his wife and children, and his head, preserved in *sake*, was sent to his brother at Kamakura. Scholars, however, are not agreed as to the manner, period, or scene of his death. Many believe that he escaped to Ezo and lived among the Ainu for many years, dying among them at the close of the twelfth century. None believe this more firmly than the Ainu themselves, who assert that he taught their fathers the arts of civilisation, with letters and numbers, and gave them righteous laws, and he is worshipped by many of them under a name which signifies Master of the Law. I have been told by old men in Biratori, Usu, and Rebunge, that a later Japanese conqueror carried away the books in which the arts were written, and that since his time the arts themselves have been lost, and the Ainu have fallen into their present condition! On asking why the Ainu do not make vessels of iron and clay as well as knives and spears, the invariable answer is, "The Japanese took away the books."

Their gods—that is, the outward symbols of their religion, corresponding most likely with the Shinto *gohei*—are wands and posts of peeled wood, whittled nearly to the top, from which the pendent shavings fall down in white curls. These are not only set up in their houses, sometimes as many as twenty, but on precipices, banks of rivers and streams, and mountain passes, and such wands are thrown into the rivers as the boatmen descend rapids and dangerous places. Since my baggage horse fell over an acclivity on the trail from Sarufuto, four such wands have been placed there. It is nonsense to write of the religious ideas of a people who have none, and of beliefs among people who are merely adult children. The traveller who formulates an Ainu creed must evolve it from his inner consciousness. I have taken infinite trouble to learn from themselves what their religious notions are, and Shinondi tells me that they have told me all they know, and the whole sum is a few vague fears and hopes, and a suspicion that there are things outside themselves more powerful than themselves, whose good influences may be obtained, or whose evil influences may be averted, by libations of *sake*.

The word worship is in itself misleading. When I use it of these savages it simply means libations of *sake*, waving bowls and waving hands, without any spiritual act of deprecation or supplication. In such a sense and such alone they worship the sun and moon (but not the stars), the forest, and the sea. The wolf, the black snake, the owl, and several other beasts and birds have the word *kamoi*, god, attached to them, as the wolf is the "howling god," the owl "the bird of the gods," a black snake the "raven god." But none of these things are now worshipped, wolf worship having quite lately died out. Thunder, "the voice of the gods," inspires some fear. The sun, they say, is their best god, and the fire their next best, obviously the divinities from whom their greatest benefits are received. Some idea of gratitude pervades their rude notions, as in the case of the worship paid to Yoshitsune, and it appears in one of the rude recitations chanted at the Saturnalia which in several places conclude the hunting and fishing seasons:

> To the sea which nourishes us,
> to the forest which protects us,
> we present our grateful thanks.
> You are two mothers that nourish the same child;
> do not be angry if we leave one to go to the other.

> The Ainu will always be
> the pride of the forest and of the sea.

The solitary act of sacrifice which they perform is the placing of a worthless, dead bird, something like a sparrow, near one of their peeled wands, where it is left till it reaches an advanced stage of putrefaction. "To drink for the god" is the chief act of "worship," and thus drunkenness and religion are inseparably connected, as the more *sake* the Ainu drink the more devout they are, and the better pleased are the gods. It does not appear that anything but *sake* is of sufficient value to please the gods. The libations to the fire and the peeled post are never omitted, and are always accompanied by the inward waving of the *sake* bowls.

The peculiarity which distinguishes this rude mythology is the worship of the bear, the Ezo bear being one of the finest of his species. It is hard to understand the feelings by which it is prompted, for they worship it after their fashion, and set up its head in their villages, yet they trap it, kill it, eat it, and sell its skin. There is no doubt that this wild beast inspires more of the feeling which prompts worship than the inanimate forces of nature, and the Ainu may be distinguished as bear worshippers, and their greatest religious festival or Saturnalia as the Festival of the Bear. Gentle and peaceable as they are, they have a great admiration for fierceness and courage. The bear, which is the strongest, fiercest, and most courageous animal known to them, has probably in all ages inspired them with veneration. Some of their rude chants are in praise of the bear, and their highest eulogy on a man is to compare him to a bear. Thus Shinondi said of Benri, the chief, "He is as strong as a bear," and the old Fate praising Pipichari called him "The young bear."

In all Ainu villages, especially near the chief's house, there are several tall poles with the fleshless skull of a bear on the top of each, and in most there is also a large cage, made grid-iron fashion, of stout timbers, and raised two or three feet from the ground. At the present time such cages contain young but well-grown bears, captured when quite small in the early spring. After the capture the bear cub is introduced into a dwelling house, generally that of the chief, or sub-chief, where it is suckled by a woman, and played with by the children. When it grows too big and rough for domestic ways, it is placed in a strong cage, in which it is fed and cared for, as I understand, till the autumn of the following year, when, being strong and well-grown, the Festival of the Bear is celebrated. The customs of this festival vary considerably, and the manner of the bear's death differs among the mountain and coast Ainu, but everywhere there is a general gathering of the people, and it is the occasion of a great feast, accompanied with much *sake* and a curious dance, in which men alone take part.

Yells and shouts are used to excite the bear, and when he becomes much agitated a chief shoots him with an arrow, inflicting a slight wound which maddens him, on which the bars of the cage are raised, and he springs forth, very furious. At this stage the Ainu run upon him with various weapons, each one striving to inflict a wound, as it brings good luck to draw his blood. As soon as he falls down exhausted, his head is cut off, and the weapons with which he has been wounded are offered to it, and he is asked to avenge himself upon them. Afterwards the carcass, amidst a frenzied uproar, is distributed among the people, and amidst feasting and riot the head, placed upon a pole, is worshipped, i.e. it receives libations of *sake*, and the festival closes with general intoxication. In some villages it is customary for the foster- mother of the bear to utter piercing wails while he is delivered to his murderers, and after he is slain to beat each one of them with a branch of a tree.

Afterwards at Usu, on Uchiura Bay, the old men told me that at their festival they despatch the bear after a different manner. On letting it loose from the cage two men seize it by the ears, and others simultaneously place a long, stout pole across the nape of its neck, upon which a number of Ainu mount, and after a prolonged struggle the neck is broken. As the bear is seen to approach his end, they shout in chorus, "We kill you, O bear! come back soon into an Ainu." When a bear is trapped or wounded by an arrow, the hunters go through an apologetic or propitiatory ceremony. They appear to have certain rude ideas of the transmigration at death of the soul of an animal into a human body, as is evidenced by the Usu prayer to the bear and certain rude traditions. But whether these are indigenous, or have arisen by contact with Buddhism at a later period, it is impossible to say.

They have no definite ideas concerning a future state, and the subject is evidently not a pleasing one to them. Such notions as they have are few and confused. Some think that the spirits of their friends go into wolves and snakes. Others believe that they wander about the forests and they are much afraid of ghosts. A few think that they go to "a good or bad place," according to their deeds. But Shinondi said, and there was an infinite pathos in his words, "How can we know? No one ever came back to tell us!" On asking him what were bad deeds, he said, "Being bad to parents, stealing, and telling lies." The future does not occupy any place in their thoughts, and they can hardly be said to believe in the immortality of the soul, though their fear of ghosts shows that they recognize a distinction between body and spirit.

Their social customs are very simple. Girls never marry before the age of seventeen, or men before twenty-one. When a man wishes to marry he thinks of some particular girl, and asks the chief if he may ask for her. If leave is given, either through a go-between or personally, he asks her father for her, and if he consents the bridegroom gives him a present, usually a Japanese curio. This constitutes betrothal, and the marriage, which immediately follows, is celebrated by carousals and the drinking of much *sake*. The bride receives as her dowry her earrings and a highly ornamented dress. It is an essential that the husband provides a house to which to take his wife. Each couple lives separately, and even the eldest son does not take his bride to his father's house. Polygamy is only allowed in two cases. The chief may have three wives, but each must have her separate house. Benri has two wives, but it appears that he took the second because the first was childless. The Usu Ainu told me that among the tribes of Uchiura Bay polygamy is not practised, even by the chiefs. It is also permitted in the case of a childless wife, though there is no instance of it in Biratori, and the men say that they prefer to have one wife, as two quarrel.

Widows are allowed to marry again with the chief's consent; but among these mountain Ainu a woman must remain absolutely secluded within the house of her late husband for a period varying from six to twelve months, only going to the door at intervals to throw *sake* to the right and left. A man secludes himself similarly for thirty days. So greatly do the customs vary, that round Uchiura Bay I found that the period of seclusion for a widow is only thirty days, and for a man twenty-five; but that after a father's death the house in which he has lived is burned down after the thirty days of seclusion, and the widow and her children go to a friend's house for three years, after which the house is rebuilt on its former site.

If a man does not like his wife, by obtaining the chief's consent he can divorce her; but he must send her back to her parents with plenty of good clothes. Divorce is impracticable where there are children, and is rarely if ever practised. Conjugal fidelity is a virtue among Ainu women, but "custom" provides that, in case of unfaithfulness, the injured husband may bestow his wife upon her paramour, if he be an unmarried man. In that case the chief fixes the amount of damages which the paramour must pay; and these are usually valuable Japanese curios. The old and blind people are entirely supported by their children, and receive until their dying day filial reverence and obedience. If one man steals from another he must return what he has taken, and give the injured man a present besides, the value of which is fixed by the chief.

Custom enjoins the exercise of hospitality on every Ainu. They receive all strangers as they received me, giving them of their best, placing them in the most honorable place, bestowing gifts upon them, and, when they depart, furnishing them with cakes of boiled millet.

They have few amusements, except certain feasts. Their dance, which they have just given in my honor, is slow and mournful, and their songs are chants or recitative. They have a musical instrument, something like a guitar, with three, five, or six strings, which are made from sinews of whales cast up on the shore. They have another, which is believed to be peculiar to themselves, consisting of a thin piece of wood, about five inches long and two and a half inches broad, with a pointed wooden tongue, about two lines in breadth and sixteen in length, fixed in the middle, and grooved on three sides. The wood is held before the mouth, and the tongue is set in motion by the vibration of the breath in singing. Its sound, though less penetrating, is as discordant as that of a Jew's harp, which it somewhat resembles. One of the men used it as an accompaniment of a song; but they are unwilling to part with them, as they say that it is very seldom that they can find a piece of wood which will bear the fine splitting necessary for the tongue.

They are a most courteous people among each other. The salutations are frequent—on entering a house, on leaving it, on meeting on the road, on receiving anything from the hand of another, and on receiving a kind or complimentary speech. They do not make any acknowledgments of this kind to the women. The common salutation consists in extending the hands and waving them inwards, once or oftener, and stroking the beard. The formal one in raising the hands with an inward curve to the level of the head two or three times, lowering them, and rubbing them together. The ceremony concludes with stroking the beard several times. The latter and more formal mode of salutation is offered to the chief, and by the young to the old men.

They have no medicine men and, though they are aware of the existence of healing herbs, do not know their special virtues or the manner of using them. Dried and pounded bear's liver is their medicine, and they place much reliance on it in colic and other pains. They are a healthy race. In this village of three hundred souls, there are no chronically ailing people; nothing but one case of bronchitis, and some cutaneous maladies among children. Neither is there any case of deformity in this and five other large villages which I have visited, except that of a girl, who has one leg slightly shorter than the other.

They ferment a kind of intoxicating liquor from the root of a tree, and also from their own millet and Japanese rice, but Japanese *sake* is the one thing that they care about. They spend all their gains upon it, and drink it in enormous quantities. It represents to them all the good of which they know, or can conceive. Beastly intoxication is the highest happiness to which these poor savages aspire, and the condition is sanctified to them under the fiction of drinking to the gods. Men and women alike indulge in this vice. A few, like Pipichari, abstain from it totally, taking the bowl in their hands, making the libations to the gods, and then passing it on. I asked Pipichari why he did not take *sake*, and he replied with a truthful terseness, "Because it makes men like dogs."

Except the chief, who has two horses, they have no domestic animals except very large, yellow dogs, which are used in hunting, but are never admitted within the houses.

The habits of the people, though by no means destitute of decency and propriety, are not cleanly. The women bathe their hands once a day, but any other washing is unknown. They never wash their clothes, and wear the same by day and night. I am afraid to speculate on the condition of their wealth of coal-black hair. They may be said to be very dirty—as dirty fully as masses of our people at home. Their houses swarm with fleas, but they are not worse in this respect than the Japanese *yadoya*. The mountain villages have the appearance of extreme cleanliness, being devoid of litter, heaps, puddles, and untidiness of all kinds. There are no unpleasant odors inside or outside the houses, as they are well ventilated and smoked, and the salted fish and meat are kept in the godowns. The hair and beards of the old men, instead of being snowy as they ought to be, are yellow from smoke and dirt.

They have no mode of computing time, and do not know their own ages. To them the past is dead, yet, like other conquered and despised races, they cling to the idea that in some far-off age they were a great nation. They have no traditions of internecine strife, and the art of war seems to have been lost long ago. I asked Benri about this matter, and he says that formerly Ainu fought with spears and knives as well as with bows and arrows, but that Yoshitsune, their hero god, forbade war for ever, and since then the two-edged spear, with a shaft nine feet long, has only been used in hunting bears.

The Japanese government, of course, exercises the same authority over the Ainu as over its other subjects, but probably it does not care to interfere in domestic or tribal matters, and within this outside limit despotic authority is vested in the chiefs. The Ainu live in village communities, and each community has its own chief, who is its lord paramount. It appears to me that this chieftainship is but an expansion of the paternal relation, and that all the village families are ruled as a unit. Benri, in whose house I am, is the chief of Biratori, and is treated by all with very great deference of manner. The office is nominally for life; but if a chief becomes blind, or too infirm to go about, he appoints a successor. If he has a smart son, who he thinks will command the respect of the people, he appoints him; but if not, he chooses the most suitable man in the village. The people are called upon to approve the choice, but their ratification is never refused. The office is not hereditary anywhere.

Benri appears to exercise the authority of a very strict father. His manner to all the men is like that of a master to slaves, and they bow when they speak to him. No one can marry without his approval. If anyone builds a house he chooses the site. He has absolute jurisdiction in civil and criminal cases, unless (which is very rare) the latter should be of sufficient magnitude to be reported to the imperial officials. He compels restitution of stolen property, and in all cases fixes the fines which are to be paid by delinquents. He also fixes the hunting arrangements and the festivals. The younger men were obviously much afraid of incurring his anger in his absence.

An eldest son does not appear to be, as among the Japanese, a privileged person. He does not necessarily inherit the house and curios. The latter are not divided, but go with the house to the son whom the father regards as being the smartest. Formal adoption is practised. Pipichari is an adopted son, and is likely to succeed to Benri's property to the exclusion of his own children. I cannot get at the word which is translated smartness, but I understand it as meaning general capacity. The chief, as I have mentioned before, is allowed three wives among the mountain Ainu, otherwise authority seems to be his only privilege.

The Ainu have a singular dread of snakes. Even their bravest fly from them. One man says that it is because they know of no cure for their bite. But there is something more than this, for they flee from snakes which they know to be harmless.

They have an equal dread of their dead. Death seems to them very specially "the shadow fear'd of man." When it comes, which it usually does from bronchitis in old age, the corpse is dressed in its best clothing, and laid upon a shelf for from one to three days. In the case of a woman her ornaments are buried with her, and in that of a man his knife and *sake*-stick, and, if he were a smoker, his smoking apparatus. The corpse is sewn up with these things in a mat, and, being slung on poles, is carried to a solitary grave, where it is laid in a recumbent position. Nothing will induce an Ainu to go near a grave. Even if a valuable bird or animal falls near one, he will not go to pick it up. A vague dread is for ever associated with the departed, and no dream of Paradise ever lights for the Ainu the Stygian shades.

Benri is, for an Ainu, intelligent. Two years ago Dening of Hakodate came up here and told him that there was but one God who made us all, to which the shrewd old man replied, "If the God who made you made us, how is it that you are so different—you so rich, we so poor?" On asking him about the magnificent pieces of lacquer and inlaying which adorn his curio shelf, he said that they were his father's, grandfather's, and great-grandfather's at least, and he thinks they were gifts from the *daimyō* of Matsumae soon after the conquest of Ezo. He is a grand-looking man, in spite of the havoc wrought by his intemperate habits. There is plenty of room in the house, and this morning, when I asked him to show me the use of the spear, he looked a truly magnificent savage, stepping well back with the spear in rest, and then springing forward for the attack, his arms and legs turning into iron, the big muscles standing out in knots, his frame quivering with excitement, the thick hair falling back in masses from his brow, and the fire of the chase in his eye. I trembled for Itō, who was the object of the imaginary onslaught, the passion of sport was so admirably acted.

As I write, seven of the older men are sitting by the fire. Their grey beards fall to their waists in rippled masses, and the slight baldness of age not only gives them a singularly venerable appearance, but enhances the beauty of their lofty brows. I took a rough sketch of one of the handsomest, and, showing it to him, asked if he would have it, but instead of being amused or pleased he showed symptoms of fear, and asked me to burn it, saying it would bring him bad luck and he should die. Itō pacified him, and he accepted it, after a Chinese character, which is understood to mean good luck, had been written upon it. But all the others begged me not to make pictures of them, except Pipichari, who lies at my feet like a staghound.

The profusion of black hair, and a curious intensity about their eyes, coupled with the hairy limbs and singularly vigorous physique, give them a formidably savage appearance, But the smile, full of sweetness and light, in which both eyes and mouth bear part, and the low, musical voice, softer and sweeter than anything I have previously heard, make me at times forget that they are savages at all. The venerable look of these old men harmonizes with the singular dignity and courtesy of their manners, but as I look at the grand heads, and reflect that the Ainu have never shown any capacity, and are merely adult children, they seem to suggest water on the brain rather than intellect. I am more and more convinced that the expression of their faces is European. It is truthful, straightforward, manly, but both it and the tone of voice are strongly tinged with pathos.

Before these elders Benri asked me, in a severe tone, if I had been annoyed in any way during his absence. He feared, he said, that the young men and the women would crowd about me rudely. I made a complimentary speech in return, and all the ancient hands were waved, and the venerable beards were stroked in acknowledgment.

These Ainu, doubtless, stand high among uncivilized peoples. Yet they are as completely irreclaimable as the wildest of nomad tribes, and contact with civilisation, where it exists, only debases them. Several young Ainu were sent to Tokyo, and educated and trained in various ways, but as soon as they returned to Ezo they relapsed into savagery, retaining nothing but a knowledge of Japanese. They are charming in many ways, but make one sad, too, by their stupidity, apathy, and hopelessness.

They are certainly superior to many aborigines, as they have an approach to domestic life. They have one word for *house*, and another for *home*, and one word for husband approaches very nearly to house-band. Truth is of value in their eyes, and this in itself raises them above some peoples. Infanticide is unknown, and aged parents receive filial reverence, kindness, and support, while in their social and domestic relations there is much that is praiseworthy.

I must conclude this chapter abruptly, as the horses are waiting, and I must cross the rivers, if possible, before the bursting of an impending storm.

A Drunken Revel

I left the Ainu yesterday with real regret, though I must confess that sleeping in one's clothes and the lack of ablutions are very fatiguing. Benri's two wives spent the early morning in the laborious operation of grinding millet into coarse flour. Before I departed, as their custom is, they made a paste of it, rolled it with their unclean fingers into well-shaped cakes, boiled them in the unwashed pot in which they make their stew, and presented them to me on a lacquer tray. They were distressed that I did not eat their food, and a woman went to a village at some distance and brought me some venison fat as a delicacy. All those of whom I had seen much came to wish me good-bye, and they brought so many presents (including a fine bearskin) that I should have needed an additional horse to carry them had I accepted but one-half.

I rode twelve miles through the forest to Hidaka Monbetsu, where I intended to spend Sunday, but I had the worst horse I ever rode, and we took five hours. The day was dull and sad, threatening a storm, and when we got out of the forest, upon a sandhill covered with oak scrub, we encountered a most furious wind. Among the many views which I have seen, that is one to be remembered. Below lay a bleached and bare sandhill, with a few grey houses huddled in its miserable shelter, and a heaped-up shore of grey sand, on which a brown-grey sea was breaking with clash and boom in long, white, ragged lines, with all beyond a confusion of surf, surge, and mist, with driving brown clouds mingling sea and sky, and all between showing only in glimpses amidst scuds of sand.

At a house in the scrub a number of men were drinking *sake* with much uproar, and a superb-looking Ainu came out, staggered a few yards, and then fell backwards among the weeds, a picture of debasement. Before I left Biratori, I inveighed to the assembled Ainu against the practice and consequences of *sake*-drinking, and was met with the reply, "We must drink to the gods, or we shall die." But Pipichari said, "You say that which is good; let us give *sake* to the gods, but not drink it," for which bold speech he was severely rebuked by Benri.

Hidaka Monbetsu is a stormily-situated and most wretched cluster of twenty-seven decayed houses, some of them Ainu, and some Japanese. The fish oil and seaweed fishing trades are in brisk operation there now for a short time, and a number of Ainu and Japanese strangers are employed. The boats could not get out because of the surf, and there was a drunken debauch. The whole place smelled of *sake*. Tipsy men were staggering about and falling flat on their backs, to lie there like dogs till they were sober, Ainu women were vainly endeavoring to drag their drunken lords home, and men of both races were reduced to a beastly equality. I went to the *yadoya* where I intended to spend Sunday, but, besides being very dirty and forlorn, it was the very centre of the *sake* traffic, and in its open space there were men in all stages of riotous and stupid intoxication. It was a sad scene, yet one to be matched in a hundred places in Scotland every Saturday afternoon. I am told by the village chief here that an Ainu can drink four or five times as much as a Japanese without being tipsy, so for each tipsy Ainu there had been an outlay of six or seven shillings, for *sake* is eight pence a cup here!

I had some tea and eggs in the *daidokoro*, and altered my plans altogether on finding that if I proceeded farther round the east coast, as I intended, I should run the risk of several days' detention on the banks of numerous "bad rivers" if rain came on, by which I should run the risk of breaking my promise to deliver Itō to Maries by a given day. I do not surrender this project without an equivalent, for I intend to add a hundred miles to my journey, by taking an almost disused track round Uchiura Bay, and visiting the coast Ainu of a very primitive region. Itō is very much opposed to this, thinking that he has made a sufficient sacrifice of personal comfort at Biratori. He plies me with stories that there are "many bad rivers to cross," that the track is so worn as to be impassable, that there are no *yadoya*, and that at the government offices we shall neither get rice nor eggs. An old man who has turned back unable to get horses is made responsible for these stories. The machinations are very amusing. Itō was much smitten with the daughter of the house master at Muroran, and left some things in her keeping, and the desire to see her again is behind his opposition to the other route.

Monday
The horse could not or would not carry me farther than Hidaka Monbetsu, so, sending the baggage on, I walked through the oak wood, and enjoyed its silent solitude, in spite of the sad reflections upon the Ainu's enslavement to *sake*. I spent yesterday quietly in my old quarters, with a fearful storm of wind and rain outside. Pipichari appeared at noon, nominally to bring news of the sick woman, who is recovering, and to have his nearly healed foot bandaged again, but really to bring me a knife sheath which he has carved for me. He lay on the mat in the corner of my room most of the afternoon, and I got a great many more words from him.

The house master, who is the village chief of Sarufuto, paid me a courteous visit, and in the evening sent to say that he would be very glad of some medicine, for he was "very ill and going to have fever." He had caught a bad cold and sore throat, had bad pains in his limbs, and was bemoaning himself ruefully. To pacify his wife, who was very sorry for him, I gave him some anti-bilious pills and the trapper's remedy of a pint of hot water with a pinch of cayenne pepper, and left him moaning and bundled up under a pile of *futon*, in a nearly hermetically sealed room, with a *hibachi* of charcoal vitiating the air. This morning when I went and inquired after him in a properly concerned tone, his wife told me very gleefully that he was quite well and had gone out, and had left twenty-five *sen* for some more of the medicines that I had given him, so with great gravity I put up some of Duncan and Flockhart's most pungent cayenne pepper, and showed her how much to use. She was not content without some of the anti-bilious pills, a single box of which has performed six of those miraculous cures that rejoice the hearts and fill the pockets of patent medicine makers.

Horsebeaking and Cruelty

After the storm of Sunday, Monday was a grey, still, tender day, and the ranges of wooded hills were bathed in the richest indigo coloring. A canter of seventeen miles among the damask roses on a very rough horse only took me to Yufutsu, whose indescribable loneliness fascinated me into spending a night there again, and encountering a wild clatter of wind and rain. Another canter of seven miles the next morning took me to Tomakomai, where I rejoined my *kuruma*, and after a long delay, three trotting Ainu took me to Shiraoi, where the clear shining after rain, and the mountains against a lemon-colored sky, were extremely beautiful. The Pacific was as unrestful as a guilty thing, and its crash and clamor and the severe cold fatigued me so much that I did not pursue my journey the next day, and had the pleasure of a flying visit from Von Siebold and Diesbach, who bestowed a chicken upon me.

I like Shiraoi very much, and if I were stronger would certainly make it a basis for exploring a part of the interior, in which there is much to reward the explorer. Obviously the changes in this part of Ezo have been comparatively recent, and the energy of the force which has produced them is not yet extinct. The land has gained from the sea along the whole of this part of the coast to the extent of two or three miles, the old beach with its bays and headlands being a marked feature of the landscape. This new formation appears to be a vast bed of pumice, covered by a thin layer of vegetable mold, which cannot be more than fifty years old. This pumice fell during the eruption of the volcano of Tarumai, which is very near Shiraoi, and is also brought down in large quantities from the interior hills and valleys by the numerous rivers, besides being washed up by the sea. At the last eruption pumice fell over this region of Ezo to a medium depth of three feet six inches. In nearly all the rivers good sections of the formation may be seen in their deeply-cleft banks, broad, light-colored bands of pumice, with a few inches of rich, black, vegetable soil above, and several feet of black sea sand below. During a freshet which occurred the first night I was at Shiraoi, a single stream covered a piece of land with pumice to the depth of nine inches, being the wash from the hills of the interior, in a course of less than fifteen miles.

Looking inland, the volcano of Tarumai, with a bare grey top and a blasted forest on its sides, occupies the right of the picture. To the left and inland are mountains within mountains, tumbled together in most picturesque confusion, densely covered with forest and cleft by magnificent ravines, here and there opening out into narrow valleys. The whole of the interior is jungle penetrable for a few miles by shallow and rapid rivers, and by nearly smothered trails made by the Ainu in search of game. The general lie of the country made me very anxious to find out whether a much-broken ridge lying among the mountains is or is not a series of tufa cones of ancient date. Applying for a good horse and Ainu guide on horseback, I left Itō to amuse himself, and spent much of a most splendid day in investigations and in attempting to get round the back of the volcano and up its inland side. There is a great deal to see and learn there. Oh that I had strength!

After hours of most tedious and exhausting work I reached a point where there were several great fissures emitting smoke and steam, with occasional subterranean detonations. These were on the side of a small, flank crack which was smoking heavily. There was light pumice everywhere, but nothing like recent lava or scoriae. One fissure was completely lined with exquisite, acicular crystals of sulphur, which perished with a touch. Lower down there were two hot springs with a deposit of sulphur round their margins, and bubbles of gas, which, from its strong, garlicky smell, I suppose to be sulphuretted hydrogen. Farther progress in that direction was impossible without a force of pioneers. I put my arm down several deep crevices which were at an altitude of only about five hundred feet, and had to withdraw it at once, owing to the great heat, in which some beautiful specimens of tropical ferns were growing. At the same height I came to a hot spring— hot enough to burst one of my thermometers, which was graduated above the boiling point of Fahrenheit. Tying up an egg in a pocket-handkerchief and holding it by a stick in the water, it was hard boiled in eight and a half minutes. The water evaporated without leaving a trace of deposit on the handkerchief, and there was no crust round its margin. It boiled and bubbled with great force.

Three hours more of exhausting toil, which almost knocked up the horses, brought us to the apparent ridge, and I was delighted to find that it consisted of a lateral range of tufa cones, which I estimate as being from two hundred to three hundred and fifty, or even four hundred feet high. They are densely covered with trees of considerable age, and a rich deposit of mold, though their conical form is still admirably defined. An hour of very severe work, and energetic use of the knife on the part of the Ainu, took me to the top of one of these through a mass of entangled and gigantic vegetation. I was amply repaid by finding a deep, well-defined crateriform cavity of great depth, with its sides richly clothed with vegetation, closely resembling some of the old cones in the island of Kauai. This cone is partially girdled by a stream, which in one place has cut through a bank of both red and black volcanic ash. All the usual phenomena of volcanic regions are probably to be met with north of Shiraoi, and I hope they will at some future time be made the object of careful investigation.

In spite of the desperate and almost overwhelming fatigue, I have enjoyed few things more than that exploring expedition. If the Japanese have no one to talk to they croon hideous discords to themselves, and it was a relief to leave Itō behind and get away with an Ainu, who was at once silent, trust-worthy, and faithful. Two bright rivers bubbling over beds of red pebbles run down to Shiraoi out of the back country, and my directions, which were translated to the Ainu, were to follow up one of these and go into the mountains in the direction of one I pointed out till I said, "Shiraoi." It was one of those exquisite mornings which are seen sometimes in the Scottish Highlands before rain, with intense clearness and visibility, a blue atmosphere, a cloudless sky, blue summits, heavy dew, and glorious sunshine. Under these circumstances scenery beautiful in itself became entrancing.

The trailers are so formidable that we had to stoop over our horses' necks at all times, and with pushing back branches and guarding my face from slaps and scratches, my thick dogskin gloves were literally frayed off, and some of the skin of my hands and face in addition, so that I returned both bleeding and swelled. It was on the return ride, fortunately, that in stooping to escape one great liana the loop of another grazed my nose, and, being unable to check my unbroken horse instantaneously, the loop caught me by the throat, nearly strangled me. In less time than it takes to tell it I was drawn over the back of the saddle, and found myself lying on the ground, jammed between a tree and the hind leg of the horse, which was quietly feeding. The Ainu, whose face was very badly scratched, missing me, came back, never said a word, helped me up, brought me some water in a leaf, brought my hat, and we rode on again. I was little the worse for the fall, but on borrowing a looking glass I see not only scratches and abrasions all over my face, but a livid mark round my throat as if I had been hung. The Ainu left portions of his bushy locks on many of the branches. Thus I made my way through the forest, preceded by this hairy and formidable-looking savage, who was dressed in a coat of skins with the fur outside, seated on the top of a pack saddle covered with a deer hide, and with his hairy legs crossed over the horse's neck—a fashion in which the Ainu ride any horses over any ground with the utmost serenity.

It was a wonderful region for beauty. I have not seen so beautiful a view in Japan as from the riverbed from which I had the first near view of the grand assemblage of tufa cones, covered with an ancient vegetation, backed by high mountains of volcanic origin, on whose ragged crests the red ash was blazing vermilion against the blue sky, with a foreground of bright waters flashing through a primeval forest. The banks of these streams were deeply excavated by the heavy rains, and sometimes we had to jump three and even four feet out of the forest into the river, and as much up again, fording the Shiraoi River only more than twenty times, and often making a pathway of its treacherous bed and rushing waters, because the forest was impassable from the great size of the prostrate trees. The horses look at these jumps, hold back, try to turn, and then, making up their minds, suddenly plunge down or up. When the last vestige of a trail disappeared, I signed to the Ainu to go on, and our subsequent exploration was all done at the rate of about a mile an hour. On the openings the grass grows stiff and strong to the height of eight feet, with its soft reddish plumes waving in the breeze. The Ainu first forced his horse through it, but of course it closed again, so that constantly when he was close in front I was only aware of his proximity by the tinkling of his horse's bells, for I saw nothing of him or of my own horse except the horn of my saddle. We tumbled into holes often, and as easily tumbled out of them. But once we both went down in the most unexpected manner into what must have been an old bear-trap, both going over our horses' heads, the horses and ourselves struggling together in a narrow space in a mist of grassy plumes. Being unable to communicate with my guide, the sense of the ridiculous situation was so overpowering that, even in the midst of the mishap, I was exhausted with laughter, though not a little bruised. It was very hard to get out of that pitfall, and I hope I shall never get into one again. It is not the first occasion on which I have been glad that the Ezo horses are shoeless. It was through this long grass that we fought our way to the tufa cones, with the red ragged crests against the blue sky.

The scenery was magnificent, and after getting so far I longed to explore the sources of the rivers, but besides the many difficulties the day was far spent. I was also too weak for any energetic undertaking, yet I felt an intuitive perception of the passion and fascination of exploring, and understood how people could give up their lives to it. I turned away from the tufa cones and the glory of the ragged crests very sadly, to ride a tired horse through great difficulties. The animal was so thoroughly done up that I had to walk, or rather wade, for the last hour. It was nightfall when I returned, to find that Itō had packed up all my things, had been waiting ever since noon to start for Horobetsu, was very grumpy at having to unpack, and thoroughly disgusted when I told him that I was so tired and bruised that I should have to remain the next day to rest. He said indignantly, "I never thought that when you'd got the Kaitakushi *kuruma* you'd go off the road into those woods!" We had seen some deer and many pheasants, and a successful hunter brought in a fine stag, so that I had venison steak for supper, and was much comforted, though Itō seasoned the meal with well-got-up stories of the impracticability of the Uchiura Bay route.

Shiraoi consists of a large old *yadoya* where the *daimyō* and his train used to lodge in the old days, and about eleven Japanese houses, most of which are *sake* shops—a fact which supplies an explanation of the squalor of the Ainu village of fifty-two houses, which is on the shore at a respectful distance. There is no cultivation, in which it is like all the fishing villages on this part of the coast, but fish oil and fish manure are made in immense quantities, and, though it is not the season here, the place is pervaded by an ancient and fish-like smell.

The Ainu houses here are much smaller, poorer, and dirtier than those of Biratori. I went into a number of them, and conversed with the people, many of whom understand Japanese. Some of the houses looked like dens, and. As it was raining, husband, wife, and five or six naked children, all as dirty as they could be, with unkempt, elf-like locks, were huddled round the fires. Still, bad as it looked and smelled, the fire was the hearth, and the hearth was inviolate, and each smoked and dirt-stained group was a family

The roofs are much flatter than those of the mountain Ainu, and, as there are few storehouses, quantities of fish, green skins, and venison, hang from the rafters, and the smell of these and the stinging of the smoke were most trying. Few of the houses had any guest seats, but in the very poorest, when I asked shelter from the rain, they put their best mat upon the ground, and insisted, much to my distress, on my walking over it in muddy boots, saying, "It is Ainu custom." In all those squalid homes the broad shelf, with its rows of Japanese curios, has a place. I mentioned that it is customary for a chief to appoint a successor when he becomes infirm, and I came upon a case in point, through a mistaken direction, which took us to the house of the former chief, with a great empty bear cage at its door. On addressing him as the chief, he said, "I am old and blind, I cannot go out, I am of no more good," and directed us to the house of his successor. Altogether it is obvious, from many evidences in this village, that Japanese contiguity is hurtful, and that the Ainu have reaped abundantly of the disadvantages without the advantages of contact with Japanese civilisation.

That night I saw a specimen of Japanese horse-breaking as practised in Ezo. A Japanese brought into the village street a handsome, spirited young horse, equipped with a Japanese demi-pique saddle, and a most cruel gag bit. The man wore very cruel spurs, and was armed with a bit of stout board two feet long by six inches broad. The horse had not been mounted before, and was frightened, but not the least vicious. He was spurred into a gallop, and ridden at full speed up and down the street, turned by main force, thrown on his haunches, goaded with the spurs, and cowed by being mercilessly thrashed over the ears and eyes with the piece of board till he was blinded with blood. Whenever he tried to stop from exhaustion he was spurred, jerked, and flogged, till at last, covered with sweat, foam, and blood, and with blood running from his mouth and splashing the road, he reeled, staggered, and fell, the rider dexterously disengaging himself. As soon as he was able to stand, he was allowed to crawl into a shed, where he was kept without food till morning, when a child could do anything with him. He was effectually spirit-broken, useless for the rest of his life. It was a brutal and brutalizing exhibition, as triumphs of brute force always are.

This morning I left early in the *kuruma* with two kind and delightful savages. The road being much broken by the rains I had to get out frequently, and every time I got in again they put my air-pillow behind me, and covered me up in a blanket. When we got to a rough river, one made a step of his back by which I mounted their horse, and gave me nooses of rope to hold on by, and the other held my arm to keep me steady, and they would not let me walk up or down any of the hills. What a blessing it is that, amidst the confusion of tongues, the language of kindness and courtesy is universally understood, and that a kindly smile on a savage face is as intelligible as on that of one's own countryman. They had never drawn a *kuruma*, and were as pleased as children when I showed them how to balance the shafts. They were not without the capacity to originate ideas, for, when they were tired of the frolic of pulling, they attached the *kuruma* by ropes to the horse, which one of them rode at a scramble, while the other merely ran in the shafts to keep them level. This is an excellent plan.

Horobetsu is a fishing station of antique and decayed aspect, with eighteen Japanese and forty-seven Ainu houses. The latter are much larger than at Shiraoi, and their very steep roofs are beautifully constructed. It was a miserable day, with fog concealing the mountains and lying heavily on the sea, but as no one expected rain I sent the *kuruma* back to Muroran and secured horses. On principle I always go to the corral myself to choose animals, if possible, without sore backs, but the choice is often between one with a mere raw and others which have holes in their backs into which I could put my hand, or altogether uncovered spines. The practice does no immediate good, but by showing the Japanese that foreign opinion condemns these cruelties an amendment may eventually be brought about. At Horobetsu, among twenty horses, there was not one that I would take— I should like to have had them all shot. They are cheap and abundant, and are of no account. They drove a number more down from the hills, and I chose the largest and finest horse I have seen in Japan, with some spirit and action, but I soon found that he had tender feet.

We shortly left the high-road, and in torrents of rain turned off on unbeaten tracks, which led us through a very bad swamp and some much swollen and very rough rivers into the mountains, where we followed a worn-out track for eight miles. It was *foul* weather, dark and still, with a brown mist, and rain falling in sheets. I threw my paper waterproof away as useless, my clothes were of course soaked, and it was with much difficulty that I kept my *shōmon* and paper money from being reduced to pulp. Typhoons are not known so far north as Ezo, but it was what they call a "typhoon rain" without the typhoon, and in no time it turned the streams into torrents barely fordable, and tore up such of a road as there is, which at its best is a mere water channel. Torrents, bringing tolerable-sized stones, tore down the track, and when the horses had been struck two or three times by these, it was with difficulty that they could be induced to face the rushing water. Constantly in a pass, the water had gradually cut a track several feet deep between steep banks, and the only possible walking place was a stony gash not wide enough for the two feet of a horse alongside of each other, down which water and stones were rushing from behind, with all manner of trailers matted overhead, and between avoiding being strangled and attempting to keep a tender-footed horse on his legs, the ride was a very severe one. The poor animal fell five times from stepping on stones, and in one of his falls twisted my left wrist badly. I thought of the many people who envied me my tour in Japan, and wondered whether they would envy me that ride.

After this had gone on for four hours, the track, with a sudden dip over a hillside, came down on Old Muroran, a village of thirty Ainu and nine

Japanese houses, very unpromising-looking, although exquisitely situated on the rim of a lovely cove. The Ainu huts were small and poor, with an unusual number of bear skulls on poles, and the village consisted mainly of two long dilapidated buildings, in which a number of men were mending nets. It looked a decaying place, of low, mean lives. But at a merchant's there was one delightful room with two translucent sides—one opening on the village, the other looking to the sea down a short, steep slope, on which is a quaint little garden, with dwarfed fir trees in pots, a few balsams, and a red cabbage grown with much pride as a foliage plant.

It is nearly midnight, but my bed and bedding are so wet that I am still sitting up and drying them, patch by patch, with tedious slowness, on a wooden frame placed over a charcoal brazier, which has given my room the dryness and warmth which are needed when a person has been for many hours in soaked clothing, and has nothing really dry to put on. Itō bought a chicken for my supper, but when he was going to kill it an hour later its owner in much grief returned the money, saying she had brought it up and could not bear to see it killed. This is a wild, outlandish place, but an intuition tells me that it is beautiful. The ocean at present is thundering up the beach with the sullen force of a heavy groundswell, and the rain is still falling in torrents.

The Coastal Ainu

Weary wave and dying blast
Sob and moan along the shore,
All is peace at last.

And more than peace. It was a heavenly morning. The deep blue sky was perfectly unclouded, a blue sea with diamond flash and a many-twinkling smile rippled gently on the golden sands of the lovely little bay. Opposite, forty miles away, the pink summit of the volcano of Komagatake, forming the south-western point of Uchiura Bay, rose into a softening veil of tender blue haze. There was a balmy breeziness in the air, and tawny tints upon the hill, patches of gold in the woods, and a scarlet spray here and there heralded the glories of the advancing autumn. As the day began, so it closed. I should like to have detained each hour as it passed. It was thorough enjoyment. I visited a good many of the Muroran Ainu, saw their well-grown bear in its cage, and, tearing myself away with difficulty at noon, crossed a steep hill and a wood of scrub oak, and then followed a trail which runs on the amber sands close to the sea, crosses several small streams, and passes the lonely Ainu village of Maripu, the ocean always on the left and wooded ranges on the right, and in front an apparent bar to farther progress in the form of Mount Usu, an imposing mountain, rising abruptly to a height of nearly three thousand feet, I should think.

In Ezo, as on the main island, one can learn very little about any prospective route. Usually when one makes an inquiry a Japanese puts on a stupid look, giggles, tucks his thumbs into his girdle, hitches up his garments, and either professes perfect ignorance or gives one some vague second-hand information, though it is quite possible that he may have been over every foot of the ground himself more than once. Whether suspicion of your motives in asking, or a fear of compromising himself by answering, is at the bottom of this I don't know, but it is most exasperating to a traveller. In Hakodate I failed to see Captain Blakiston, who has walked round the whole Ezo seaboard, and all I was able to learn regarding this route was that the coast was thinly peopled by Ainu, that there were government horses which could be got, and that one could sleep where one got them; that rice and salted fish were the only food; that there were many bad rivers, and that the road went over bad mountains; that the only people who went that way were government officials twice a year, that one could not get on more than four miles a day, that the roads over the passes were all big stones.

So Mount Usu took me altogether by surprise, and for a time confounded all my carefully constructed notions of locality. I had been told that the one volcano in the bay was Komogatake, near Mori, and this I believed to be eighty miles off. And there, confronting me, within a distance of two miles, was this grand, splintered, vermilion-crested thing, with a far nobler aspect than that of *the* volcano, with a curtain range in front, deeply scored, and slashed with ravines and abysses whose purple gloom was unlighted even by the noonday sun. One of the peaks was emitting black smoke from a deep crater, another steam and white smoke from various rents and fissures in its side—vermilion peaks, smoke, and steam all rising into a sky of brilliant blue, and the atmosphere was so clear that I saw everything that was going on there quite distinctly, especially when I attained an altitude exceeding that of the curtain range. It was not for two days that I got a correct idea of its geographical situation, but I was not long in finding out that it was not Komogatake. There is much volcanic activity about it. I saw a glare from it last night thirty miles away. The Ainu said that it was a god, but did not know its name, nor did the Japanese who were living under its shadow. At some distance from it in the interior rises a great dome-like volcanic group of Shikaribetsu, and the whole view is grand.

A little beyond Hidaka Monbetsu flows the Osaru River, one of the largest of the Ezo streams. It was much swollen by the previous day's rain; and as the ferry-boat was carried away we had to swim it, and the swim seemed very long. Of course, we and the baggage got very wet. The coolness with which the Ainu guide took to the water without giving us any notice that its broad, eddying flood was a swim, and not a ford, was very amusing.

From the top of a steepish ascent beyond the Osaru-*gawa* there is a view into what looks like a very lovely lake, with wooded promontories, and little bays, and rocky capes in miniature, and little heights, on which Ainu houses, with tawny roofs, are clustered. Then the track dips suddenly, and deposits one, not by a lake at all, but on Usu Bay, an inlet of the Pacific, much broken up into coves, and with a very narrow entrance, only obvious from a few points. Just as the track touches the bay there is a road post, with a prayer wheel in it, and by the shore an upright stone of very large size, inscribed with Sanskrit characters. It stands near to a stone staircase and a gateway in a massive stone-faced embankment, which looked much out of keeping with the general wildness of the place.

On a rocky promontory in a wooded cove there is a large, rambling house, greatly out of repair, inhabited by a Japanese man and his son, who are placed there to look after government interests, exiles among five hundred Ainu. From among the number of rat-haunted, rambling rooms which had once been handsome, I chose one opening on a yard or garden with some distorted yews in it, but found that the great gateway and the *amado* had no bolts, and that anything might be appropriated by anyone with dishonest intentions. But the house master and his son, who have lived for ten years among the Ainu, and speak their language, say that nothing is ever taken, and that the Ainu are thoroughly honest and harmless. Without this assurance I should have been distrustful of the number of wide-mouthed youths who hung about, in the listlessness and vacuity of savagery, if not of the bearded men who sat or stood about the gateway with children in their arms.

Usu is a dream of beauty and peace. There is not much difference between high and low water on this coast, and the lake-like illusion would have been perfect had it not been that the rocks were tinged with gold for a foot or so above the sea by a delicate species of fucus. In the exquisite inlet where I spent the night, trees and trailers drooped into the water and were mirrored in it, their green, heavy shadows lying sharp against the sunset gold and pink of the rest of the bay. Log canoes, with planks laced upon their gunwales to heighten them, were drawn upon a tiny beach of golden sand, and in the shadiest cove, moored to a tree, an antique and much-carved *bezaisen* was floating double. Wooded, rocky knolls, with Ainu huts, the vermilion peaks of Mount Usu redder than ever in the sinking sun, a few Ainu mending their nets, a few more spreading edible seaweed out to dry, a single canoe breaking the golden mirror of the cove by its noiseless motion, a few Ainu loungers, with their mild-eyed, melancholy faces and quiet ways suiting the quiet evening scene, the unearthly sweetness of a temple bell—this was all, and yet it was the loveliest picture I have seen in Japan.

In spite of Itō's remonstrances and his protestations that an exceptionally good supper would be spoiled, I left my rat-haunted room, with its tarnished gilding and precarious *fusuma*, to get the last of the pink and lemon-colored glory. Going up the staircase in the stone-faced embankment, and up a broad, well-paved avenue, to a large temple, within whose open door I sat for some time absolutely alone, and in a wonderful stillness; for the sweet-toned bell which vainly chimes for vespers amidst this bear-worshipping population had ceased. This temple was the first symptom of Japanese religion that I remember to have seen since leaving Hakodate, and worshippers have long since ebbed away from its shady and moss-grown courts. Yet it stands there to protest for the teaching of the great Buddha. Generations of Ainu heathen pass away one after another. And still its bronze bell tolls, and its altar lamps are lit, and incense burns for ever before Buddha. The characters on the great bell of this temple are said to be the same lines which are often graven on temple bells, and to possess the dignity of twenty-four centuries:

> All things are transient
> They being born must die,
> And being born are dead;
> And being dead are glad
> To be at rest.

The temple is very handsome, the baldachino is superb, and the bronzes and brasses on the altar are especially fine. A broad ray of sunlight streamed in, crossed the matted floor, and fell full upon the figure of Sakya Muni in his golden shrine. Just at that moment a shaven priest, in silk-brocaded vestments of faded green, silently passed down the stream of light, and lit the candles on the altar, and fresh incense filled the temple with a drowsy fragrance. It was a most impressive picture. His curiosity evidently shortened his devotions, and he came and asked me where I had been and where I was going, to which, of course, I replied in excellent Japanese, and then stuck fast.

Along the paved avenue, besides the usual stone trough for holy water, there are on one side the thousand-armed Kannon, a very fine relief. On the other is Buddha, throned on the eternal lotus blossom, with an iron staff much resembling a crozier in his hand, and that eternal apathy on his face which is the highest hope of those who hope at all. I went through a wood, where there are some mournful groups of graves on the hillside, and from the temple came the sweet sound of the great bronze bell and the beat of the big drum, and then, more faintly, the sound of the little bell and drum, with which the priest accompanies his ceaseless repetition of a phrase in the dead tongue of a distant land. There is an infinite pathos about the lonely temple in its splendor, the absence of even possible worshippers, and the large population of Ainu, sunk in yet deeper superstitions than those which go to make up popular Buddhism. I sat on a rock by the bay till the last pink glow faded from Mount Usu and the last lemon stain from the still water. A beautiful crescent, which hung over the wooded hill, had set, and the heavens blazed with stars:

> Ten thousand stars were in the sky,
> Ten thousand in the sea,
> And every wave with dimpled face,
> That leapt upon the air,
> Had caught a star in its embrace,
> And held it trembling there.

The loneliness of Usu Bay is something wonderful—a house full of empty rooms falling to decay, with only two men in it—one Japanese house among five hundred savages, yet it was the only one in which I have slept in which

257

they bolted neither the *amado* nor the gate. During the night the *amado* fell out of the worn-out grooves with a crash, knocking down the *shōji*, which fell on me, and rousing Itō, who rushed into my room half asleep, with a vague vision of blood-thirsty Ainu in his mind. I then learned what I have been stupid not to have learned before, that in these sliding wooden shutters there is a small door through which one person can creep at a time called the *jishindo*, or "earthquake door," because it provides an exit during the alarm of an earthquake, in case of the *amado* sticking in their grooves, or their bolts going wrong. I believe that such a door exists in all Japanese houses.

The next morning was as beautiful as the previous evening, rose and gold instead of gold and pink. Before the sun was well up I visited a number of the Ainu lodges, saw the bear, and the chief, who, like all the rest, is a monogamist, and, after breakfast, at my request, some of the old men came to give me such information as they had. These venerable elders sat cross-legged in the verandah, the house master's son, who kindly acted as interpreter, squatting, Japanese fashion, at the side, and about thirty Ainu, mostly women, with infants, sitting behind. I spent about two hours in going over the same ground as at Biratori, and also went over the words, and got some more, including some synonyms. The click of the "ts" before the "ch" at the beginning of a word is strongly marked among these Ainu. Some of their customs differ slightly from those of their brethren of the interior, especially as to the period of seclusion after a death, the non-allowance of polygamy to the chief, and the manner of killing the bear at the annual festival. Their ideas of metempsychosis are more definite, but this, I think, is to be accounted for by the influence and proximity of Buddhism. They spoke of the bear as their chief god, and next the sun and fire. They said that they no longer worship the wolf, and that though they call the volcano and many other things *kamoi*, or god, they do not worship them. I ascertained beyond doubt that worship with them means simply making libations of *sake* and drinking to the god, and that it is unaccompanied by petitions, or any vocal or mental act.

These Ainu are as dark as the people of southern Spain, and very hairy. Their expression is earnest and pathetic, and when they smile, as they did when I could not pronounce their words, their faces have a touching sweetness which is quite beautiful, and European, not Asiatic. Their own impression is that they are now increasing in numbers after diminishing for many years. I left Usu sleeping in the loveliness of an autumn noon with great regret. No place that I have seen has fascinated me so much.

A charge of three *sen* per *ri* more for the horses for the next stage, because there were such "bad mountains to cross," prepared me for what followed— many miles of the worst road for horses I ever saw. I should not have complained if they had charged double the price. As an almost certain consequence, it was one of the most picturesque routes I have ever travelled. For some distance it runs placidly along by the seashore, on which big, blue, foam-crested rollers were disporting themselves noisily. It passes through several Ainu hamlets, and the Ainu village of Abuta, with sixty houses, rather a prosperous-looking place, where the cultivation was considerably more careful, and the people possessed a number of horses. Several of the houses were surrounded by bears' skulls grinning from between the forked tops of high poles, and there was a well-grown bear ready for his doom and apotheosis. In nearly all the houses a woman was weaving bark cloth, with the hook which holds the web fixed into the ground several feet outside the house. At a deep river called the Noko, which emerges from the mountains close to the sea, we were ferried by an Ainu completely covered with hair, which on his shoulders was wavy like that of a retriever, and rendered clothing quite needless either for covering or warmth. A wavy, black beard rippled nearly to his waist over his furry chest, and, with his black locks hanging in masses over his shoulders, he would have looked a thorough savage had it not been for the exceeding sweetness of his smile and eyes. The Uchiura Bay Ainu are far more hairy than the mountain Ainu, but even among them it is quite common to see men not more so than vigorous Europeans, and I think that the hairiness of the race as a distinctive feature has been much exaggerated, partly by the smooth-skinned Japanese.

The ferry scow was nearly upset by our four horses beginning to fight. At first one bit the shoulders of another; then the one attacked uttered short, sharp squeals, and returned the attack by striking with his fore feet, and then there was a general melee of striking and biting, till some ugly wounds were inflicted. I have watched fights of this kind on a large scale every day in the corral. The miseries of the Ezo horses are the great drawback of Ezo travelling. They are brutally used, and are covered with awful wounds from being driven at a fast scramble with the rude, ungirthed pack saddle and its heavy load rolling about on their backs, and they are beaten unmercifully over their eyes and ears with heavy sticks. Itō has been barbarous to these gentle, little-prized animals ever since we came to Ezo; he has vexed me more by this than by anything else, especially as he never dared even to carry a switch on the main island, either from fear of the horses or their owners. today he was beating the baggage horse unmercifully, when I rode back and interfered with some very strong language, saying, "You are a bully, and, like all bullies, a coward." Imagine my aggravation when, at our first halt, he brought out his note-book, as usual, and quietly asked me the meaning of the words "bully" and "coward." It was perfectly impossible to explain them, so I said a bully was the worst name I could call him, and that a coward was the meanest thing a man could be. Then the provoking boy said, "Is bully a worse name than devil?" "Yes, far worse," I said, on which he seemed rather crestfallen, and he has not beaten his horse since, in my sight at least.

The breaking-in process is simply breaking the spirit by an hour or two of such atrocious cruelty as I saw at Shiraoi, at the end of which the horse, covered with foam and blood, and bleeding from mouth and nose, falls down exhausted. Being so ill used they have all kinds of tricks, such as lying down in fords, throwing themselves down head foremost and rolling over pack and rider, bucking, and resisting attempts to make them go otherwise than in single file. Instead of bits they have bars of wood on each side of the mouth, secured by a rope round the nose and chin. When horses which have been broken with bits gallop they put up their heads till the nose is level with the ears, and it is useless to try either to guide or check them. They always want to join the great herds on the hillside or seashore, from which they are only driven down as they are needed. In every Ezo village the first sound that one hears at break of day is the gallop of forty or fifty horses, pursued by an Ainu, who has hunted them from the hills. A horse is worth from twenty-eight shillings upwards. They are very sure-footed when their feet are not sore, and cross a stream or chasm on a single rickety plank, or walk on a narrow ledge above a river or gulch without fear. They are barefooted, their hoofs are very hard, and I am glad to be rid of the perpetual tying and untying and replacing of the straw shoes of the well-cared-for horses of the main island. A man rides with them, and for a man and three horses the charge is only sixpence for each two and a half miles. I am now making Itō ride in front of me, to make sure that he does not beat or otherwise misuse his horse.

After crossing the Noko River, from which the fighting horses have led me to make so long a digression, we went right up into the "bad mountains," and crossed the three tremendous passes of Rebunge Pass. Except by saying that this disused bridle track is impassable, people have scarcely exaggerated its difficulties. One horse broke down on the first pass, and we were long delayed by sending the Ainu back for another. Possibly these extraordinary passes do not exceed fifteen hundred feet in height. The track ascends them through a dense forest with most extraordinary abruptness, to descend as abruptly, to rise again sometimes by a series of nearly washed-away zigzags. At others by a straight, ladder-like ascent deeply channelled, the bottom of the trough being filled with rough stones, large and small. Or with ledges of rock with an entangled mass of branches and trailers overhead, which render it necessary to stoop over the horse's head while he is either fumbling, stumbling, or tumbling among the stones in a gash a foot wide, or else is awkwardly leaping up broken rock steps nearly the height of his chest, the whole performance consisting of a series of scrambling jerks at the rate of a mile an hour.

In one of the worst places the Ainu's horse, which was just in front of mine, in trying to scramble up a nearly breast-high and much-worn ledge, fell backwards, nearly overturning my horse. The stretcher poles, which formed part of his pack, struck me so hard above my ankle that for some minutes afterwards I thought the bone was broken. The ankle was severely cut and bruised, and bled a good deal, and I was knocked out of the saddle. Itō's horse fell three times, and eventually the four were roped together. Such are some of the diversions of Ezo travel.

Ah, but it was glorious! The views are most magnificent. This is really Paradise. Everything is here—huge headlands magnificently timbered, small, deep bays into which the great green waves roll majestically, great, grey cliffs, too perpendicular for even the most adventurous trailer to find root-hold, bold bluffs and outlying stacks cedar-crested, glimpses of bright, blue ocean dimpling in the sunshine or tossing up wreaths of foam among ferns and trailers. And inland ranges of mountains forest-covered, with tremendous gorges between, forest filled, where wolf, bear, and deer make their nearly inaccessible lairs. And outlying battlements. And ridges of grey rock with hardly six feet of level on their sinuous tops. And cedars in masses giving deep shadow. And sprays of scarlet maple or festoons of a crimson vine lighting the gloom.

The inland view suggested infinity. There seemed no limit to the forest-covered mountains and the unlighted ravines. The wealth of vegetation was equal in luxuriance and entanglement to that of the tropics, primeval vegetation, on which the lumberer's axe has never rung. Trees of immense height and girth, especially the beautiful ginko tree, with its small fan-shaped leaves, all matted together by riotous lianas, rise out of an impenetrable undergrowth of the dwarf, dark-leaved bamboo, which still attains a height of seven feet. All is dark, solemn, soundless, the haunt of wild beasts, and of butterflies and dragonflies of the most brilliant colors. There was light without heat, leaves and streams sparkled, and there was nothing of the half-smothered sensation which is often produced by the choking greenery of the main island, for frequently, far below, the Pacific flashed in all its sunlit beauty, and occasionally we came down unexpectedly on a little cove with abrupt cedar-crested headlands and stacks, and a heavy surf rolling in with the deep thunder music which alone breaks the stillness of this silent land.

There was one tremendous declivity where I got off to walk, but found it too steep to descend on foot with comfort. The deep groove being too narrow for me to get to the side of my horse, I dropped down upon him from behind, between his tail and the saddle, and so scrambled on!

The sun had set and the dew was falling heavily when the track dipped over the brow of a headland, becoming a waterway so steep and rough that I could not get down it on foot without the assistance of my hands. It terminated on a lonely little bay of great beauty, walled in by impractica-ble-looking headlands, which was the entrance to an equally impractica-ble-looking, densely-wooded valley running up among densely-wooded mountains. There was a margin of grey sand above the sea, and on this the skeleton of an enormous whale was bleaching. Two or three large dug-outs, with planks laced with stout fiber on their gunwales, and some bleached drift-wood lay on the beach, the foreground of a solitary, rambling, dilapidated grey house, bleached like all else. Three Japanese men with an old Ainu servant live there to look after "government interests," whatever these may be, and keep rooms and horses for government officials—a great boon to travellers who, like me, are belated here. Only one person has passed Rebunge this year, except two officials and a policeman.

There was still a red glow on the water, and one horn of a young moon appeared above the wooded headland. The loneliness and isolation are over-powering, and it is enough to produce madness to be shut in for ever with the thunder of the everlasting surf, which compels one to raise one's voice in order to be heard. In the wood, half a mile from the sea, there is an Ainu village of thirty houses, and the appearance of a few of the savages gliding noiselessly over the beach in the twilight added to the ghastliness and loneliness of the scene.

The horses were unloaded by the time I arrived, and several courteous Ainu showed me to my room, opening on a small courtyard with a heavy gate. The room was musty, and, being rarely used, swarmed with spiders. A saucer of fish oil and a wick rendered darkness visible, and showed faintly the dark, pathetic faces of a row of Ainu on the verandah, who retired noiselessly with their graceful salutation when I bade them good night. Food was hardly to be expected, yet they gave me rice, potatoes, and black beans boiled in equal parts of brine and syrup, which are very palatable. The cuts and bruises of yesterday became so very painful with the cold of the early morning that I have been obliged to remain here.

Ainu Canoes

Rebunge is a most fascinating place in its awful isolation. The house master was a friendly man, and much attached to the Ainu. If other officials entrusted with Ainu concerns treat the Ainu as fraternally as those of Usu and Rebunge, there is not much to lament. This man also gave them a high character for honesty and harmlessness, and asked if they might come and see me before I left. Twenty men, mostly carrying very pretty children, came into the yard with the horses. They had never seen a foreigner, but, either from apathy or politeness, they neither stare nor press upon one as the Japanese do, and always make a courteous recognition. The bear-skin covering of my saddle pleased them very much, and my boots of unblacked leather, which they compare to the deer-hide moccasins which they wear for winter hunting. Their voices were the lowest and most musical that I have heard, incongruous sounds to proceed from such hairy, powerful-looking men. Their love for their children was most marked. They caressed them tenderly, and held them aloft for notice, and when the house- master told them how much I admired the brown, dark-eyed, winsome creatures, their faces lighted with pleasure, and they saluted me over and over again. These, like other Ainu, utter a short screeching sound when they are not pleased, and then one recognizes the savage.

These Rebunge Ainu differ considerably from those of the eastern villages, and I have again to notice the decided sound or click of the "ts" at the beginning of many words. Their skins are as swarthy as those of Bedaween, their foreheads comparatively low, their eyes far more deeply set their stature lower, their hair yet more abundant, the look of wistful melancholy more marked, and two, who were unclothed for hard work in fashioning a canoe, were almost entirely covered with short, black hair, especially thick on the shoulders and back, and so completely concealing the skin as to reconcile one to the lack of clothing. I noticed an enormous breadth of chest, and a great development of the muscles of the arms and legs. All these Ainu shave their hair off for two inches above their brows, only allowing it there to attain the length of an inch. Among the well-clothed Ainu in the yard there was one smooth-faced, smooth-skinned, concave-chested, spindle-limbed Japanese, with no other clothing than the decorated bark-cloth apron which the Ainu wear in addition to their coats and leggings. Escorted by these gentle, friendly savages, I visited their lodges, which are very small and poor, and in every way inferior to those of the mountain Ainu. The women are short and thick-set, and most uncomely.

From their village I started for the longest, and by reputation the worst, stage of my journey, seventeen miles, the first ten of which are over mountains. So solitary and disused is this track that on a four days' journey we have not met a human being. In the Rebunge valley, which is densely forested, and abounds with fordable streams and treacherous ground, I came upon a grand specimen of the ginko tree, which, at a height of three feet from the ground, divides into eight lofty stems, none of them less than two feet in diameter. This tree, which grows rapidly, is so well adapted to our climate that I wonder it has not been introduced on a large scale, as it may be seen by everybody in Kew Gardens. There is another tree with orbicular leaves in pairs, which grows to an immense size.

From this valley a worn-out, stony bridle track ascends the western side of Rebunge Pass, climbing through a dense forest of trees and trailers to a height of about two thousand feet, where, contented with its efforts, it reposes. With only slight ups and downs, it continues along the top of a narrow ridge within the seaward mountains, between high walls of dense bamboo, which, for much of that day's journey, is the undergrowth alike of mountain and valley, ragged peak, and rugged ravine. The scenery was as magnificent as on the previous day. A guide was absolutely needed, as the track ceased altogether in one place, and for some time the horses had to blunder their way along a bright, rushing river, swirling rapidly downwards, heavily bordered with bamboo, full of deep holes, and made difficult by trees which have fallen across it. There Itō, whose horse could not keep up with the others, was lost, or rather lost himself, which led to a delay of two hours. I have never seen grander forest than on that two days' ride.

At last the track, barely passable after its recovery, dips over a precipitous bluff, and descends close to the sea, which has evidently receded considerably. Thence it runs for six miles on a level, sandy strip, covered near the sea with a dwarf bamboo about five inches high, and farther inland with red roses and blue campanula.

At the foot of the bluff there is a ruinous Japanese house, where an Ainu family has been placed to give shelter and rest to any who may be crossing the pass. I opened my *bentōbako* (lunch box) of red lacquer, and found that it contained some cold, waxy potatoes, on which I dined, with the addition of some tea, and then waited wearily for Itō, for whom the guide went in search. The house and its inmates were a study. The ceiling was gone, and all kinds of things, for which I could not imagine any possible use, hung from the blackened rafters. Everything was broken and decayed, and the dirt was appalling. A very ugly Ainu woman, hardly human in her ugliness, was splitting bark fiber. There were several *irori*, Japanese fashion, and at one of them a grand-looking old man was seated apathetically contemplating the boiling of a pot. Old, and sitting among ruins, he represented the fate of a race which, living, has no history, and perishing leaves no monument.

By the other *irori* sat, or rather crouched, the *missing link*. I was startled when I first saw it. It was—shall I say?—a man, and the mate, I cannot write the husband, of the ugly woman. He was about fifty. The lofty Ainu brow had been made still loftier by shaving the head for three inches above it. His hair hung, not in shocks, but in snaky wisps, mingling with a beard which was grey and matted. His eyes were dark but vacant, and his face had no other expression than that look of apathetic melancholy which one sometimes sees on the faces of captive beasts. His arms and legs were unnaturally long and thin, and he sat with his knees tucked into the armpits. His limbs and body, with the exception of a patch on each side, were thinly covered with fine black hair, more than an inch long, which was slightly curly on the shoulders. He showed no other sign of intelligence than that evidenced by boiling water for my tea. When Itō arrived he looked at him with disgust, exclaiming, "The Ainu are just dogs. They had a dog for their father," in allusion to their own legend of their origin.

The level was pleasant after the mountains, and a canter took us pleasantly to Oshamanbe, where we struck the old road from Mori to Sapporo, and where I halted for a day to rest my spine, from which I was suffering much. Oshamanbe looks dismal even in the sunshine, decayed and dissipated, with many people lounging about in it doing nothing, with the dazed look which over-indulgence in *sake* gives to the eyes. The sun was scorching hot, and I was glad to find refuge from it in a crowded and dilapidated *yadoya*, where there were no black beans, and the use of eggs did not appear to be recognized. My room was only enclosed by *shōji*, and there were scarcely five minutes of the day in which eyes were not applied to the finger-holes with which they were liberally riddled. During the night one of them fell down, revealing six Japanese sleeping in a row, each head on a wooden pillow.

The grandeur of the route ceased with the mountain-passes, but in the brilliant sunshine the ride from Oshamanbe to Mori, which took me two days, was as pretty and pleasant as it could be. At first we got on very slowly, as besides my four horses there were four led ones going home, which got up fights and entangled their ropes, and occasionally lay down and rolled. Besides these there were three foals following their mothers, and if they stayed behind the mares hung back neighing, and if they frolicked ahead the mares wanted to look after them, and the whole string showed a combined inclination to dispense with their riders and join the many herds of horses which we passed. It was so tedious that, after enduring it for some time I got Itō's horse and mine into a scow at a river of some size, and left the disorderly drove to follow at leisure.

At Yurappu, where there is an Ainu village of thirty houses, we saw the last of the aborigines, and the interest of the journey ended. Strips of hard sand below high-water mark, strips of red roses, ranges of wooded mountains, rivers deep and shallow, a few villages of old grey houses amidst grey sand and bleaching driftwood, and then came the Yurappu, a broad, deep stream, navigable in a canoe for fourteen miles. The scenery there was truly beautiful in the late and splendid afternoon. The long blue waves rolled on shore, each one crested with light as it curled before it broke, and hurled its snowy drift for miles along the coast with a deep booming music. The glorious inland view was composed of six ranges of forest-covered mountains, broken, chasmed, caverned, and dark with timber. Above them bald, grey peaks rose against a green sky of singular purity. I longed to take a boat up the Yurappu, which penetrates by many a gorge into their solemn recesses, but had not strength to carry through my wish.

After this I exchanged the silence or low musical speech of Ainu guides for the harsh and ceaseless clatter of Japanese. At Yamakoshi, a small hamlet on the seashore, where I slept, there was a sweet, quiet *yadoya*, delightfully situated, with a wooded cliff at the back, over which a crescent hung out of a pure sky. Besides, there were the more solid pleasures of fish, eggs, and black beans. Thus, instead of being starved and finding wretched accommodation, the week I spent on Uchiura Bay has been the best fed, and certainly the most comfortable, week of my travels in northern Japan.

Another glorious day favored my ride to Mori, but I was unfortunate in my horse at each stage, and the Japanese guide was grumpy and ill-natured—a most unusual thing. Otoshibe and a few other small villages of grey houses, with an ancient and fish-like smell, lie along the coast, busy enough doubtless in the season, but now looking deserted and decayed. Houses are rather plentifully sprinkled along many parts of the shore, with a wonderful profusion of vegetables and flowers about them, raised from seeds liberally supplied by the Kaitakushi Department from its Nanai experimental farm and nurseries. For a considerable part of the way to Mori there is no track at all, though there is a good deal of travel. One makes one's way fatiguingly along soft sea sand or coarse shingle close to the sea, or absolutely in it, under cliffs of hardened clay or yellow conglomerate, fording many small streams, several of which have cut their way deeply through a stratum of black volcanic sand. I have crossed about a hundred rivers and streams on the Ezo coast, and all the larger ones are marked by a most noticeable peculiarity: on nearing the sea they turn south, and run for some distance parallel with it, before they succeed in finding an exit through the bank of sand and shingle which forms the beach and blocks their progress.

On the way I saw two Ainu land through the surf in a canoe, in which they had paddled for nearly a hundred miles. A river canoe is dug out of a single log, and two men can fashion one in five days. But on examining this one, which was twenty-five feet long, I found that it consisted of two halves, laced together with very strong bark fiber for their whole length, and with high sides also laced on. They consider that they are stronger for rough sea and surf work when made in two parts. Their bark-fiber rope is beautifully made, and they twist it of all sizes, from twine up to a nine-inch hawser.

Beautiful as the blue ocean was, I had too much of it, for the horses were either walking in a lather of sea foam or were crowded between the cliff and the sea, every larger wave breaking over my foot and irreverently splashing my face. The surges were so loud and incessant, throwing themselves on the beach with a tremendous boom, and drawing the shingle back with them with an equally tremendous rattle, so impolite and noisy, bent only on showing their strength, reckless, rude, self-willed, and inconsiderate. This purposeless display of force, and this incessant waste of power, and the noisy self-assertion in both, approach vulgarity!

Towards evening we crossed the last of the bridgeless rivers, and put up at Mori, which I left three weeks before, and I was very thankful to have accomplished my object without disappointment, disaster, or any considerable discomfort. Had I not promised to return Itō to his master by a given day, I should like to spend the next six weeks in the Ezo wilds, for the climate is good, the scenery beautiful, and the objects of interest are many.

Another splendid day favored my ride from Mori to Togeshita, where I remained for the night. I had exceptionally good horses for both days, though the one which Itō rode, while going at a rapid scramble, threw himself down three times and rolled over to rid himself from flies. I had not admired the wood between Mori and Lake Onuma on the sullen, grey day on which I saw it before, but this time there was an abundance of light and shadow and solar glitter, and many a scarlet spray and crimson trailer, and many a maple flaming in the valleys, gladdened me with the music of color. From the top of the pass beyond the lakes there is a grand view of the volcano in all its nakedness, with its lava beds and fields of pumice, with the lakes of Onuma and Konuma, and Junsai, lying in the forests at its feet, and from the top of another hill there is a remarkable view of windy Hakodate, with its headland looking like Gibraltar. The slopes of this hill are covered with the monkshood, of which the Ainu make their arrow poison.

The *yadoya* at Togeshita was a very pleasant and friendly one, and when Itō woke me yesterday morning, saying, "Are you sorry that it's the last morning? I am," I felt we had one subject in common, for I was very sorry to end my pleasant Ezo tour, and very sorry to part with the boy who had made himself more useful and invaluable even than before. It was most wearisome to have Hakodate in sight for twelve miles, so near across the bay, so far across the long, flat, stony strip which connects the headland upon which it is built with the mainland. For about three miles the road is rudely macadamized, and as soon as the bare-footed horses get upon it they seem lame of all their legs; they hang back, stumbling, dragging, edging to the side, and trying to run down every opening. When we got into the interminable main street I sent Itō on to the consulate for my letters, and dismounted, hoping that as it was raining I should not see any foreigners. I was not so lucky, for first I met Dening, and then, seeing the consul and Dr. Hepburn coming down the road, evidently dressed for dining in the flag-ship, and looking spruce and clean, I dodged up an alley to avoid them. But they saw me, and did not wonder that I wished to escape notice, for my old *bettō*'s hat, my torn green paper waterproof, and my riding skirt and boots, were not only splashed but caked with mud, and I had the general look of a person fresh from the wilds.

Bezaisen

This is my last day in Ezo, and the sun, shining brightly over the grey and windy capital, is touching the pink peaks of Komogatake with a deeper red, and is brightening my last impressions, which, like my first, are very pleasant. The bay is deep blue, flecked with violet shadows, and about sixty *bezaisen* are floating upon it at anchor. There are vessels of foreign rig too, but the wan, pale *bezaisen* lying motionless, or rolling into the harbour under their great white sails, fascinate me as when I first saw them in Edo Bay. They are antique-looking and picturesque, but are fitter to give interest to a picture than to battle with stormy seas.

Most of the *bezaisen* in the bay are about a hundred and twenty tons burthen, a hundred feet long, with an extreme beam, far aft, of twenty-five feet. The bow is long, and curves into a lofty stem, like that of a Roman galley, finished with a beak head, to secure the forestay of the mast. This beak is furnished with two large, goggle eyes. The mast is a ponderous spar, fifty feet high, composed of pieces of pine, pegged, glued, and hooped together. A heavy yard is hung amidships. The sail is an oblong of widths of strong, white cotton artistically puckered, not sewn together, but laced vertically, leaving a decorative lacing six inches wide between each two widths. Instead of reefing in a strong wind, a width is unlaced, so as to reduce the canvas vertically, not horizontally. Two blue spheres commonly adorn the sail. The mast is placed well abaft, and to tack or veer it is only necessary to reverse the sheet. When on a wind the long bow and nose serve as a head sail. The high, square, piled-up stern, with its antique carving, and the sides with their latticework, are wonderful, together with the extraordinary size and projection of the rudder, and the length of the tiller. The anchors are of grapnel shape, and the larger *bezaisen* have from six to eight arranged on the fore-end, giving one an idea of bad holding-ground along the coast. They really are much like the shape of a Chinese small-footed woman's shoe, and look very unmanageable. They are of unpainted wood, and have a wintry, ghastly look about them.

I have parted with Itō finally today, with great regret. He has served me faithfully, and on most common topics I can get much more information through him than from any foreigner. I miss him already, though he insisted on packing for me as usual, and put all my things in order. His cleverness is something surprising. He goes to a good, manly master, who will help him to be good and set him a virtuous example, and that is a satisfaction. Before he left he wrote a letter for me to the governor of Muroran, thanking him on my behalf for the use of the *kuruma* and other courtesies.

Caught in a Typhoon

H. B. M.'s legation, Tokyo, September 21
A placid sea, which after much disturbance had sighed itself to rest, and a high, steady barometer promised a fifty hours' passage to Yokohama. When the Hepburns and I left Hakodate by moonlight, on the night of the 14th, as the only passengers in the *Hyōgo-maru*. Captain Moore, her genial, pleasant master, congratulated us on the rapid and delightful passage before us, and we separated at midnight with many projects for pleasant intercourse and occupation.

But a more miserable voyage I never made, and it was not until the afternoon of the 17th that we crawled forth from our cabins to speak to each other. On the second day out, great heat came on with suffocating closeness, the mercury rose to 85 degrees, and in lat. 38 degrees 0' N. and long. 141 degrees 30' E. we encountered a typhoon, a revolving hurricane, that lasted for twenty-five hours, and jettisoned the cargo. Captain Moor has given me a very interesting diagram of it, showing the attempts which he made to avoid its vortex, through which our course would have taken us, and to keep as much outside it as possible. The typhoon was succeeded by a dense fog, so that our fifty-hour passage became seventy-two hours. We landed at Yokohama near upon midnight of the 17th, to find traces of much disaster, the whole low-lying country flooded, the railway between Yokohama and the capital impassable, great anxiety about the rice crop, the air full of alarmist rumors, and paper money, which was about par when I arrived in May, at a discount of thirteen percent! In the early part of this year (1880) it has touched forty-two percent.

Late in the afternoon the railroad was reopened, and I came here with Wilkinson, glad to settle down to a period of rest and ease under this hospitable roof. The afternoon was bright and sunny, and Tokyo was looking at its best. The long lines of *yashiki* looked handsome. The castle moat was so full of the gigantic leaves of the lotus, that the water was hardly visible. The grass embankments of the upper moat were a brilliant green. The pines on their summits stood out boldly against the clear sky. The hill on which the legation stands looked dry and cheerful. And, better than all, I had a most kindly welcome from those who have made this house my home in a strange land.

Tokyo is tranquil, that is, it is disturbed only by fears for the rice crop, and by the fall in Japanese currency. The military mutineers have been tried, popular rumor says tortured, and fifty-two have been shot. The summer has been the worst for some years, and now dark heat, moist heat, and nearly ceaseless rain prevail. People have been "rained up" in their summer quarters. "Surely it will change soon," people say, and they have said the same thing for three months.

An Awkward Question

H. B. M.'s legation, Tokyo, December 18

I have spent the last ten days here, in settled fine weather, which should have begun two months ago if the climate had behaved as it ought. The time has flown by in excursions, shopping, select little dinner parties, farewell calls, and visits made with Chamberlain to the famous groves and temples of Ikegami, where the Buddhist bishop and priests entertained us in one of the guest rooms. And to Enoshima and Kamakura, vulgar resorts which nothing can vulgarize so long as Fuji-*san* towers above them.

I will mention but one sight, which is so far out of the beaten track that I ascertained its whereabouts only after prolonged inquiry. Among Buddhists, especially of the Monto sect, cremation was largely practised till it was forbidden five years ago, as some suppose in deference to European prejudices. Three years ago, however, the prohibition was withdrawn, and in this short space of time the number of bodies burned has reached nearly nine thousand annually. Sir Harry Parkes applied for permission for me to visit the Kirigaya ground, one of five, and after a few delays it was granted by the governor of Tokyo at Mori's request.

So yesterday, attended by the legation linguist, I presented myself at the fine *yashiki* of the Tokyo governor, and quite unexpectedly was admitted to an audience of the governor. Kusumoto Masataka is a well-bred gentleman, and his face expresses the energy and ability which he has given proof of possessing. He wears his European clothes becomingly, and in attitude, as well as manner, is easy and dignified. After asking me a great deal about my northern tour and the Ainu, he expressed a wish for candid criticism. But as this in the East must not be taken literally, I merely ventured to say that the roads lag behind the progress made in other directions, upon which he entered upon explanations which doubtless apply to the past road-history of the country. He spoke of cremation and its necessity in large cities, and terminated the interview by requesting me to dismiss my interpreter and *kuruma*, as he was going to send me to Meguro in his own carriage with one of the government interpreters, adding very courteously that it gave him pleasure to show this attention to a guest of the British ambassador, for whose character and important services to Japan he has a high value.

An hour's drive, with an extra amount of yelling from the *bettō*, took us to a suburb of little hills and valleys, where red camellias and feathery bamboo against backgrounds of cryptomeria contrast with the grey monotone of British winters. Alighting at a farm road too rough for a carriage, we passed through fields and hedgerows to an erection which looks too insignificant for such solemn use. A longish building of wattle and dab, much like the northern farmhouses, a high roof, and chimneys resembling those of the oast houses in Kent, combine with the rural surroundings to suggest farm buildings rather than the funeral pyre, and all that is horrible is left to the imagination.

The end nearest the road is a little temple, much crowded with images, and small, red, earthenware urns and tongs for sale to the relatives of deceased persons, and beyond this are four rooms with earthen floors and mud walls. There is nothing noticeable about them except the height of the peaked roof and the dark color of the plaster. In the middle of the largest are several pairs of granite supports at equal distances from each other, and in the smallest there is a solitary pair. This was literally all that was to be seen. In the large room several bodies are burned at one time, and the charge is only one yen, about three shillings and eight pence, solitary cremation costing five yen. Faggots are used, and one shilling's worth ordinarily suffices to reduce a human form to ashes.

After the funeral service in the house the body is brought to the cremation ground, and is left in charge of the attendant, a melancholy, smoked-looking man, as well he may be. The richer people sometimes pay priests to be present during the burning, but this is not usual. There were five "quick-tubs" of pine hooped with bamboo in the larger room, containing the remains of laborers, and a few oblong pine chests in the small rooms containing those of middle-class people.

At eight p.m. each coffin is placed on the stone trestles, the faggots are lighted underneath, the fires are replenished during the night, and by 6 a.m. that which was a human being is a small heap of ashes, which is placed in an urn by the relatives and is honorably interred. In some cases the priests accompany the relations on this last mournful errand. Thirteen bodies were burned the night before my visit, but there was not the slightest odor in or about the building, and the interpreter told me that, owing to the height of the chimneys, the people of the neighborhood never experience the least annoyance, even while the process is going on. The simplicity of the arrangement is very remarkable, and there can be no reasonable doubt that it serves the purpose of the innocuous and complete destruction of the corpse as well as any complicated apparatus (if not better), while its cheapness places it within the reach of the class which is most heavily burdened by ordinary funeral expenses. This morning the governor sent his secretary to present me with a translation of an interesting account of the practice of cremation and its introduction into Japan.

SS. Volga, Christmas Eve, 1878
The snowy dome of Fuji-*san* reddening in the sunrise rose above the violet woodlands as we steamed out of Yokohama harbour on the 19th, and three days later I saw the last of Japan—a rugged coast, lashed by a wintry sea.

Glossary

amado:	Siding shutter.
amainu:	Heavenly dogs.
andon:	Paper-covered lamp stand.
bentōbako:	Lunch box.
betsu:	Ainu word for river.
bettō:	Footman.
bezaisen:	Edo period coastal trader.
chaya:	Teahouse.
daidokoro:	Kitchen.
daimyō:	Feudal lord.
dashi:	Float.
doma:	Earth floor.
dōsha:	Ammonium chloride.
fundoshi:	Undergarment for adult males, made from cotton.
fusuma:	Sliding door covered with thick paper.
fukinuke:	Aperture in the roof of a traditional house for the escape of smoke from open fires.
futon:	Quilt.
gaijin:	Alien.
geta:	Wooden clogs.
gohei:	Sacred wand.
hakama:	Skirt-like trousers.
haiden:	Chapel.
haori:	Lightweight silk jacket originally meant to be worn by men.

harakiri:	Ritual suicide through disembowelment.
hibachi:	Small Japanese charcoal heating appliance somewhat resembling a brazier.
ichibu(-gin):	Silver coins with a contemporary exchange rate of three *ichibu-gin* to one Mexican dollar.
irori:	Fireplace.
itama:	Board space.
jinrikisha:	Rickshaw.
jishindo:	Earthquake escape door.
jorōya:	Brothel.
kago:	Litter.
kaimyō:	Posthumous (Buddhist) name.
kakemono:	Hanging scroll.
kakke:	Beriberi.
kamoi:	Ainu word for god.
kata:	River.
kekkō:	splendid, delicious, wonderful.
kimono:	Traditional female garment.
kirin:	Unicorn.
koto:	Thirteen-stringed musical instrument resembling a horizontal harp.
kura:	Storehouse.
kuruma:	Vehicle, drawn by either by man or animal.
kurumaya:	Person who draws a kuruma.
mago:	Packhorse driver.
matsuri:	Festival.
mekake:	concubine.
mikoshi:	Portable shrine.
mochi:	Rice cake.
mon:	Gate.
obi:	Broad sash for a kimono.
ri:	3.9 km.
rin:	One-thousandth of a yen.
sake:	Japanese rice wine.
sakura:	Cherry blossom.

satsu:	Paper money.
sen:	One-hundredth of a yen.
shamisen:	Three-stringed musical instrument.
shide:	Zigzag-shaped paper streamers used in ropes at Shintō shrines or used in Shintō rituals.
shimenawa :	Twisted straw rope with stripes of zigzag-shaped white paper streamers (shide) that are hung around an object to ward off evil spirits.
shōgun:	Hereditary military ruler during Japan's feudal era.
shōji:	Lightweight sliding doors covered with paper.
shōmon:	Certificate.
tabakobon:	Tray with charcoal-holder and ash-pot.
tabi:	Traditional socks with pouches separating the big toe from the four other toes.
Tanabata:	Festival of the Weaver Star and the Cowherd Star.
taro:	*Colocasia esculenta*, or taro root.
tatami:	Straw mat roughly six by three feet.
tomoe:	Crest in the shape of three swirling commas.
torii:	Gateway built at the entrance to a Shinto shrine.
yadoya:	Inn.
yashiki:	Samurai mansion.
yukata:	Informal light cotton *kimono*.
zen:	Small lacquered table.

Index

TOYO PRess: Explore Dream Discover

Editorial supervision: William de Lange. Book and cover design: Chōkei Studios. Printing and binding: IngramSpark. The typefaces used are Perpetua, Prescript, and Herculanum.

www.ingramcontent.com/pod-product-compliance
Lightning Source LLC
Chambersburg PA
CBHW020437130626
46549CB00001B/180